Writing in InDesign
Second Edition:
Including Design, Typography, ePUB, Kindle, & InDesign CS6

Writing In InDesign

SECOND EDITION

INCLUDING DESIGN, TYPOGRAPHY, EPUB, KINDLE, & INDESIGN CS6

David Bergsland

Written and published in March, 2012
© David Bergsland • All Rights Reserved
ISBN-13: 978-1469924281
ISBN-10: 1469924285
Mankato, Minnesota • http://radiqx.com • info@radiqx.com

Please let us know if there is anyway I can help you in your publishing endeavors.

I dedicate this to my best friend
& soul mate, Pastor Pat
& the Lord whom we both serve
who has adopted us
into the Chosen People
whom we love

Contents

Introduction

I want to say some brief words of welcome as you start though this second edition of *Writing in InDesign*. You will discover that what I am doing is working creatively within InDesign to produce completed books almost as a fine art exercise while maintaining excellence and production needs.

What I want to share with you is a method, an attitude, a ministry of service to the reader which is enabled by the typographic power of InDesign. I am discussing one-person self-publishing, direct communication from author to reader.

One of the wonderful things about the new publishing paradigm is the control we get as artists, authors, and designers over the entire package. A modern book is released in multiple sizes, versions, and formats. The content and design remain fluid as we shape the book while we learn and grow. We can easily adjust content, layout, and presentation of our books after they are released in response to emails, FaceBook friends, tweets, and the whole host of contemporary social networking online.

Who is this book written for?

The focus of this book is very sharp. It is designed for people who are writing books and booklets, non-fiction in specific—beginning with very limited capital and few personnel resources. The good news is that you can start with an able computer, the software I mention, and a vision. Money is not required to start, and little is required as you grow.

I'm sharing techniques for the new wave of author/publishers who are not (and do not intend to be) large publishing houses. It is designed to help those of you without the resources and connections nor inclination to intrigue the large, mass-market media houses with their incredible capital requirements and insane marketing needs that look more like addicted gambling than actual communication through book production.

One of the trials of the new paradigm is the incredible amount of knowledge and the various skills necessary to do all of this. The good news is that the Design Edition of Adobe's Creative Suite enables you to use these skills and gain the knowledge necessary quite easily. It is the only software available which gives you the power you need to publish creatively and professionally in one package.

I have been uniquely positioned to take advantage of the new workflow. I began as a fine artist in the 1960s and early 1970s. I learned typesetting and graphic design at the hands of a masterful art director in the late 1970s. I spent a decade as an art director myself within the largest commercial printer in Albuquerque, New Mexico.

I began teaching these materials in 1991. Within a couple of years a large traditional publisher was asking me to convert my handouts to a book on the new digital printing. I used that opportunity to develop the first all digital printing and design curriculum in the country (as far as I can tell). I wrote a book a year for them on typography, FreeHand, Illustrator, Photoshop, and finally InDesign. *Publishing with InDesign* was one of the first books on the new software that would eventually take over the industry.

Becoming a teaching pastor as well as church administrator for my wife's church in Albuquerque in 1993 enabled me to use my skills in a whole new way. Materials for Bible studies, spiritual dramas, and worship services were a new joy for me.

While all of this was going on, in 1996, I took all my coursework online. I became involved with the distance learning initiative at my community college. I continued to write new instructional materials. I was supplying them to my students on the class Website as downloadable PDFs.

Then I found Lulu. With Lulu, then Createspace, then Scribd, then Zazzle, then Kindle, and then ePUBs, my world changed. Writing books became a real joy to me as InDesign kept getting better and better. More and more I was doing everything in InDesign except the photos.

If you have a designer working with you

It is possible you have decided to use a professional editor and/or designer to help you. If so, you will need to get a copy of this book to him or her so that you are on the same page. Book design knowledge is rare among designers today. Design knowledge is far outside the knowledge of most editors. They will need to appropriate the more technical knowledge found in the appendixes, if you decide not to do these things yourself.

Book design must be a specialty of your designer

You still need to read the materials so that you can talk the same language as your designer and understand their needs. If you are working with someone else, it will take many sharing sessions for you to come to the same mind about how these things should be done. They are not you and they will not put the book together the way you would. But you are using them because of their expertise. Respect their advice. Support each other in this process.

This book contains an extravagant amount of additional training in the appendixes

To keep the reading experience of the book intact and comfortable I moved six major sections into appendixes.

A: Basic Typography Part One [60 PAGES]

Here you get the information you need to use fonts professionally. This covers why and how typesetting (what we do in InDesign) differs from typewriting (what you might do in Word and Office [I don't use them anymore, at all]).

B: Setting up styles: Typography Part Two [32 PAGES]

Here is the conceptual knowledge on how to set up a functional default set of paragraph and character styles, plus an intro to object styles. You'll modify these for your use.

B2: A set of default styles [6 PAGES]

Here are step by step instructions for setting up a set of defaults which will get you started. You will modify these many times as you proceed in your book design journey. But, You must start somewhere.

C: Image production & formats [24 PAGES]

The difference between vector and bitmap. How to make a graphic in InDesign. How to convert them in Photoshop for use in ebooks. What formats should used and why.

C2: Cover design [6 PAGES]

You increasingly need to be concerned about how readable your cover is when reduced to thumbnail size on a Website. This is true of your print covers as well as your ebook covers.

D: Uploading your finished book [17 PAGES]

This covers step by step procedures at Lulu and Createspace for print books and for downloadable PDFs at Lulu and Scribd with tips and techniques learned.

E: InDesign and ePUB [29 PAGES]

Here are design tips and techniques for converting your printed book to an ePUB—ready to upload to iBooks and NookBooks. Included is a simple conversion process for your Kindle version.

F: Repairing the XHTML and CSS [15 PAGES]

This mainly applies to those of you still using CS5.5 or earlier. If you are earlier, you need much more than what is contained here. For those of you comfortable in these two coding languages, here are instructions on how to crack open your ePUB and make it fancy.

What about fiction?

Novels, and the like, are much more simple in structure, but what we talk about in this book certainly applies. This is the reason why I put a lot of the more technical knowledge in the appendices. It's there if you need it.

Poetry truly needs this knowledge because this is pure communication with words and typography. You are painting word pictures and that requires tools which are simply not available in a word processor.

The New Publisher

Here we are—well into the second decade of the new millennium and we now have a new method of publishing which truly helps individuals. The new changes are almost designed for those of us who feel called to share our vision with our trainees, students, and sheep. The new methodologies work better for teachers and leaders in small unique niches than anyone else.

But who cares about books?

Most of us start out our personal publishing efforts as bloggers these days—short, pithy writing offering a conversation with those we serve. These writings are easily compiled into books and ebooks. Even though the writing style will need a large transformation, the content is largely written and needs only copyediting to make it work in a book. You can't just collect, rewrite, and print, however.

On the other hand, in a world gone mad for the flashy immediacy (and minimal content) of video, why should we worry about books anyway? The key lies in the parenthetical phrase above *"and minimal content"*. We all know the difference between reading the book and seeing the movie. With an excellent novel, you enter an entire world, directed by the wordsmithing of the author. With an excellent movie you are handed a very intense (but brief & limited) slice of the life of that world you entered in the book.

But even this misses the entire point of a good non-fiction book. The depth of knowledge, subtle word definitions, language studies, historical insights, maps, and all the rest provided by a book could only be handled [if it's even possible] by a very lengthy, ridiculously expensive movie. And these exceedingly lengthy explanatory movies are simply a waste of resources to produce for a relatively nonexistent [small niche] audience. A four page, explanatory handout for the Seder meal during Holy Week becomes a fifteen minute to an hour video. This is a major production requiring many new skills and large expenses—and there is often subtle information available in the printed materials that simply cannot be translated into moving visuals.

Though it is true that videos might get us better numbers when we offer a class, it is also true that the students learn less from videos than they do from books, writing, and research. Lectures and teachings are converted to books relatively easily. It is easy to add reference materials. Illustrations and graphics are commonly developed by the author for the oral presentation.

Even so, things have radically changed. As a writer, most of my research and reference materials are now online. To be forced to return to printed reference works would really slow me down and I would miss many opportunities to cross reference and discover new insights.

But the core is still the book.

Books have been the major source of knowledge ever since our culture was torn apart by this new technology at the beginning of the Renaissance. Readily available books completely transformed our civilization.

The new digital production techniques have stirred up the pot. Smartphones seem to have taken over the world. But have they really? The new magazine apps for the iPad and other tablets are visually exciting. But none of them have been really successful—probably because reading on a screen is still not as easy and comfortable—yet. However, the new digital world presents us with many new opportunities. I could be making this book into course work using iBook Author, for example—which just came out in February as I was editing this book. But that seems to be a false hope after careful review (which I blogged about).

How have things changed?

The entire definition of a book has been revised: This piece you are reading did not appear as a book in the traditional sense at first. These paragraphs were first released as the first posting of a new series on my blog, *The Skilled Workman*, in April of 2011. There was a link to a free downloadable PDF version at Scribd. The intention was a fully developed book after I was given the complete vision to share. I ended up with six of these postings, as I recall. The book which resulted from this process was a synergistic improvement to the process. The first edition of *Writing In InDesign* was released through Createspace to Amazon at the end of July, 2011.

But a whole host of new options came into play as soon as that first part was posted on my blog. I made a downloadable PDF for Scribd. I tweeted about it. I shared it on FaceBook. But if I thought it would help, I could have easily released a Kindle, an ePUB, and several other ebook variations. I could have also offered it as a printed booklet. The new paradigm of publishing enables me to easily offer it in a wide variety of formatted options to attract and communicate with various types of readers. Most of these options are free. All they take is a little bit of effort on my part. But the final results are much better than what could be done in the old paradigm. The capabilities change weekly.

Desktop publishing has reached its potential

I clearly remember how excited I was in the early 1990s when I realized that what I had been doing (designing printing materials) with a team of forty highly skilled people and millions of dollars of equipment could now be done by a single person working at their desk.

It is true that I have taken things a little further than most by designing my own fonts, doing all my own illustrations, and so on. However, the concept is clear and the freedom to communicate in words from your computer is exhilarating. Books, blogs, ebooks, brochures, emails and much more can be directed to your readers to help communicate the message you have been given.

A teacher/trainer/prophet/leader can now have a world-wide influence from his or her office. We are no longer limited by locale. As a practical example, The Wisdom of the Tanakh and the Gospel of the Messiah can now be presented to the entire world, and the author can help the people he or she is called to serve no matter where they live. More than that, it can be done professionally and compellingly without the immense barriers erected by traditional publishing.

Here are some of the things that have changed in publishing since Y2K

- **Printing is now just an option:** The multi-million dollar printing presses have become an output option. The same is true of the expensive bindery equipment. All of the front end design and preproduction processes are given to us as software to be loaded into our computer and used in our office.

  It's all part of InDesign and Photoshop: They are now part of the creative process leading to many different types of fulfillment. The art department and prepress department of the printing companies are long gone as are the $100,000 copy cameras, the $500,000 scanners and color separators, the extremely skilled (& expensive) typesetters, layout specialists, camera operators, film assemblers, and all the rest. We, the document creators, now control all of that.

- **No expensive proofs:** Before the digital revolution a true proof, an actual copy of the finished product, cost hundreds or even thousands of dollars. Now we can simply have a single copy of our book printed—usually for ten dollars or less. Plus we can print proofs of individual pages for pennies. The ebooks are used as their own proofs and revised as necessary.

- **Lengthy lead times are eliminated:** I can remember the shock when my first book was published. It took so long to actually get it into print. It was common, back then, to spend a year writing a book and then another year to get it actually printed and released. This is the old paradigm.

  Now I write fully formatted. So, as soon as the book is finished, I can give it to the proofer, and it can be released within a day or two. I released one last Thursday and now have print, ePUB, and Kindle out and available.

- ❦ No minimum orders: In traditional publishing, just setting up the plates to be printed cost at least $50 a page and usually closer to $100. Plus you had to run a couple hundred copies through the press to get the first usable copy. Additionally, there was no real way to bind a single book on a practical level. As a result you could easily spend a thousand dollars to get the first copy of each sheet of paper (which usually held four to thirty two pages of a book) and less than fifty dollars to get the next 2,000 copies as they were printed at 10,000 to 50,000 copies an hour. You no longer need to print hundreds or thousands of documents to get the cost per unit price down to the place you can afford. **You can print a single book.**

- ❦ Not limited to brick and mortar bookstores: This is why they are all dying. You can publish what you need when you need it. You can service a very small niche effectively and profitably. You can use the mammoth online bookstores to distribute your documents and books—as well as email and your own Websites. You can even serialize your new book in your blog—getting reader feedback as you go. All you need to do is give your readers a link to the finished book in Lulu, Amazon, and Barnes and Noble for them to get a copy.

- ❦ Not limited to print: You can offer your book in the iBookstore on the iPad, NookBooks at Barnes & Noble, the Kindle store on Amazon, at Scribd, and many more ebook venues.

- ❦ Changes and corrections are normally free: You are no longer dependent on your copyediting budget to get a professional book. You can upload a new version with typo fixes without interrupting the availability of the book. Once a book is released with an ISBN#, you can still change everything except the title and author of the book. But even if you want to change that, all you need to do is publish the book as a new book or a new edition. You can leave the old book for sale if you like, building separate readerships for similar content.

- ❦ Targeted editions are no problem: You can make specialized versions for various movements, denominations, synagogues, churches, areas, countries, and/or targeted audiences with little effort required.

- ❦ Existing pieces from multiple books and documents can be assembled for special programs: you can take your work and make it into a custom curriculum or special presentation at the conference or service to which you are called to share your work.

That's what this book is: It is a targeted version of my basic digital publishing writings directed at authors, non-fiction primarily (though this knowledge will help a novel just as well). There are many things here that would not appeal to non-writers or that they could not comprehend. I am using pieces from *InDesign 7.5 On-Demand*, *Practical Font Design*, *Publishing with InDesign*, & *Introduction to Digital Publishing*—as well as pieces from various blog postings, gift designs, and so on. It is a natural extension of my life and work as an illustrator, typographer, art director, font designer, author, teacher, and publisher.

Writing within InDesign

Here I am again recommending a road less traveled by—not unusual in my life and work. Before the choruses rise up in defense of other workflows, let me tell you my reasonings. I fully recognize that most people write in Word. What these people do not realize [in most cases] is this simple fact starts their book under a great handicap. If Word users are publishing their own book, they are missing out on the best tools for communicating with readers.

Books are not entirely about words

Of course as a writer this may not make much sense to you. But hear me out. For years I have taught graphic designers that the content is all that matters. Now I am teaching writers that presentation and layout are a big part of your book. For designers, this has been a major fight because many never read the copy they design into books and printed materials. Now I am dealing with writers who do not see the need for typography and layout skills. In the publishing world there is a real disconnect between the writers and the book designers. They are treated as two entirely separate skill sets. It is better for them to merge, as much as possible.

Most designers do not deal well with words

Graphic designers [and this includes most book designers] are visual people, focused on how things look. One of my major concerns as I started to write books in the mid-1990s was my experience in my classes of using published textbooks as examples of poor communication. As a pastor, commercially available Bible studies were just as bad. They rarely had any meaning to our little flock because they were not explanations of scripture, but mere human examinations of men's ways. The examples are endless.

My pursuit of functional, reader-centered books has been fraught with trials. I was constantly bumping up against standardized procedures of traditional publishers which really made their books hard to read or use effectively. This goal is so far outside the norm in publishing today that there is no room at all for an author who even cares about these things (except in the brand new world of on-demand publishing—**the focus of this book**).

Let's talk about some simple examples of this lack of concern for the reader

- ❦ Illustrations listed by number with no connection to the copy which talks about what is illustrated: Most traditional non-fiction publishers require this typographic horror. In many cases, authors are not allowed to even pick out the images because they are not considered professional enough to understand what is required of an graphic.

  But the result is illustrations, maps, charts, and photos listed by number which are often not on the same page (or even the same chapter) as the content they illustrate. *Why bother to even have them?* Few readers will find them or take the time to look for them. The result is frustrated readership and readers who simply quit reading in disgust.

  For fiction, it is equally bad to have an illustration or map which cannot be easily referenced by the reader. In my attempts at novels I added maps where they were needed in the copy to help the reader understand what is going on a little better.

- ❦ Heads and subheads generated by designers: In many cases over the years I spent as a graphic designer, I wrote all the subheads, developed all the lists, wrote all the captions, and even wrote most of the headlines.

  I developed them out of a need to help direct the reader through the copy I was formatting.

The author commonly had no clue that they were desirable or necessary. I wrote them as a service to the reader. But I was a real minority as mentioned. Many designers [and it may well be most designers] do not even read the copy they layout, as I said.

As a writer, you must be aware of these issues and realize that they are a primary method of clearing up communication with the reader. Heads, subheads, list design, and all the rest are key elements of your support of the reader.

❧ Page layout determined by fashion and visual concerns: Fonts are chosen because they look good. Layouts are determined by fashion. Columns, margins, sidebars and the like are chosen to stimulate visual interest and provoke excitement instead of being chosen to communicate the content effectively, clearly, and accessibly. Clarity and accuracy are rarely considered.

The most glaring example of this is seen in the books where content is broken up into small pieces—supposedly to help people with short attention spans. We recently bought a book on creationism that is virtually unreadable. The gorgeous, fancy illustrations push the copy into bits and pieces that randomly appear out of the visual clutter of the pages' backgrounds. My wife gave up on it.

But it goes much further than that. Here's a quote from Wikipedia about the normal traditional editorial process (please force yourself to read it, I realize it is difficult to read):

"(Once) a decision is taken to publish a work, and the technical legal issues resolved, the author may be asked to improve the quality of the work through rewriting or smaller changes, and the staff will edit the work. Publishers may maintain a house style, and staff will copy edit to ensure that the work matches the style and grammatical requirements of each market. Editors often choose

or refine titles and headlines. Editing may also involve structural changes and requests for more information. Some publishers employ fact checkers, particularly regarding non-fiction works."

Notice that there is nothing here about serving the readers. The readers' needs are not part of the process. It's all about sales and the marketing decisions of the publisher. This is equally true for secular and spiritual publishers. Textbooks are some of the worst examples of editorial damage.

In most cases they will not even talk to you unless you can convince them that you have a large enough following to guarantee enough sales to cover the costs. Once you've passed that hurdle, they will normally insist that you fit your content into their style—even if that style hinders your book. Authors are taken captive—used as tools to make the publisher money.

Let's take a brief look at this world of traditional publishing—that relic of the information age which came before the digital desktop on-demand world in which we live now. In general, these traditionalists are extremely confused by what is taking place in the new digital publishing world. In fact, by reading this book you will commonly know more about the new on-demand publishing options than they will.

Large company publishing

The traditional model is completely bound up [or broken up] into areas of expertise that are assembled production style into the finished product. This works relatively well for mass-market content where the audience is understood by everyone in the process. The list of people with whom you, as an author, are required to interact in this scenario is incredible. Several types of editors (-in chief, acquisition editors, copyeditors), proofers, marketers, illustrators, art departments, production departments, assistants, preflightists, IT specialists, and the list goes on. This is often delegated by authors with clout to agents, publicists and the like. I am assuming that you do not have that type of clout—yet. More than that, do you want it?

The basic large company process

1. Manuscript submission: maybe with an agent "to grease the skids"

2. Editor (-in-Chief?): Acceptance of project and contract signing: setting up royalties, rights, and so on; Fitting project into publisher's production plans and series developments

3. Acquisition editors: Setting up the work team, with veto authority over both concept and content (often expecting you to change your concept to meet their perceived need)

4. Marketing team: determines focus, market, and demographics (this information is also used to convince you to change your concept or focus)

5. Technical editors: make sure that technical details are accurate and instructions actually work

6. Copyeditors: fix grammar, rearrange copy, regulate consistency; (they often have full veto authority over content)

7. Illustrators: Fix up rough sketches from authors, converting them to professional graphics (often drawn by people who do not understand either the content or the audience)

8. Peer review: manuscript is sent to peers in the field to determine relevance and acceptability. These peers are determined by the examination of their existing customers through the marketing department (often they are your competitors with contrary ideas).

9. Art department: determines layout, typography, sets up digital workflow to conform to the publisher's current standards (with no say or input by the author)

10. Cover designer: Authors are rarely consulted and never allowed to do the cover—it's just never done

11. Page layout: a production job within the art department after manuscript approval. This

is normally completely outside the author's control—the realm of "professional design".

12. Proofers: typos and typography errors which must be "fixed" in the copy even if the author knows they are converting standard niche usage into actual content error.

13. Print-ready file production: Magic done by pros to the bafflement of the author (as far as they are concerned).

14. Production proof: author often does not even see this

15. Production: outside author's control

16. Packaging: outside author's control

17. Marketing: outside author's control

Once the book is published you rarely hear from the publisher again except to get the yearly royalty checks. Hat they do is completely outside your knowledge or control.

This process is long and expensive

It's all about money. Books must support this huge bureaucratic infrastructure. Production costs run from tens of thousands of dollars on up to millions. If you cannot count on selling thousands or millions of books, they cannot afford to publish your work. It commonly takes a year after the manuscript is completed to produce the book. For time-sensitive work, this does not work well. The need can be fulfilled and gone before this type of traditionally published book reaches the marketplace.

These specialists commonly do not understand your content

I have had copyeditors flag something that was standard industry usage because he/she did not speak the industry lingo. I was writing on printing and publishing and they had no idea what a separation is for an image, or a signature is for a book, or that leading is a specific measurement (and speaks of the metal not a person). Imagine finding editors and proofers for a book on a capella choir music, Hebrew word studies, corn genetics, liturgical dance, Hauge Synod theology, how occult practices have entered modern religion, contemporary prophecy, or whatever your niche is. It's not going to happen.

But you can write a book to your niche that will help your readers, sell well, and help support the work in which you are involved. You know your niche and you understand your readers much better than the publishing houses do. It will take some real effort on your part and quite a bit of work. But you can do it.

Niche writers to limited markets

Here we begin to see the modern reality of publishing. The change is of the same type as we saw with the conversion in television from three, then four, gargantuan mass-market networks to the current reality of thousands of channels on cable and satellite. The same thing has happened in magazines where there are now over 10,000 magazines in the US alone. There are now millions of active blogs. We are currently publishing over a million different book titles per year. Obviously things have changed a little.

In a typical niche, the overhead of traditional publishing is not good stewardship

Many of the new books are developed for very small niches when dealing with a global scale of things. Let's take this book you are reading on writing and creating books within InDesign. Statistics are hard to find. In the USA, the labor department says there are nearly 300,000 graphic designers but only 26,000 desktop publishers. They say that there are a little over 150,000 authors which are about 70% self-employed.

Smashwords works with 18,000 writers. Lulu claims to have worked with over a million creators. But there are no stats on the number of InDesign users, the number of authors using InDesign, or anything like that. When I start checking keyword searches on Google in this area, I am left with the notion that there may be a few thousand people doing this. That's my niche.

How does the publishing world handle a niche this small? **It doesn't.**

So, what is a writer to do? You do not have many options unless you have enough money to pay for all the services of a traditional publisher. Here are some rough and probably minimal cost figures if you go traditional:

1. Copyeditor: $1000
2. Book formatter: $1000
3. Proofer: $500
4. ISBN #: $125 per book unless you buy a large block
5. Cover designer: $500
6. Printer: $2000 or much more
7. Press release: $500
8. Book review: $1000
9. Marketing package: $2,000 to $10,000
10. Books to give away: $1000
11. Website: $2000 plus $50 to $100 a month for ISP, Web access, site maintenance, et al
12. & on & on & on

So, what do you do if you do not have ten to fifteen thousand dollars with which to gamble? I've been challenged on the book designer blog with figures closer more like $2,000–$4,000. But that's still a lot of money. I'm expecting to sell 500-1,000 copies with a gross profit of well under $5,000. I'd be a fool to spend it all up front.

You must learn to produce your own books.

For the past two decades, I have taught digital publishing skills. For the past fifteen years I have written and published books, both traditionally and on-demand. I have taught skills to present digital content transparently, effectively, and gracefully. I've learned how to present reader-centered books to my students and followers. But Word [and word processors in general] cannot do this. There are skills and capabilities that are necessary which are simply not available in Office. Here's a short list:

- **Typography:** The skill to use fonts, paragraph styling, and page layout to invisibly communicate content—using point size, leading, small caps, ligatures, oldstyle figures, lining figures, ems, ens, discretionary hyphens, tracking, kerning, and much more. All of these things are controlled with styles: paragraph, character, and object. For this you need a professional page layout program. (See Appendixes A, B, and B2 for more directed study in this area)

- **High resolution images:** You want vector graphics if possible. Printing requires 300 dpi minimum for photos and bitmapped images. You'll need Photoshop for the high resolution images. JPEGs, GIFs, and PNGs won't work. They need to be PDFs, EPSs, AIs, PSDs, or TIFFs for printing quality work. (See Appendix C & C2 for more directed study about these things as well as cover design.)

- **PostScript (or PDF):** This is a page description language that is required by book printers. You must be able to create and proof in PDF. This requires InDesign, Photoshop, and Acrobat Pro. All printing companies now require a PDF to print from. If you give them anything less, they make their own PDF and you have no control over what results from that conversion.

- **Page layout:** A thorough understanding of columns, margins, alignments, indents, gutters, lists, tables, headlines, subheads, sidebars, running heads, drop caps, and much more is required.

I'll do my best to define all these terms as I go. Many of you already know quite a bit of this—if you've been using InDesign before. That's another reason why much of explanation will be done in the Appendices, especially A, B, and C. However, for those of you coming from Word, this will be a radical revising of your existing knowledge.

Writing in InDesign gives you layout power

You can use a subhead for clarity, a kicker as a small lead-in style to emphasize a header, lists to recapture the reader's attention with their rhythmic order, a sidebar for peripheral information to entertain the good readers, a table for overly complex lists, and much more. I know you can do some of these things in Word, but not to the typographic level required.

You can see on the page, as you write, how clearly the content is being communicated—or not. It helps you change your content into something that communicates clearly and easily to your readers. It lets you see boring areas and fix them as you write. It provides the control you need to speak to your specific niche—emphasizing unique niche concepts as you go. You can also see when you've gone too far and lapsed into mere busyness and clutter.

Basically writing in a page layout program gives you tools that word processors have a hard time even imagining—which could not be accomplished in that glorified typewriter even if you perceived the need. You will learn to communicate much more clearly.

I focus on you, the reader, and on what I can do to help you. I try to put myself in your shoes and answer your questions. Obviously that is difficult for me as a daily InDesign user for well over a decade (plus a decade of Page-Maker and Quark use before that). I can easily forget my many questions which nearly overwhelmed me as I started out. (Plus InDesign and the Adobe engineering team have provided answers to most of those original questions with updates providing these features to the application itself).

If I miss something, email me so I can add it into the third edition (which I will produce as soon as I find it necessary to do so). I'll do my best to answer you immediately. Use david@radiqx.com, @davidbergsland on Twitter, or radiqxpress on FaceBook.

When you're done, it's ready to print!

If you print on-demand, it can be available to your readers in a couple weeks or less (even today, depending on the suppliers you use). If you produce an ePUB or downloadable PDF, they can have it to read this afternoon. A Kindle book might take another hour or so. All from the same content. In most cases, you can do it at very little cost to you—other than charges to see a proof and minimal distribution costs.

As an example, I released a book over the weekend.

It is a short book called, *Basic Book Typography*. In it I took out the typographic teachings from this books (and others) to make a more directed version for a wider audience. I did this while I was waiting for the general release of CS6 on April 23, 2012. The typography book avoided any of the version-specific areas.

I finished editing and proofing last Thursday. I finished the conversion to Kindle on Friday. I uploaded the printed book to Createspace on Friday. I uploaded the Kindle version Friday. The files were approved by Createspace on Saturday and I approved them.

On Monday I made the changes necessary to convert the formatting to a version that would work better for ePUBs—which are required by Nook and iBooks. By Monday night I was getting Amazon to repair some of the linkages for the printed and Kindle versions.

On Tuesday morning I checked out the new book page in NookBooks at the Barnes & Noble site. It takes a while longer to get things approved for the iBookstore.

Next I'd normally go get a new section set up on my Website, post release notices in my blogs, and start tweeting about the new book. However, today I have gone back to this book you are reading to get it ready for release next week.

This type of rapid release cycle is now normal

It will become second nature to you after you do it few times. It is really fun as well. Now that the book is nearly ready for release, I can begin to ramp up my marketing efforts. I've already written some friends who might be willing to read and review it.

I'll cover the current options of the various suppliers available now at the time of release for this edition. You'll find this information in the body of this book and in Appendix D. For updates, you should follow my blog and twitter feed.

The conversion process for ePUBs is in a great deal of flux at present as the industry stabilizes on standards. There are not even ereaders for many of the new, proposed ideas for standards. As a result, this area will be changing a lot in the near future. But currently, there is no tool that is nearly as good as InDesign CS6 for the entire process.

Where do you start?

My assumption is that this is something you are already doing. You have been writing and you have a body of work you want to publish. If you are not writing, you are not a writer. This is not for people who say "*I really want to write a book about...*" some day in the undefined future.

This is for people who have done a lot of writing. You may have a lot of the book written, or a completed book. You want to get it published so you can share what you have written. This is for the rabbi who is constantly writing teachings, columns, blogs, and the like. This is for the teacher who is constantly writing handouts, lesson plans, and curriculum. This is for the conference speaker who wants to leave his thoughts with the audience. The list goes on.

So, this is the free lunch

Nope! For me—even with my skills, training, and background—it takes work, perseverance, and a willingness to take risks and simply put my stuff out there for the world to see. I'm certain that is different for you. I'd like to hear your stories. This is not simple or even easy, but it is fun. You need to find your routine. I write two to six hours a day, six days a week as my normal practice. When I was teaching full-time, I wrote an hour and a half every morning.

You will need to develop your own routine. But as I mentioned, I am certain you already have done this. You will need to do some additional reading, studying, and practicing as you turn the corner into professionalism. It is not instant success. This would be the type of thing to start in your first year of college or grad school—hoping you will have become a producing writer by the time you graduate.

Reality orientation

But let's face it, kids don't normally have the foresight to do something like this—in most cases. In fact, there is little cause to inflict the kingdom or the world with immature work. By the time you are considering doing something like what we are discussing, you are commonly well on the way to maturity. It takes experience [and character] to produce anything worth sharing. It also takes time to learn how to write, how to communicate clearly, how to convert the vision you've been given, adding the nuts and bolts required to work in reality. This is grown-up work (no matter what your actual physical age is).

But you learn by doing...

Plus, there is a lot to learn: typography, page layout, printing limitations, ebook limitations, and much more. BUT! You can do it simply, line upon line, precept upon precept, as you grow into the publisher you need to be. *How long will it take?* That depends on how seriously you take the assignments. I used to teach this stuff in two intense semesters to people starting from scratch who were not interested in writing. Most just wanted to draw. As a writer this will come more easily.

You can be up and running in a week or so, competent in a matter of months, and producing excellent work within a year.

But you will need to work at it and practice. In this new publishing paradigm, we can publish blog postings, white papers, books, booklets, essays, teachings, Bible studies, prophecies, forecasts, guides, brochures, and more. Of course, this assumes that you are writing on your computer. That is required, of course.

If so, you already have a computer and some software. The question is whether or not it can do what you need it to do. Some upgrades may be necessary, though you'll be surprised at how little is actually required.

Let's start with the computer. The main thing to understand is that ebooks and on-demand publishing are so new that current software is required. This requires a relatively new computer. What I am listing as minimums are based on the assumption that you will be using the Adobe Creative Suite in a fairly recent version. This is especially true for ebooks.

Computer minimums

- **You really need a Mac:** but I won't argue about it. You'll need a 64-bit Intel CPU, a monitor at least 1600 pixels wide, 2 GB or more of RAM (4GB for CS6, though 8 GB is better), Mac OSX.5.8 or better (OSX.6.8 or better for CS6), a 100 GB hard drive or better, and safe backup storage. You'll need a full extended keyboard with a numerical keypad. If you have a laptop with all its limitations, you'll need a wired USB or Bluetooth keyboard with a full set of function keys, editing keys, and a numerical keypad.

- If you already have a PC: you can use it providing it meets the criteria above. Plus you'll need to be able to calibrate your monitor. You'll need Windows XP (service pack 3) or better (Windows 7 is pretty much necessary and Vista is no longer supported for CS6).

- These are all minimums: You'll actually want at least 4 GB RAM to keep working at speed and to avoid crashes. Each book will add at least a large portion of a Gigabyte into storage. So a 300–500 GB hard drive is not out of line at all.

- You'll also need high-speed internet and a PostScript printer for proofing: You will be uploading and downloading PDFs that are often dozens of megabytes in size. Sometimes this needs to be done many times in a day. It often cannot be done at all with a slow internet connection.

  You cannot get along without the PostScript printer. However, your printed proofs can done elsewhere—as they require PostScript. (Warning: HP's PostScript clone is not very good. So, be careful of that.)

Creative Suite 5.5 minimum, but CS6 is better

> You should get the Design Premium software bundle, at least. Actually, you can get by with CS4 or even CS3 for almost everything else, but you need InDesign 7.5 or better (found in CS5.5). You can simply upgrade InDesign.
>
> Only with CS5.5 can you export an ePUB from InDesign that will validate so that iBookstore and NookBooks will accept it. Increasingly, ePUBs are leading the sales of ebooks. The 5.5 upgrade from CS5 is all about easier production for ebooks. CS6 has stabilized things even more and writes better code.

Get the non-profit or academic versions: (if you qualify). A good resource for these discounts and information on whether you qualify or not is found at the AcademicSuperstore Website. They just need a valid school ID or a scan of your non-profit paperwork, certificate, or whatever. Yes, it is worth taking an accredited class to access academic pricing.

Current non-profit/academic pricing (CS6 PRICING IS NOT RELEASED YET):

- ❦ InDesign 7.5: less than $200
- ❦ Creative Suite 5.5 Design Standard: under $200, but no Dreamweaver or Flash
- ❦ Creative Suite 5.5 Design Premium: In the low $400 range or better

C6 has made things much more complicated with the subscription model. But I do not have the details yet. It's a bit of a snarl—you know what the world is like. But you can do it if you persevere.

- ❦ You will need InDesign, Photoshop, and Acrobat Pro: You may need Dreamweaver. Illustrator is handy. But as I mentioned, older versions of this software will do fine for you—except for InDesign.

In this field you must keep up

If you do not have CS5.5, you'll need to get CS6—in fact, because of all the changes coming with HTML5, CSS3, and ePUB3 you'll probably need to keep current regardless. CS6 is quite a bit better, plus there are all the changes tied in with the new subscription model Adobe is foisting off on us. CSNext promises to be a major event also.

Plus, make sure you have a recent computer. I had to buy a new computer to work with CS5. You need to plan on a new computer every couple of years. My old computer with its G4 CPU and 1 GB RAM still runs fine. My wife is using it. But I can no longer use it for my work.

You need your own publishing house

On the practical side, you need to think about how you are going to handle your sales. You should do this very early on in the process. For some reason, one of the more difficult areas for an author to get a hold of is the business aspect of writing. If you only have one book of memoirs you are going to give as gifts to your family, then maybe you do not be concerned about these things.

But even then you need to consider the benefits of having a business. Your computer, smartphone, software, writing supplies, research materials, travel expenses for research, and much more can be legitimate business expenses. The time to find out about these things is not after you collect a lot of money and have a huge tax bill. The time to do it is before the tax bill becomes an issue.

You'll need a business account to collect and disperse money. If you are just starting out, I recommend a PayPal business account. It is free (they collect fees from sales) and it will let you collect income, make payments, and all the other things you need to do as a publisher. Several suppliers prefer PayPal and some require PayPal for royalty payments.

You must start up a business to handle all the legalities. A sole proprietorship is usually free in most states and takes almost no time to set up. You may use a dba for your sole proprietorship, set it up as a subsidiary of your corporate identity, or of a 501(3)c if you are a non-profit.

Picking a good name

Regardless of your personal legal necessities dealing with your local governments, you need a name to use. This is not the Big Idea—that great phrase that everyone will remember forever and always associate positively with you, the author. But if you can do that—wonderful. What you need a name that makes sense to you, which you are proud of, that people recognize as your business.

More than that, you need a name which can be trademarked, which does not infringe on any other publisher, person, or company. The best advice is to use your own name, if possible. After all, as an author you are selling yourself, your ideas, and your communication skills. If you have an unusual name, this is an easy and simple way to go. However, if your last name is John and you write about evening entertainments you might need to be creative.

You need a logo, business card, letterhead, invoice, and all the normal accoutrement of any real business. As you know, InDesign is the preferred tool for designing these things as well. Maybe, like me, publishing is just part of what you do. Regardless, you need some legal method of dealing with the IRS [or whatever tax authority exists in your country], if nothing else.

To be recognized by the industry as a publisher

This is more complex. The best description of this process I have seen is a posting in The Book Designer. Joel has laid it out for us here:

http://www.thebookdesigner.com/2009/12/how-to-create-your-publishing-company/

You will need to buy a minimal block of ISBN#s for a few hundred dollars and then go to Bowker (where you bought the ISBNs) and register your company name at BowkerLink. That's all free, once you have bought your block of numbers. But you will need an official name, a real address, a bank account number, and probably a business phone and email accounts. In fact, you'll probably need a good domain name for your business. How far you go with this is up to you. Just remember the first rule of building your publishing business. Be professional. But there is one final, very important piece of advice [just my opinion, understand].

Do not borrow money to build the business!

What is On-Demand publishing?

The concept is simple. The printer or distributor stores the book on their hard drive (server farm). It is printed or downloaded only after it is ordered and paid for. So, unless there is a demand, it is not printed or downloaded. Much like just-in-time manufacturing, your book is delivered up**on demand**.

- ❦ You upload the digital files: They are stored on the servers of the on-demand printer or ebook distributor.

- ❦ They print the document or enable downloads: after they receive an order. There is no warehousing and no storage issues with cartons of printed books.

- ❦ Your royalty is large: You commonly get 70% to 80% of the money received after printing costs are deducted. For the ebooks, the maximum production costs are 99¢ (commonly nothing). Even with retail books you do much better than you would if you got a contract with a traditional publisher—where a 10% royalty is respectable.

- ❦ You receive your royalties quickly: In most cases, you get the money the next month. Some suppliers delay things up to two months, and a few only pay quarterly. All of those options are far superior to the once a year payments of traditional publishers.

- ❦ You do not have to deal with wholesale orders and returns: One of the worst parts of traditional publishing comes after your book sales taper off. The retailers return unsold inventory to the publisher for a refund, and you take a loss.

- ❦ Sales continue to grow: Unless you are publishing very unique time-limited work, on-demand sales slowly grow and continue to grow. Because there are no warehousing issues, there are no reasons to stop selling your books. In many cases, your sales will continue to build for a decade or more.

With traditional publishing, there is a huge marketing push and shipments to all the stores, and then all the sales happen very quickly. When that initial rush is over—so is your book. There is no shelf room for books that might sell some day.

It's basically a very simple process

The complexity is added by the fact that the individual on-demand printers and suppliers all have different requirements for artwork. The differing formats have unique limitations. The result is that you usually have to layout your book several times to get it in the different formats. In this way, you can have many printers and distributors selling your work at the same time.

You can add new versions as needed: As new distributors appear in the world, it is usually very easy to make up a version for them to sell. As you hear of them, you can try them out. All of these changes were relatively frantic during the early parts of the new millennium. But they have settled down. It has been a while since a new supplier came out who captured any large portion of the market.

Well, that's not really true either. The iPad has only been out two years (I'm writing in the early spring of 2012) and it is already a major player. Its sales are getting close to matching those of the 500# gorilla, Amazon. There is no real competition to the iPad. But then Amazon is not sitting around. The Fire, for a couple hundred bucks, kicked it up a notch. At this point, Fires are selling very well—plus they are the only ebook provider who accepts books with embedded fonts at this point. Nook is becoming a player, and their sales are growing rapidly.

This industry is rapidly growing & changing: The good news is that it is changing in our direction. The era of author-controlled publishing is here—just as designer-controlled printing emerged in the mid-1990s. This trend will continue and grow for those of us who are ready.

30

I only cover the free options

You need to be careful! It is very easy to waste a huge amount of money needlessly. For example, I'm not going to cover the vanity press options. In this old scenario, you (the author) pay for all the production costs. Several of these "subsidy printers" do on-demand printing, but the upfront costs are in the thousands of dollars—so in reality they are merely remnants of the old way of doing things.

My focus is on helping non-profits, ministries, and individuals to get their message to the people they serve and the readers they need.

The new on-demand paradigm is publishing with very few upfront costs. You may choose to pay for marketing and distribution—but they are not required services. Most of you already have good, functional mailing lists of followers—a built-in market for your work. I will talk about some of those options with the services I recommend.

The benefits of the new paradigm

It is very fast!

One of the real changes in the new paradigm is the speed with which you can release books, booklets, posters, and so on. If you have proofed copy that is ready to format, you can get it published and released in a day or so. The limitation is only your formatting speed.

With the techniques and workflow explained in this book, you will be able to write, formatting as you go, ending up with finished formatted documents that are ready to publish and distribute to your readers and supporters in a wide variety of formats: printed and digital.

It is very easy to revise into a new edition

New editions of existing works take a little bit of time because they are usually substantially rewritten. But even a radically revised new edition can be done in a week to a month. This 2ⁿᵈ edition book is a major rewrite of my *Writing In InDesign* book—adding a great deal (nearly 150 pages). But even then I only spent a few months—mostly waiting for the CS6 release. I could have released it two months ago except for that fact.

Typo fixes are commonly done in a day—unless you have purchased a distribution package that requires a new proof. Even in that case you can get a new proof printed, shipped to you, and approved in around a week. If you have bought a distribution plan which charges you for reworking or making changes, release it as a new edition or under a new name.

You can revise all versions of your book in this time frame **IF** you have your application set up well and **IF** you use the formatting techniques I will share in this book. InDesign CS6 has added some capabilities which make this process even more convenient.

You can publish in multiple formats

Some of the new possibilities really rock your traditionalist world the first time you realize what can be done. For example, with many of my latest books I begin with a coil-bound workbook edition. Because of the vagaries in the on-demand world, spiral-bound books cannot be distributed. Therefore they do not require a proof.

Because they cannot be distributed, there is no massive markup for retail. This means I can offer these books at near cost and still make the same royalty as I will with the distributed retail book released later. This means that the workbooks can be sometimes be listed at a lower price than the retail books and come close to the price of mainstream mass market books.

At this point I publish in many formats, depending on the book type.

The different suppliers are listed just before the end of the book—before the appendices.

What skills do you need?

The idea is that InDesign can be learned and you can become comfortable enough with the software so that it becomes an extension of your creativity. For example, as I started this chapter, I hit the shortcut to set my headline. This started the chapter on the next odd page (which is the norm). When I wrote the headline and hit the Return key, InDesign changed to the body copy paragraph style with no indent and a little extra space before paragraph to set this paragraph. Now when I hit Return again, it automatically changes to my normal body copy style with a .4" first line indent. But there was some learning, experience, and setup time required to prepare for this.

I need to talk a bit about skill sets you will want to have to do this well. Obviously, this new publishing paradigm is radically intruding upon areas held by editors, copy-editors, illustrators, typographers, and graphic designers. It has taken over the skill sets of camera operators, separators, and the rest of the prepress world. That's a pretty daunting list of knowledge and skills.

The key is to realize that like all personal growth it comes line by line, precept by precept. There is help available. Plus, a lot of it is covered naturally by the design of InDesign itself. Yet, several of the things you need to know are almost completely unknown outside the industry.

Typography is a good example

This was an assumed baseline skill of any graphic designer in the late 20th century. But that has been eroded by our modern video-centered world. Many modern graphic designers can barely read—if you can imagine that. This is a larger problem than you might think because much of our typographic knowledge comes from all the excellent typography we have been reading since we learned to read.

For us this is no problem

I've never known a writer who didn't love to read. Before 1990, there was nothing printed that was not typeset to a relatively high level. Typewriter output was obviously not typeset, but word processor output had not reached the general public for reading materials like it has now. The Web with its poor font choices and horrible typography was not a factor until the late '90s. The result is that you subconsciously recognize excellence in typographic design (unless you're under 30).

These lines will be further blurred as HTML5 and CSS3 come online. Right now, these things are limited to people who keep upgrading to current equipment. But it is likely that these standards will be the norm soon.

But some things will not change. Word processors will still produce obviously non-professional typography and layouts. Good typography on the Web will become possible, but it will still be rare. The major change will probably be in the better ereaders, like the new iPad with Retina Display. Maybe the Fire will get there, and who knows about the Nook?

At present, ereaders are contributing to the dulling of the typographic sense of our culture. But excellent typography contributes so much to readability and trustworthiness that adding this capability to ereaders will hopefully happen fairly soon. Our hope is in the common use of ePUB3. InDesign C6 moves us in that direction. The iPad and Kindle Fire both support at least portions of ePUB3. Apple's release of iBooks 2 is an excellent step up as the process to ePUB3 becomes more prevalent.

This is good because your readers expect excellent typography and will consider your output untrustworthy (subconsciously, at least) if you do not provide them with it. All of us who read have been trained by the fact we've seen nothing that is not professionally typeset until the last decade—except for bureaucratic stuff.

The good news is that InDesign has relatively good typography built in—with few modifications needed. I'll cover some of those capabilities in a bit. But before I get into that you need to learn some terminology.

34

What is typography?

Here are some dictionary definitions. In truth, they are helpful only to show us what typography is not. You will quickly discover that outside of our industry, publishing, almost no one really knows what type is. Even graphic designers rarely know what the art of setting type is all about.

Dictionaries talk about process not purpose

Webster's: The craft of composing type and printing from it; art and technique of printing with movable type.

Random House: the art or process of printing with type; the work of setting and arranging types and of printing from them; the general character or appearance of printed matter

Cambridge: the style, size and arrangement of the letters in a piece of printing

Wikipedia: art of arranging letters on a page to be printed, usually for a combination of aesthetic and functional goals

Wikipedia does the best job of word definition here.

What we are about as typographers is directing reader responses with our craft. To reword things, I would call the art of using letters calligraphy—the craft of using letters is typography. My focus here is the craft of typesetting on a professional level—and its relationship to the number one virtue of book design: readability.

What's unusual is that none of the dictionaries really get it. First of all, they are all tied to printing. Online typography is not considered. Secondly, they describe the physical act, but typography is only secondarily concerned with the physical act of arranging letters on paper for printing.

Obviously physical considerations and traditional shapes play a huge role in font design. But typography goes far beyond the actual shapes of the letters, paragraphs, columns, and pages into the cultural and subjective responses of individual readers. Our concern must be presenting the content easily to be effortlessly comprehended. It must be reader-centered or it is a fine art exercise.

Not surprisingly, one of the best quotes is from Hermann Zapf, one of the 20th century's outstanding type designers

This is the purpose of typography: *The arrangement of design elements within a given structure should allow the reader to easily focus on the message, without slowing down the speed of his reading.*

My definition is simple:
Typography is the art of communicating clearly and easily with type

Typography is built with fonts. There are well over a hundred thousand fonts available now. Most of them are merely decorative and of little use in book design. What you need to know is relatively simple.

Picking fonts

Now that we have briefly discussed what typography is, it is time to look at type styles and the actual design of the fonts you use. In an attempt to get a handle on the different styles, many different classification systems have arisen. Most of these are of mere historical interest though, in truth, many of you will find these distinctions increasingly important as you grow further as a digital publisher.

One of the things you will discover early on is that traditional typographers really ought to get a life. I can say that because *I are one*. Even from the inside, I find most typographic wranglings to be far beyond nitpicking and well into anal and/or compulsive. Some of the lists and forums I have been on spend months wrangling over insignificant details that will never be noticed by the reader.

My goal in this book is to give you a quick handle on what you have available in our tools of choice: InDesign and a Mac (it's more difficult on a PC). Plus, I want you to end up with the beginnings of a procedure to pick fonts on purpose to help with communication. Font choice is one of the prime determinants of your personal publishing style.

In the broad spectrum of available fonts, there are four general classifications: serif, sans serif, handwriting, and decorative. It would probably be a bit better to split handwriting into script and text; but these four have served well over the years. I will only be covering fonts that work well for book design. So, for our purposes in this book, there are two classifications: serif and sans-serif

Font design books will give you many more classes. For example, they'll break serif into three to nine subcategories; the same with sans serif. These breakdowns are mainly historical. The functional differences between fonts designed for book design are minimal. We'll leave the more complete categorizing to those who care (you can see a more complete synopsis with a reader's focus in Appendix A).

 Historical appropriateness is usually only important to historians: If it makes you happy, do it. However, readers are looking for comfort and ease while reading. Because design is often best when spontaneous rather than structured, this book avoids the legalistic approach as much as possible while still trying to make your choices clear. After all, they are **your** choices.

Bringing it into perspective

Out of the tens of thousands of typefaces available now through Websites like MyFonts, Fonts.com, and many more, only 1,000 or so are used all the time by many people. Out of those, there are a couple hundred fonts or so used by traditional book designers. Plus, there are probably thousands of multiple-derivative, differently named copies of these popular fonts. So it isn't as scary as it sounds—quite.

First, we must define a serif.

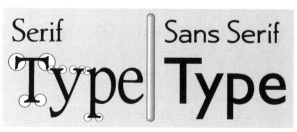

A serif is a flare, bump, line, or foot added to the beginning or end of a stroke in a letter. Originally, they were the finishing touches added to the end of strokes produced

by pens in the hands of scribes. They have become very stylized over the centuries. There are hundreds of different serif stylings, but do you know their importance?

They seem totally insignificant, but they certainly are not. They strongly influence how we react to type. In fact, on a subconscious level, serifs can be one of the most powerful influences on the reader's reaction to your writing.

Reading has many habitual associations. The type read during an event or about an occasion takes on the flavor of those events. Many of these typographic reactions are very personal. For example, you may find that your favorite script font happens to be the font on the menu the night you became engaged. Your favorite serif probably comes from that book you read as a teenager which changed your life. Your favorite sans serif probably comes from marketing pieces about a great, well-loved product you bought.

"Reading has many habitual associations."

In our homogeneous, franchised, marketing society, most of us see the same things every day. The result of all of this is that virtually every person in the United States has similar reactions to various type styles. However, there are large differences between the habitual viewers of CBS and Disney when compared to the habitual viewers of Hallmark and the History Channel. The fonts used help identify these differences. The fonts used to promote Ford pickups are very different from those used for Lexus and Cadillac touring sedans.

The dominance of serif

Almost every good book you have ever read was set in serif type. Virtually every textbook was also. This one is set in a font I designed called Contenu Book. Virtually all body copy before the 1950s was serif. Because of these things, serif typefaces are perceived as warm, friendly, nostalgic, and easy to read. Some of the more modern serif fonts have that edge which was in style in the 1990s, but most are beautiful, quiet, and comfortable. Designers began to use these connections consciously during the 1950s and 1960s. The marketing research boom in the 1970s simply reinforced this trend.

As a result, serif faces are used almost exclusively: in ads and marketing pieces promoting quality, stability, good value, integrity, and warmth. They are also used to reinforce family values, patriotism, and the emotional content of character traits considered positive by our culture. They are the main choice for the body copy of books—especially fiction.

Sans serif is relatively new

Even though sans serif faces (without a serif) have been around since at least the early nineteenth century and were popular around the start of the 20th century, they were never mainstream until the 1950s. Up until the 1950s, sans serif faces were used extensively only by groups like the modernist, Bauhaus movement in Germany during the 1930s, where geometric type was promoted as modern. Futura, Bauhaus, and Kabel are classic examples of this style. Most people saw them as plain and unadorned. Often they were aggressively modern.

There was quite a bit of large extra-bold sans serif used in the wood typefaces cut for the Victorian explosion of advertising. But those connotations again had little to do with readable copy. Hucksters shouting at us like they did in those broadsides with that huge type usually do not bring pleasant memories except perhaps nostalgia.

In the late 1950s, Helvetica became extremely popular. It was designed by Max Miedinger in 1957, though the name was not chosen until 1960 (it simply means Swiss as Max was Swiss). It was quickly accepted as a new standard type style by many in the business, scientific, and advertising communities. Sans serif faces, in general, became de rigeur for scientific and business publishing.

Most of the reading associations of sans serif type are anything but warm and friendly. The only exception would be within the youth cultures like extreme jocks who, in cultivating rebellion and adrenaline rushes, have made sans serif their "normal" type classification. But that is all changing. In fact, more recently, humanist sans serif faces have become quite popular. Books, however, are rarely in sans serif—except non-fiction.

These usage normals were almost unanimous until very recently as desktop publishing brought in designers with no design education. So the reactions are predictable enough to be very useful.

- ❦ Sans serif faces are clean and modern.

- ❦ Serif faces, in general, are more elegant and beautiful.

As mentioned, these distinctions are being greatly muddied by new trends toward very readable sans serif fonts designed for body copy. For my headers and sidebar copy, the sans serif fonts I am using are Buddy—a companion sans I designed to go with Contenu.

The Times/Helvetica problem

One of the more interesting phenomena of digital publishing is the use of Times and Helvetica. Although these are fairly well-designed typefaces, their excessive usage resulting from their specification as the default fonts in so many nonprofessional applications and operating systems has completely changed their perception in the mind of the typical reader.

Most professional typographers avoid these two fonts families like the plague. As a result, the only place people see them is in output by people who are untrained in publishing and simply use the software defaults—think schools, bureaucracies, the IRS, collection agencies, and the like. Because of this uncaring usage, Times, Times New Roman, Helvetica, and Arial have been virtually ruined for serious use by designers. They bring up too many bad associations.

Typically, you should pick a serif for body copy & a sans serif for heads and subheads.

However, this is simply the norm. You need to pick font combinations which appeal to the readers of your book within the limited niche of that book. As mentioned earlier, these choices are fairly limited. I will give you some choices as we go. You will definitely find your own as you develop as a publisher. Time spent at MyFonts.com will be great fun for you and a wonderful help to your font style education!

Our needs are specific

As book designers, we need fonts which are easy and comfortable to read in large quantity—without strong personality. Our font choices cannot get in the way of the content. If the reader notices the fonts used, that fact takes away from our writing. After all, we are writers. In addition, we need something else—variety for emphasis. What we need, to do what we do, are font families. These are sets of fonts with different styles and weights.

The typical font family

Ah ha! You think you know this one, right? Well, maybe. In the word processor world, especially on PCs, fonts come in regular, italic, bold, and bold italic. But you will discover that this is a modern word processor limitation. It is true that there are many four-font families. However, there are also many 2-font, 3-font, 5-font, 6-font, and 8-font families. There are even some 30+ font families.

Contenu Book
Contenu Book Italic
Contenu Medium
Contenu Italic
Contenu Book Bold
Contenu Book Bold Italic
Contenu Black
Contenu Black Italic

The body copy family I am using for the printed version of this book is Contenu (one of my most recent designs). It comes in eight fonts, as you just saw. But font families can be much larger than this. Adobe Jenson Pro comes with 32 fonts. Helvetica and Helvetica Neue (a recently updated version) have a total of nearly 80 fonts in the two families. The fonts that are installed with the Creative Suite that are designed for reading and books commonly have six fonts. This is true of Caslon, Garamond, and Minion. But Chapparal has eight and Myriad has ten.

What you will find, is that the system fonts which come with your operating system, and fonts which were installed with Office usually only have four.

As writers and book designers, we need a minimum of three: regular, italic, and bold. Italic is necessary for periodical names and emphasis. Bold is used for proper names and headers, As you saw at the start of this paragraph I used a sans serif through the colon to emphasize an important point. But regardless of which font family you choose it must satisfy several basic requirements of book design.

What do you need in a font family to make it exceptional for designing books?

That is what we need to cover here. Good font families for book design are relatively rare. I'm prejudiced toward my designs (after all I designed them to meet my needs), but you need to be aware of which fonts might work for you and why. These fonts are a careful choice. Let's start with some basic criteria for book design fonts.

- ❦ Readability: Body copy set with the fonts you choose must be exceptionally easy and comfortable to read. Reading comfort is imperative to help the reader enjoy your writing.

- ❦ Extremely smooth type color: Type set with the font you choose must have excellent letterspacing and produce a smooth even texture when the type is set in paragraphs. That smooth, medium gray type color generated by the body copy is the background that you must have to easily contrast the headers—to make heads & subheads pop off the page, as it were.

* Legibility: The fonts chosen need to be quickly absorbed when being used for headlines, subheads, captions, pull quotes, and the like. This is not the place for fancy scripts, or wild decorative typefaces. You need to be sure your readers can quickly comprehend your fonts.

* Oldstyle figures: It would probably help if I called them what they are: lowercase numbers. 1234567890 They are essential for good type color—where lining figures [1234567890] are shouting just like all caps shout in an email.

* Variety of weights: You will really need regular & bold weights, but light & black weights will help immensely.

* True small caps: Small caps are capital letters that are the same size as the x-height but the same weight as regular capitals. MOST FONTS USE CAPS REDUCED IN SIZE FOR SMALL CAPS AND THEY LOOK VERY LIGHT & THIN. HERE ARE TRUE SMALL CAPS. You should also choose a font which has small cap figures like 1234567890 TO GO WITH THE SMALL CAP TYPE.

Studying Studying

Here's a comparison of oblique & italic in Garamond

* True, but readable, italics: Obliques *[slanted letters]* simply look wrong to an educated reader. *Many italics are closer to a script with all of the attendant readability issues.*

I could add more to this list, but that should be enough for now. In the 1980s and 1990s, fonts which could supply these things were not common. What I saw in the textbooks perpetrated on my students angered me. Most of the textbooks I was given to use were useful for little other than readily available examples of terrible typography. My students all complained how hard they were to read.

So, I made student reading comfort the primary focus of my textbook designs. I started designing fonts to help me in that quest. I started hearing student comments like: "I started reading my assignment for the first week and read five chapters before I noticed how far I had read." Actually, I've only heard that particular comment once—but it was (and is) really gratifying... It's one of my motivations to write.

Readability

I've talked about this already, but you must remember the importance of this characteristic of book design typography. Here's a little graphic to show you some of the things that influence how easily you can read a font.

Readability comparisons

	Helvetica	Gill Sans	Caslon	Jenson	Bodoni	Brinar
Writing Axis	Op	Op	Op	Op	Op	Op
	No axis	No axis	Varied Axes	Humanist	Modern	Humanist
Aperture	ace	ace	ace	ace	ace	ace
	Closed	Mostly Open	Mostly Open	Open	Closed	Mostly Open
Modulation	RN	RN	RN	RN	RN	RN
	No	No	Yes	Yes	Excessive	Yes
Slanted crossbars	Ae	Ae	Ae	Ae	Ae	Ae
	No	No	No	Yes on e	No	Yes
Double story	ag	ag	ag	ag	ag	ag
	a only	a&g	a&g	a&g	a&g	a&g
Circle/Oval	OG	OG	OG	OG	OG	OG
	Slight Oval	Circle	Barely Oval	Slight Oval	Oval	Slight Oval
Calligraphic	rag	rag	rag	rag	rag	rag
	No	No	No	Yes	No	Vaguely

I've seen my wife throw novels away because they were too hard to read. Difficult to read books have become commonplace, One of the attractions of ebooks is the ability to change the type to make it more comfortable to read (although their true typographic control is minimal).

Everyone has too much to read. *If you give them any excuse, they will quit reading your work and go on to the next piece in their long list of things they have to read.*

If you ever took one of my classes, you know how much I harp on readability—especially the importance of aperture and other factors concerning readability. There are many technical font design issues that control this.

It's not important that you understand the seven characteristics on the previous page at this point: What matters is that you see that Jenson, Brinar, and Caslon (in that order) are the most readable out those six font choices.

But before I can go further, I need to define some terms. There are some basic terms used to describe type that you must understand. This is mainly true because I cannot talk about type without using these terms.

 I'm trying to keep this as brief as possible: Typography is really a lifetime study, but you need to get into the basics quite quickly for our purposes in this book. My goal is to show you enough to get you started. In Appendix A I have placed some basic differences between word processing and typesetting (like never double-space). You might check that out to make sure we're on the same page.

Appendix A is actually required reading, but some of you may already know the information (though I doubt that this is true for many of you).

The basic parts of type

Again, this goes further than you need to go. However, you can see on the next page how the point size of the type relates to the ascender, cap height, x-height, baseline, and descender. More importantly, you get a glimpse of things that are important in the world of typography.

These two illustrations are from my font design books, *Practical Font Design: Third Edition*, and *Fontographer: Practical font Design for Graphic Designers* which are available in print at Lulu (for better printing), Amazon, FontLab & B&N and as ebooks at iBookstore, NookBooks, Scribd, and Kindle. For an introduction to typography in publishing read Appendices A & B.

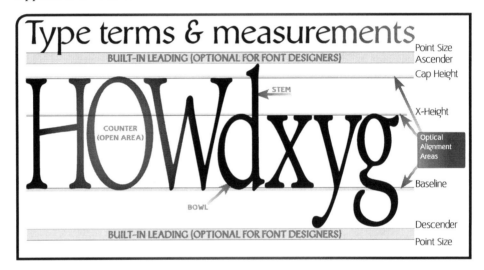

Other good books on typography

- *InDesign Type* by Nigel French: This is the best basic book I have seen on setting up type in InDesign

- *The Elements of Typographic Style* by Robert Bringhurst: This is the industry classic. It's pretty heavy-duty but an excellent read.

- *Stop Stealing Sheep* by Erik Speikermann: The title comes from an old quote by Frederic Goudy who said that anyone who would letterspace lowercase would steal sheep. It's a very entertaining yet highly informative read.

Not surprisingly, because book designers are typographers, there are many books on the subject. The sad thing is that most of them are very dry, ridiculously technical, and full of strong opinions stated as facts (been guilty of that m'self). As you grow in skill as book designer, you'll probably read several of them.

Check out your local library.

What fonts should you use?

One of the goals of this book is to teach you good stewardship. You can spend a lot of money on fonts. The good news is that the Creative Suite comes with some excellent fonts for book design. Included are four good fonts for body copy.

- ❦ Adobe Caslon Pro—6 weights
- ❦ Adobe Garamond Pro—4 weights
- ❦ Chaparral Pro—4 weights
- ❦ Minion Pro—6 weights

The Mac OSX software gives you several more—including those used on the iPad (we talk about what's available on the iPad in Appendix E about ePUB design). They are quite pretty.

- ❦ Baskerville—6 weights
- ❦ Cochin—4 weights
- ❦ Hoefler Text—4 weights
- ❦ Optima—5 weights

Many of you will also have others installed by various hardware and software you have purchased over the years.

What you are looking for is a professional quality serif font face. Check Font Book on the Mac. It is a free piece of software that comes with OSX to install and view the fonts you have installed on your computer. You may be surprised at some of the gems. A couple you probably have are

- ❦ Adobe Jenson Pro—4 weights
- ❦ Palatino—4 weights

Any of these font families will work for you as you get into the industry and learn your craft. Eventually you will probably buy something special for your taste and style—but it certainly not necessary. If you like the fonts I am using in this book, email me and ask. I will sell you the 12 Fonts used: Contenu Book (4), Contenu (4), and Buddy (4) for $50. List price is $25 each for the twelve fonts and that's below average. Fifty dollars for twelve OpenType Pro fonts is probably a ridiculously cheap offer, but I want you to get a good start on your publishing efforts.

Typography is probably the major skill set you will be adding as you learn to publish your own books. As mentioned, InDesign naturally tends to produce good typography—unlike Word. In Word it is very difficult to do excellent typography. In fact, many of the things you need are impossible in Word.

I will mention these things as I remember them, but don't hold me to a complete list. I do not use Word or word processors unless forced to do so. Their documents were a horror when I received them as raw copy when I was working full-time as a graphic designer. In fact, I developed a relatively extensive list of steps to completely strip out word processor formatting to enable good typography to be added within InDesign. I cannot state it too forcefully.

Word processors cannot do what we need to do as book designers!

Page layout basics
Setting up your book to be read

One of the more daunting aspects of book design for the inexperienced is page layout. Most people have Word experience and as I have said countless times already—Word cannot do professional page layout. In fact, it is worse than that because Word's feeble attempts give you bad habits and poor expectations—which must be corrected.

Many settings have to be covered for every document. Many of these are set up as you go through the Preferences in InDesign. You might want to consider setting your measuring system to inches or millimeters, for example. You should work in whatever measurement system works best for you. Every application has important decisions to be made in Preferences. To repeat, the point is to set up your applications so they work best for you.

Let's put it together

By now we should have most of the pieces. Make sure you have the graphics, if possible. If you do not know what is required for professional work, please read Appendix C on graphic production to find out. If you are like me, some of the graphics are written or designed on the spot to fill in a blank page portion. But let's go through an assembling and formatting session. Of course we start with file management.

Before you start your document

Again, this is just my procedure. Feel free to use or discard as you find necessary to fit your personal workflow. However, many of these things are there to solve problems I have had with previous books.

  - ❧ Make a book folder: You'll need a folder to hold all the pieces. This is critical. You will be taking these pieces and modifying them as you reformat for the different versions. It is crucial to have all your pieces in one place so you can keep track of them. You should make this folder first or as you open your new document to get started.

☙ Make a links folder: You'll need this sooner or later so you might as well start right. This will hold all the graphics you actually use in the document. Make sure your links are set up as you see below, in your preferences.

All your graphics will be linked. You cannot paste in graphics. They must be imported (either placed or dragged in from the links folder).

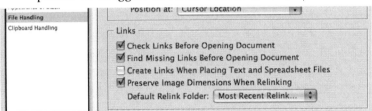

☙ Make an originals folder: Because I will be making so many InDesign PDFs, I always need a folder to hold the original full-color InDesign files and the original high-resolution color Photoshop files. These are important to use when you convert your print version to use in ebooks. Color costs a lot in print, but it is free in many ebooks (depending on the ereader used).

 If you have an original word doc: I would put it in the originals folder—especially if you have more than one. It is also a good time to check that your preferences for file handling are set to NOT create a link when placing text or spreadsheets (You can see I have it unchecked in the capture above). Very quickly you will have edited your book to the place where updating a link to the Word doc eliminates all your laboriously made changes.

Keeping track of your graphics

As you go through all the different versions you will be making for your book, there will be differing requirements for your graphics. Your printed versions require high resolution, black and white, grayscale, or full-color CMYK images that are either vector or 300 dpi or better. Your downloadable PDFs can handle full-color CMYK with no cost to you. Your ePUBs require better resolution color RGB JPEGs. Even Kindle uses color images for those people using their Mac, PC, iPad, or Fire to read your Kindle ebook—but they must be Web-compatible (72 dpi RGB).

Full-size color graphics: You will need a place to store the full-resolution, full-color versions of your graphics. Remember, the printed versions will probably have black & white interior pages and grayscale images of the maps, photos, and so forth. I always make a large color version of my graphics and save it in the Originals folder of my new book. This gives me what I need for the various versions. For example, the Scribd PDF can take full color RGB versions of the graphics at high resolution. The ePUB needs color versions (though at a lower resolution). You need someplace to keep those color graphics. Of course, you could just call it [BookName] Color Graphics—maybe that's too obvious ;-)

From my color art I then save grayscale versions for print to exact size, which I then save in my links folder for placing: I assume you are beginning to see the problem. There are so many versions that you must establish a clear, simple folder structure to hold them all. If not, you will quickly lose track of what you are doing and what goes where.

> ❦ Make a place or find the place on your backup hard drive to back up the folder: drag your new folder into the backup location to make a copy of it. You must backup your work consistently and often. I have had a hard drive die with an unbacked-up book on it, just before the deadline of the publisher. That's a nightmare, believe me. Remember, in reality it is always *when* your hard drive fails, never *if* it does so. Sooner or later they all fail.

A slight aside for management

Here is a screen capture of the setup of my hard drive when I originally wrote this book in 2011. My publishing company is Radiqx Press. So I have a RadiqxPress folder. In the left favorites bar of my hard drive window, just below

RadiqxPress, you can see TMRadiqxPress. That is the identical folder on my external hard drive currently called Time
Machine (though I do not use Apple's automatic backup
software because it interferes with my work). It is quicker
and easier to do it manually. I can drag'n'drop all the work
I do today into the backup folder very easily. You can see
all the recent books or folders holding recent series in the
Radiqx Lulu folder. I find I fill up my comfortable storage
in about three months. At that point I need more subfolders
to be able to find things quickly.

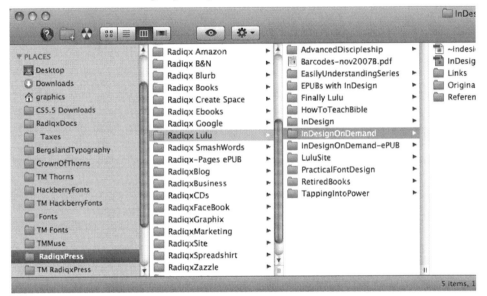

Within my publishing folder I have set up the following folders:
Obviously, this is just my procedure, but I'll give you
the reasons so you'll have a good idea how to begin setting
up your file management.

- 🍎 Radiqx Lulu: for the original book and their
  versions, as I always start there. This is
  where I sell the most downloadable PDFs.

- 🍎 Radiqx Createspace: for their version. I package
  the Lulu book into a folder here. Then I
  usually change the size of the book and
  make the new version to sell on Amazon.
  This sells most of my printed books.

- ❦ Radiqx Scribd: Their version of the PDF uses color graphics and colored styles. This is one of the best places I have found to spread the news.

- ❦ Radiqx ePUBs: For Lulu, this is a recent addition as the iPad has become one of my major sellers. The ePUB requires a radical reformatting (which is discussed in Appendix E).

- ❦ Radiqx Amazon: for the Kindle version. This is the third best seller after printed books and downloadable PDFs.

- ❦ Radiqx Smashwords: for their version if I can. Their requirement of a Word file and the 5 MB limit mean that many of my books won't work here.

- ❦ Radiqx Zazzle: for giftware and marketing pieces

- ❦ Radiqx B&N: for the PubIt version. I don't use this any more because PubIt can use the same ePUB I give to Lulu for the iBooks version.

- ❦ Radiqx Blurb: for the Blurb version (This is also dropped at this point because I am not using Blurb.) This is a good resource for photo books and high-quality coffee table books..

- ❦ Plus: several more as you can see

It does not matter what you call them, but you will need folders like these and more for any other suppliers you use. As you can see, within the Lulu Folder I have made an InDesignOnDemand folder (this was captured before I wrote the first *Writing in InDesign*). Inside of that I have the folders I have already mentioned—plus a Reference pieces folder to hold my research and references that are not on the Web. This was the book I was working on when I made the screen capture.

I am certainly not telling you to do it like I do.

But you will find a similar setup essential eventually—hopefully not too late after you've lost some crucial piece of your work [been there—done that—many times].

My backup hard drive has exactly the same folder structure. I keep two windows open on the desktop with the Computer hard drive on top and the backup hard drive on the bottom. Throughout the day [and certainly before I shut down at the end of the day] I drag all the folders I worked on today into their duplicate on the backup hard drive. It asks if I want to replace the older one and I agree that would be a good idea—fast, easy, and easy to remember once it becomes a habit. This is an essential practice.

As mentioned, I learned to be careful when I lost a hard drive a month before the deadline while writing one of my early textbooks. With it I lost over a third of the book and all the graphics upon which I had just spent the previous two months. (That's such a bad memory—I just backed up the folder again ;-) Remember, the warnings from the computer geeks about backing up your data are never written, "**IF** you lose a hard drive". They write (and I reaffirm) "**WHEN** you lose your hard drive do you have a backup copy?" You will have hard drives die.

You must have your books backed up

There will come a day when you lose it all and must rebuild from your backup. It should be off site also. The latest thing is the cloud, but that takes a monthly charge in many cases. Make your plans now. A fire or flood could wipe you out.

Starting at the beginning: Document Setup...

This is the dialog box that opens when you choose New from the file menu or type Command+N. Many of the choices found in this dialog box are based on your experience. I'll use my choices. The first choice is that I always start with print chosen as my intent.

There are many reasons for this. But I can state it simply as I start out. Print has the high quality abilities necessary to make a printed book. Web and ebook design are much more restricted. It is easy to lower the quality to ebook standards. It is impossible to raise many things like graphic quality from ebook up to print standards.

A new standard: color

As mentioned, I always start with high resolution, full color graphics. You need that beginning point for graphics to cover all the versions you will be making. Except for the greyscale Kindles and Nooks, all of our ebooks will be in color. Even there, Kindle Fire & apps on other machines support color. For years printing and color were mutually exclusive when publishing books because printing in color is normally too expensive to be good stewardship.

 In this new publishing world, all documents will be done in print and in color: This is due to the wide variety of formats and media you will be using. BUT, you can severely damage your relationship with your readers if they think you are wasting money on color printing. Color is for the monitor. Print comes first because of the high quality and resolutions required. Designing at that level allows use in the lower levels. Printing in color is commonly a simple squandering of resources and can offend your readers. So you will need to save greyscale versions of the graphics for your print files.

Some of the things are obvious

In this book we are concerned about book publishing so several of the options are predetermined. Let's go through these choices quickly:

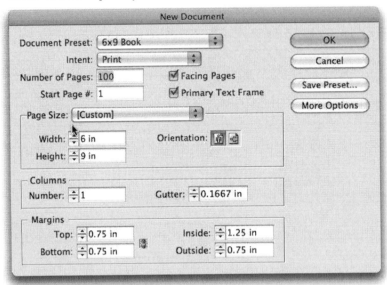

🐛 Facing pages: Yes, we are doing multiple page documents. This gives us a workspace that mimics a book.

Here's a major change for CS6!

🐛 Master text frame (CS5.5): No. It doesn't do what you want it to do. We never use it here. A procedure for 5.5 is a bit complex.

🐛 Primary Text Frame (CS6): It is essential to check this to enable easy page size and margin conversions.

This is the first portion we see that really impacts us in the massive conversion to more the more fluid layouts necessary for on-demand books and especially ebooks. It actually adds pages as you write! It's a wholly new capability!

🐛 Intent: Print. Always. There are three choices: Print, Web, Digital Publishing. Only print uses 300 dpi full color images and supports vector images. Only the Print Intent and PDFs can handle the fonts and styles we need to do excellent typography.

Even when ePUB3 comes fully online, I will still always start with Print. It is easily converted to Digital publishing or Web. It is usually impossible to convert the other way from ebook to print.

🐭 Number of pages: This can range from 12 to 100 pages to start. You'll be adding more later. You need 24 pages minimum to publish. It should be divisible by 4 to facilitate bindery operations on the printed book. As you can see, I start with 100 pages in 5.5. **Change:** In CS6, I start with a single (1) page and Facing pages plus Primary Text Frame checked. It can add pages automatically.

🐭 Save Preset: You'll probably end up saving several document presets at various sizes. Just click this button and name your setting. As you can see, this is the Preset for my 6x9 Book starting point.

If you are going to have images which touch the edge of the paper, you need to click the More Options button. Here you will find the **bleed** (see next page) settings. To make an image go to the edge of the paper you must print it an eighth inch beyond the trimmed edge to cover unavoidable variances in cut locations when trimming the books after they are printed. I'll talk about this more in a couple of pages.

Document size [page size]

In traditional publishing, there were many more options. This is one reason why traditional publishing costs so much more. Virtually all traditional printing is custom work—to meet the needs of the individual designer & various paper and press sizes. We give up some of that freedom to control costs as we move into on-demand printing.

For the on-demand print publisher, many costs are controlled by limiting the options. Plus, the equipment itself has limitations in the type of paper used and paper sizes available. As a result, document size is a given with few options. Here the concern is distribution. The fact that we can publish free is wonderful, but we must live with some restrictions. You need to make wise choices.

Amazon accepts 13 standard page sizes in early-2012

Size	Lulu	Amazon	B&W	Color
5 x 8 inches		√	√	
5.06 x 7.81 inches		√	√	
5.25 x 8 inches		√	√	
5.5 x 8.5 inches		√	√	√
6 x 9 inches (trade)	√	√	√	√
6.14 x 9.21 inches (royal)	√	√	√	√
6.69 x 9.61 inches		√	√	
7 x 10 inches		√	√	√
7.44 x 9.69 inches (Crown)	√	√	√	
7.5 x 9.25 inches		√	√	
8 x 10 inches		√	√	
8.5 x 8.5 inches	√	√		√
8.5 x 11 inches (letter)	√	√	√	√

There are only certain sizes acceptable to Amazon (and the other retailers offered by our on-demand print suppliers). You must make at least one version of your book in a size that can be distributed through Amazon (unless you have no intention of selling any printed copies). They are the 500# gorilla at this point, and by far the best at marketing and selling self-published, on-demand printed books. The other options are all expensive and should be used only if you have a clear, demonstrated audience. The standard trade paperback (as close to normal as you can get) is 6×9.

🐚 In general: I would always release a 6×9 version (or royal or crown). They fit bookshelves best—if nothing else. There are quite a few more sizes that cannot or will not be distributed by Lulu and Createspace, like Lulu's choices starting with the pocket book at 4.25×6.875 up to the 12×12 premium casewrap. Createspace also provides for custom sizes with no distribution. The free options are limited. If you need a special size, you will need to become "official", buy your own ISBN#s, and use a different printer.

Remember, it only costs a proof to release another version (if that)

Some of Lulu's sizes work well with comb binding and saddle-stitching. These cannot be distributed through Amazon, but they can work really well to add workbook varieties to the mix, for example. They might not have the larger distribution, but they can be real handy to offer as low price releases on your media table at seminars.

Come along with me through the reasoning behind book sizing

Today I had a discussion with a friend of mine about some decisions he is making about his new book—which happens to be a new Bible translation. It will help you to see the types of considerations necessary to determine page size and layout for your project. I'll cover the basic requirements for bleeds, margins, columns, master pages, and so on after this little step by step examination of the decision process.

We start with the inspiration

My friend asked:

"I am using a book by Malcolm Gladwell for a sample. Its cover is 5 and 7/16 wide, but it is 8 and 7/32 tall. It's using your guidelines for the top to bottom, but the inside pages are 5 and 3/8 in wide. I really like the heft and feel of the book,

but wonder if they only trimmed the outside edge and left the inside folded and uncut, then glued. If this is possible, can I have it done this way? say by CreateSpace? And since the Bible is such a mass market item, I will probably have many set ups, including an audio. Will this affect how the book is handled?"

There are many questions here. Let's take a look at them to come to some conclusions. This is a very practical process, but it does take some careful thought and wise decisions. This is a normal procedure as you start any book. I don't seem to do this any more, but that is only because I have made my decisions, based on experience, over a period of several decades.

The bindery issues

Modern books, unless you have a large printing budget, are glued together with square spines. The term for this is perfect bound. If you can see the fold on the inside bound edges of a leather-bound book, it was probably smyth-sewn. This hand sewing technique has gone the way of almost all good handcrafting—very rare. In most cases, it is far too expensive to be considered. Plus, the people who formerly sewed these books are now gone.

At this point large sheets of paper containing many pages, called signatures, are folded, stacked, and then trimmed on all four sides to be glued and covered. The cover includes the front cover, back cover, and spine. It is printed oversize with the printed portion extended an eighth inch beyond the actual final size of the book (this is called a bleed) on all four sides. The printed cover is wrapped around the book covering the glued spine edge of the assembled book. The oversized areas are trimmed off with the same knife strokes used to cut the interior pages of the book. I realize this implies that an interior bleed would be used, but in practice it rarely is. My guess is gluing problems with ink on the paper make spine-edge bleeds difficult. Regardless, inked areas at the spigne stop at the trim size. Plus, I would always ask before I did it, to get permission.

Now I have to ask several more questions

Does the Gladwell book bleed? I'll cover that process after this description is completed. For now all you need to know is that bleed means the ink touches the edges of the paper. I'll assume it does not. It rarely does for books, and it's hard to find a compelling reason to use a bleed.

Does it have sidebars? I would doubt it because of the narrow width. With minimal margins of a half inch (and those are very small), a 5⅜" page only has room for a 4⅜" text area. With a 3¾" main column and a quarter inch gutter this makes for a ⅜" wide sidebar area. With the normal 10/12 body copy, you'll need to find a slightly condensed font to handle even a 3¾" column while maintaining the readable standard of 9-12 words per line.

There are several other considerations which I haven't mentioned which are common attributes of a book like a Bible. It could have a list of cross-references for nearly every verse. It could have commentaries in a separate area at the bottom of the page. It will have footnotes (and translators notes). But that is outside our discussion here.

Next I examine comparable books

For my friend, I went through a quick analysis of my favorite bibles. I do not have any idea, at this point, about how he sees his bible; but an examination of my preferences gives him a place to begin his decision making process.

My favorite bible (though it is too worn for study use) is the old Harper Study Bible using the Revised Standard Version [RSV] (no longer in print). It is single column (which makes for excellent readability). It uses an interior margin of .75", a column width of 3.65" (22 picas), then a tenth inch (half pica) gutter on each side of a half-point vertical rule with an exterior sidebar of a half inch for cross references. It has a ⅜" exterior margin. The page size is 5⅜" wide by a skosh under 8½" tall.

My current study bible is an NASB Inductive which I love for the wide margins on the outside for notes. It uses a half inch interior margin with a four and a half pica (¾") sidebar for cross references. Then comes the vertical rule with a half pica gutter on both sides, a 24 and half pica wide column (4.1"), and a 1.75" exterior margin. It uses a slightly condensed book font and the column width is bit too large as it runs 11-14 words wide. So it is not quite as easy to read as the Harper Study Bible. The page size is 7⅛" wide by 9³/₁₆" tall . It has no commentary to direct reader response—and that's a good thing .

For a reading Bible I use a NRSV (though I don't like the translation) which is two-column and designed for reading. The Bible is basically square at 7½" wide by 8" tall , with two 3 . 1" (18 and a half pica) columns and a one pica gutter. It has half inch inside and outside margins, and fills the page very tightly. It appears to have been done in InDesign because the justification is superb. The word count per line stays very close to nine words. It is very comfortable to read, but there are no references or sidebars and few footnotes.

Why did I cover all this for my friend? Because, size and proportions can vary widely. The key is the column width, font choices, and the words per line. You do not get any choices in how the printing company sets up your pages on their paper. That is all done by computer (half the pages are upside down when printed). The computer puts your pages (the trim size including a bleed) where they need to go. The printing layout is designed to fit their bindery equipment.

Modern perfect binding uses a lot more glue and much thicker paper than traditional bible design. This necessitates larger interior margins. I would say .75" minimum. To get the readability of the older books, I suggested he probably needed to be talking to the Bible printers of central Michigan. However, you are now talking about major expenditures and probably a couple thousand bibles, minimum. For that, your size limitations will be very different. They use web presses (huge rolls of much thinner paper). This makes the printing much cheaper. But the simple setup (before the first page is printed) will cost you a $1000 or so.

My recommendation to my friend

He had made another need known to me. *"Another issue is the guideline set ups for side bars. I want to have small comments that run along with the text. If I use an inset sidebar..."*

My recommendation (based on the excellent 6x9 sample layout he had sent to me earlier) is that he needed a wider book to give the room necessary for a sidebar. Createspace offers a 7x10, for example. I use Lulu's 7.44" wide by 9.69" tall page for my spiral-bound workbooks and that works very well. But that does not distribute because of the binding. I would try the various distributable options offered by Createspace. I would do several dummy setups, cut to size, so you can see how they feel in your hand—and how well they read.

6x9 is an ugly size, but it is the trade standard. For a bible, I don't know if that matters. The Gladwell book has nearly a 2 by 3 proportion which is the same as the 6x9. You need to decide how the various books feel in your hand. I suggest a trip to the library with a ruler. Then you pick the size that comes closest to your ideal while leaving space for readability and a sidebar.

This is the type of decision-making process you need to go through for your book. I tend to gloss over these things because I have made many firm decisions based on years of experience. When I started, I had the bindery department of the printing company I worked for at the time make me dummies of the books. You probably do not have that option. So, your process will be based on checking out the book size and feel you really like. Then you can make the decisions necessary to work within the limitations of on-demand printers.

All printers have limitations. You choose the best options available.

The other thing my friend mentioned was the necessity of publishing in various sizes and formats. Once you have your book formatted to your first size, the other sizes are relatively easy. Your copy will all be in one piece, everything will be formatted with editable styles, and all graphics will be attached to a location in the copy. This makes it very quick and easy to reflow and reformat your book into any new format you need.

If you need special sizes

I know I'm repeating myself here. But for special sizes, spiral or wire-o binding and so forth, you will need to find a supplier to do it for you. Places like Snowfall Press can give you retail distribution for free, BUT you must have your own ISBN# (at this point).

Remember the pricing for buying ISBN#s: A single ISBN# today costs $125, ten ISBN#s cost $250, one hundred cost $575, and a thousand cost $1000. This means the cost per ISBN drops from $125 to $25 to $5.75 to $1. You can get the price per number much lower by buying a million or more (as Lulu and Createspace probably did).

This actually means that you must set yourself up as a "professional publisher" by getting your ISBN#s from Bowker and registering your company with them. You'll also need to get a barcode made of that ISBN on a free site (Google one) or pay around $25 each. But it will give you maximum distribution to any bookstore interested. For Christian authors, for example, this is the only way to get your books in places like Lifeway, CBD, and the rest of the Christian retail marketplace.

Bleeds

A bleed is needed when you produce a design where the ink goes to the edge of the paper. (On-demand printers will normally not allow type to come any closer than .375" or .5" from the edge of the trim size.) To produce a bleed, you make everything that reaches to the edge of the page extend one-eighth inch beyond the edge and then trim the piece back to finished size after printing. That's one-eighth inch, nine points, or a little less than four tenths of a millimeter (.375 mm to be precise). As you can see on the next page, any place that touches the edge requires a bleed—so the example is a four-side or full bleed, even though three of the sides only have ink touching the edge in narrow areas.

The power cutters used in the industry are the reason a bleed is necessary. These huge guillotine cutters slide their knives through stacks of paper several inches thick. They can cut 1,000 to 3,000 sheets at a time. Those huge cuts force the paper to slide around a bit—no matter how tightly they are clamped. The result of these limitations is that cuts are only accurate to plus or minus a sixteenth of an inch or so.

Saturday Only!
CLEARANCE SALE!

The typical temptations to spend more money than you have! Plus luscious pictures and supposed cash savings.

Logo/address

The dashed line is the actual trimmed size of the document.
BLEED   **TRIM**

Margins

This seems to be too obvious, but many ruin their job here. The most common amateur mistake is to make margins too small. You can assume that you need to leave .5" margins, minimum—and that is tight in a book.

In addition, margins are often a large part of style. If you are trying for the elegant look of an old book, for example, you will need huge margins. There are many formulas, but here's one you can try: 100% inside, 125% top, 150% outside, and 200% bottom (for example, 1.25″ top; 1.5″ outside; 2″″ bottom; and 1″ inside). *"Look at all that empty paper. I can't afford to waste that space!"* It's not wasted space, but room to breathe. You might want to keep some old books to remind yourself. Very high-priced products (or very cultured clients) commonly use designs with one inch to two inch margins or much more.

 Extra-wide margins: If you are producing a book that will be studied—where readers will be taking notes—margins of a couple of inches (at least on the outside) are a real service to the reader. If you remember (and we will cover this in a bit) that the column width rarely goes much above four inches, you'll find plenty of room in an 8″ width.

Conversely, if you need to convey the maximization of your money—fundraising materials and the like—you need small margins, gutters, and a lot of rules and boxes. You need to fill every open white space, making the page look like everything is crammed in to save money. Even if it is not strictly true, readers will think it is.

The point to remember is:
the smaller the margins,
the cheaper the look.

Minimal professional standards: basically you want the margins to be large enough to engender trust. Most readers have a subconscious reaction to cheapness—making it synonymous with unreliability and many other negatives. You need to be careful to make your work look professional. It really helps your readers relax and open up.

For the new publisher: I would assume a three-quarter inch (.75″) margin as my minimum. The gutter margin (toward the spine of the book) should be at least an inch. The on-demand printers tend to cut slightly undersize and even half-inch margins can look very cheap and too tight for your work in the final delivered product. If you are going to err, do it on the side of larger margins than you think are necessary.

Columns

Be very careful with your column choices. Your focus must be easy, comfortable readability. Generally, the more asymmetrical (off-center) and the more open you can lay out the piece, the better. Of course, you can go crazy and make things totally illegible. Modern style tends to be chaotic, splashy, and overly complex. But your innate taste and discretion should keep these tendencies in check. The problem, of course, is that taste and discretion have become rare. I know you are working hard to learn taste and reduce that trend. ***Thank you.***

The basic concept is to focus on the reader: You are writing to serve your reader. If you are not doing this, you need to have a little talk with yourself about why you are writing in the first place. Books are a very conservative piece of design. The typography needs to be invisible. Your goal is to present the content as irresistible to read and easy to understand. That is the essence of good typography.

 Be very careful of using cheap clip art and supplied templates: Art and layouts from sources like Office are instantly recognizable, and subconsciously cause most readers to reject your work as bad quality, bureaucratic, official, or any number of similar horrible epithets. InDesign's templates are stylized and probably for a different demographic than the one to which you are writing. There are now several Websites with excellent stock photos to download for free or for a couple dollars each: morguefile, fotolia, bigstock, and many more. All of us use stock art. The important thing is to locate high quality images, with unlimited use.

Column width: The first assumption is that you have column widths in good, readable range. Basically you are shooting for seven to eleven words per line. Once you have a few pages written, then you adjust your font sizes to get the right number of words per line. The formula I use for column width is very simple and gives you a good starting point for readability.

Here's a practical rule of thumb that's less complex than most:

40% of the body copy point size in inches or the point size in centimeters

So, 10 point type works well in a column that is four inches or 10 cm wide. 12-point type may need nearly five inches (40% is 4.8"). This assumes a normal x-height of about 50% of the cap height or a third of point size. If the x-height or width of the letters is radically different than the norm you will need to make adjustments.

Adjust your margins to leave an appropriate column width

This can be tricky with smaller books. There is a real limit to the smallness of body copy type (about 8 point). This gives us problems with the smaller book sizes.

The normal body copy size is 10 point type with 12 point leading. I'll talk about that elsewhere. But it is a fairly rigid norm. This normally requires a four inch column. For a five inch wide book, this only allows for half-inch margins on the sides. As mentioned that is very tight. You can probably take the column down to 3.5" with no readability issues, but you dare not go more narrow than that (just be sure to keep the 9 to 10 words per line).

On the other hand, an 8"x 10" book leaves you with four inches of margins. This is not a bad thing. One inch margins on all sides leaves you with an extra two inches for the gutter. This makes excellent room for a sidebar and to hold graphics up to six inches wide.

For two-column books: it should be easy to see that you need a page that is at least ten inches wide for any visual comfort. Books this wide become difficult to hold and read comfortably—no matter what you do. It is rarely a good solution (though adding a narrow sidebar can be a real benefit in an 8" wide book).

For a 6x9 book: my normal setup is .75" top and outside. I set the bottom at an inch to leave a quarter inch to hold my page numbers. I use the resultant 1.25" inside margin to help keep the copy out of the gutter and make reading more comfortable.

For a low price workbook to help your students, a two-column letter-sized book might help: You can set it up with three-quarter inch outside and 1" inside margins, and two 4" columns with a quarter-inch gutter between the columns. This will enable you to convert a 200 page 6×9 book to eighty pages or less—enabling a cheap workbook for group studies. Make it spiral-bound to be even more useful.

Guides

Guides are the non-printing lines that enable designers to line up graphic pieces to keep their designs tidy. More than that, it is assumed that text blocks will line up with each other; that graphics will line up to an assumed grid; that headlines and subheads will relate to that inferred grid.

 Especially when you are learning your craft, shut the guides off on a regular basis (there's a shortcut and a tool bar choice): Until you get used to the fact that these lines appearing in your design on the screen do not print, you will tend to leave room for them. As a result, many of your white spaces will be surprisingly large. Proofing a printed hard copy helps a lot, but simply turning off the guides and frame edges occasionally will tend to keep you on track—simply with the clean preview that presents itself.

Master pages

Some might think that this fantastic ability requires at least a larger subhead, or something. Really, all that master pages do is place repeating elements automatically. Unless you have a graphically intensive book with placeholder graphics for sidebars, headers, footers, and the like or a repeating task like a monthly magazine, a journal, or a large newsletter, master pages are only used to place automatic numbering markers for page numbers.

Major change for CS6: you must use Primary Text Frames [PTF]

This is true if you ever want to change the page size. Layout Adjustment does not work any more. This is a major change to the InDesign interface. The Document setup dialog will no longer give you what you expect unless you use a PTF to hold your body copy. In 5.5 Layout Adjustment is turned on in the Margins dialog box. It works very well (with some minor adjustments required every time you use it). I've had to develop an entirely new technique for CS6.

Automatic page numbering

You insert an automatic page number into an insertion point in the text by right-clicking and choosing: Insert Special Character>> Markers>> Current Page Number. If you insert a page number on a normal page, the number will be on that page only. It will always be correct, no matter how many pages you add, delete, duplicate, or rearrange. If you add these special characters on a master page, the page number will appear on all pages where that master page is applied. You can see mine below.

Remember! You cannot use page numbers for ebooks: The only exception is the print-ready downloadable PDF. Some of the ePUB distributors offer a page location indication so the readers can keep track of things, but that is not what we are talking about here.

Table of Contents and Index

Tables of contents are created by collecting selected paragraph styles. Indexes are created by hand-flagging the entries and then automatically gathering them into an index.

Tables of contents are used quite a bit. Newsletters, magazines, books, and so on all need tables of contents. You simply collect the heads and subheads into a new story and then reformat as desired. The TOC paragraph styles can be generated automatically.

Indexing is a tedious task: It's considered a specialized skill. In most cases, if an index is needed, a pro is needed to write it according to industry wisdom. But if you're a one-person shop (like me) you simply do the best you can. You simply go through your book from front to back adding words and phrases as you go.

Indexing is all done with the Index panel. You need to look up the instructions in InDesign Help. It is not difficult. As I said, you do everything with the Index panel. You can also add shortcuts to various commands as needed.

But, it is a slow process. You need to hand flag every entry (except for the fact that you can add all the instances of a particular selection at the same time). There is an shortcut to add the entries one by one, also. I found it helped me a lot to go under the Panel Menu shortcuts and add a shortcut for Delete, so I could delete entries that didn't work. For example, I had an entry for InDesign which was stupid because the word, InDesign, is on every page in this book. So I deleted that.

Be prepared to do it twice (or more) to get it right. Remember, index references are case sensitive. So, you'll need to decide how you are going to enter ones that are used in several different capitalizations. Look at other indexes to see what you like. Most of all, focus on what the reader will want to be looking up. Make sure you have entries for what you know they'll be looking for.

 The Table of Contents and the Index are a very nice service you provide the reader: It is important that you take some time to examine what you do in these stories added to the front and back if your book. If you can make them very comfortable to use, and make sure it is easy for the reader to find what he or she needs to find in your book, you have gone a long way toward reader satisfaction. They are essential.

Sidebars

In general, sidebars are a wonderful idea. By definition, sidebars contain interesting data that is not essential to the document. They add reader interest. They add graphic interest. They alleviate boredom. They contain graphic and typographic aberrations that are added merely for aesthetic reasons. As you have probably figured out by now, making room for sidebars will usually require a larger book size. There is very little room for them in a 6x9 book, for example. You need to design room for them.

Sidebars in ebooks: I have little doubt that these will be implemented fairly soon in ebooks. They are simply to helpful when creating a better reader experience—and Kindle Fire finally supports it, too. However, at the time of the writing of this book, they are a very iffy proposition. You need to mess with the HTML and CSS code of your ePUB.

In addition, depending on the type of book you are writing and producing, it may well be read on a smartphone. This is not too large a problem for iPhones with their Retina Display, but the others are severely handicapped in this regard. Novels, and the like, have no need for sidebars. A book like this can put them to good use. But they take a wide screen to handle things.

These capabilities are now possible in CSS3 and HTML5, but as of CS6 there is no easy and reliable way to implement any of them from within InDesign. However, InDesign CS6 is getting very close and I'm hoping for good controls in CSNext.

Folios or apps from InDesign

You can use Abobe's Digital Publishing Suite to create a magazine app. However, the expense of that is far outside the parameters of this particular book. There is a large initial fee and ongoing charges. My guess is that the capabilities of ePUB3 and beyond will wipe out apps.

Of course, this may change. But being able to add videos and sound fundamentally changes the nature of a book. My focus is to help you with books as they are presently understood. This is certainly going to change in the future, but there are many directions that change can go. I will do my best to keep you up to speed in The Skilled Workman and in my typography blog on Blogger.

Formatting basics

Before I get started with this, I need remind you about the goal: ***a beautiful book which is comfortable to read***. You need a customized set of styles to enable you to keep your book consistent and give you global control over the entire book as you format. You can see the benefits to the left. This is only possible if you first understand how to design paragraphs. I will help you through the basic set up of styles (to implement your paragraph designs). But before we can go there, I need talk about some underlying concepts.

Designing your paragraphs

You need to know some basics about setting up your paragraphs. Most of this knowledge is assumed by software manuals and publishing Websites. Somehow they seem to believe that your little psyche will be stifled if any opinion on normalcy is mentioned—or some such idiocy like that. It's not magic or luck when you produce reading materials that are enjoyable to read. It is the result of setting up your copy (formatting it) in a manner that the reader instantly recognizes and comfortably understands.

You must lead the reader through your writing effortlessly—completely unaware of your guidance. You need to make your writing feel natural, comfortable, and obvious to help the reader receive the content.

My way is not the only way: As I go through this little presentation, I will be simply sharing what I use. My hope is that you can look at my usage for conceptual understanding. Then convert that for your use. I will attempt to give you the arguments that have convinced me to do things in this manner. But, there is no right or wrong (once you are inside the relatively wide parameters of normalcy).

The need for comfort

Our basic problem is that we have too much to read. Subconsciously we all look for ways to eliminate content (in order to keep our reading requirements within a tolerable range). We might miss a lot of good content this way—but that is the way it is.

In our modern culture, huge numbers of people have difficulty reading. People often know how to read (technically) but they hate to actually do it. I've heard stats as high as 60% of Americans are functionally illiterate. Most people agree it is a huge percentage even if it is as low as a third of adults. They may be able to read but: it is difficult for them, in a second language, or they just hate reading. The social media users go far beyond that, of course. I know young men and women (fifty years old or less) who avoid reading entirely [as much as possible]—even though they are considered fully literate by polls and testing.

The result is that we need to go out of our way to make our books accessible to poor readers. Reading is hard to avoid. But many do. We have a large and growing portion of our middle class who get all of their information from social media, TV, movies, and videos.

 Modern interactive features: This is an area you need to thoroughly examine. My opinion is that adding video and such to a book changes it into something entirely different. The non-reader may be more attracted to the video content, BUT would they ever buy a "book" in the first place? If you feel the need for video, you should consider whether you actually need a "book" at all.

We can argue all we want about these media options and their limited amount of actual content. But, this fact remains: even those who buy our books may well have trouble reading. We must help them as much as we can with our formatting and layout. We must be kind to our readers—gentle and loving.

If our readers experience any discomfort or reading difficulty we have probably lost them. They will simply not finish reading our content.

I am a very good and very fast reader. Yet I simply put books aside that are difficult to read—unless the content is required or very compelling. I am not talking about difficult content (though that can be a problem). I am talking about poor layouts, columns that are too wide, fonts that are too styled, overly busy layouts, and all the rest.

I am currently struggling with a book on creationism (I mentioned already that my wife gave up and asked me to brief her on it when I finished reading it). The content is exciting. The layout is so poor with photographic backgrounds, glossy paper, excessive line lengths and a host of other problems—I am having to force myself to read it. The only difference with me is that I am tuned into this problem so I often notice when I do this with a book. Most people are not conscious of why they put down a book. They simply do not read it.

The poetry filter

Here's another example. I wonder how many of you are like me? I probably shouldn't admit this, but anything in a book which is formatted as poetry I skip (except in scripture). I simply pass over that portion of the copy and continue on. My experience over the years is that the content in poetry is very limited and far too open to interpretation. I am almost always looking for facts—easily accessible facts. In a novel, I am looking for plot and character development. Poetry has never provided this for me. So, I have developed reading habits that keep me from wasting time. I jump to the explanation of the poetry that inevitably follows.

I am sure this horrifies many of you. I am not saying that this poetry filter of mine is good or desirable. I am simply saying that it exists. Again, the only thing strange is that [as a typographer] I am more aware of my reading habits—so I noticed this behavior.

What reading filters do you have?

I suspect you need to examine yourself. It's hard to say what you have been missing all these years. We all have things we just do not read—often for subconscious reasons. As typographers we try to limit those reactions.

Writing in InDesign—adding words

Before we cover this, I must talk briefly (for new users of InDesign) about getting your document set up to handle the new copy. This has changed radically from Cs5.5 to CS6. Received this comment the other day.

> *I still cannot write into InDesign without manually creating text frames and threading them together* [By hand].

Getting set up in CS5.5: This is what you are stuck with in CS5.5. You can put text frames on your master page and link them, but I've never been able to get that done easily. The best way is to simply write until you've gone over and the frame overflows. Switch to your Selection tool and you'll see the little red plus in the lower corner of the text frame. Click on that and then drop it on the next page.

Building threaded frame easily

The way I commonly get around all of this in CS5.5 is to place (import) a long story onto a page with AutoFlow (hold down the Shift key when you click to drop the story). This will add enough pages to hold the entire story. Then I click in the story, select all, and delete it. I end up with the insertion point in the first frame of many pages of threaded frames. If I am adding more copy to the end of a story like this, I go to the beginning of what I just added and hold down the Command and Shift keys, then type the End key. This selects everything to the end of the story—which I then delete. This gives me a bunch of additional threaded text frames to work with.

For CS6 it is much better and far more simple: Use a Primary Text Frame [PTF]. Set up your document as a one page document with a PTF. Command+Shift+Click to release your PTF from Master page control. Click in the frame with your text tool to set the insertion point and start from there. All copy added will add pages as necessary when needed.

There are basically three scenarios for adding copy to your book

When we start talking about the design of your book, we must come to grips with reality in a new way. All books have limitations. Many of these boundaries are a result of the equipment used by the printer or distributor. For example, Apple currently does not allow for ePUBs with book names which are not in title case (at least through Lulu).

We are not talking about that type of thing yet—though we will. Here, at the beginning, we are discussing how to deal with the raw copy. In the modern world, it is rare to have copy which is clean enough to use as is. You want copy entirely formatted with styles. But you'll need to sort out how you deal with copy from these three sources.

One: Using copy written elsewhere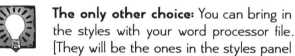

Usually we are talking about a Word document. But it could be copy from your blog (as I am doing in this book), quotes from a Website, copy from BBEdit, or several other sources. InDesign can place .doc files, .docx, .rtf, and .txt. In most cases, RTF (Rich Text Format) is best.

Here is the basic step by step scenario.

1. Strip out all the formatting: You can do it before you import into InDesign or after, but word processing formatting is such a major problem that it is almost never usable. I commonly open word processing documents in the word processor of choice, select all and style all the paragraphs with normal.

    The only other choice: You can bring in the styles with your word processor file. [They will be the ones in the styles panel with the little floppy disk icon behind them.] You can then simply convert the bad styles to ones you have set up in InDesign by deleting them one by one. InDesign will ask you which style you want to use instead—replacing all of them in the entire book.

2. Place or paste the copy: Place (under the File menu) is InDesign's import command. To make it flow from page to page, we always needed to autoflow the copy (up to version CS5.5). This means you hold down the Shift key while clicking to drop the copy into your document.

For CS6, using the Primary Text Frame, you simply place an insertion point in the PTF and paste. Additional pages are added as necessary.

3. Start checking the formatting at the beginning of the copy (even if you don't think it's necessary).

4. Put the Type tool's insertion point in the first paragraph

5. Type the short cut for the headline style.

6. Type Command+Down Arrow to go to the beginning of the next paragraph.

7. Type the shortcut for that style.

8. Type Command+Down Arrow to go to the beginning of the next paragraph.

9. Type the shortcut for that style.

10. Type Command+Down Arrow to go to the beginning of the next paragraph.

11. Type the shortcut for that style.

12. Type Command+Down Arrow to go to the beginning of the next paragraph.

13. Type the shortcut for that style.

14. And so on...

We'll talk about setting up the shortcuts and styles to do this in the next chapter on styles. You can literally format an entire book in just a few minutes using this method. It is amazingly fast and efficient. In fact, it is more efficient than you might think as the style shortcuts often use the Command key also. So you simply hold down the Command key with your left hand and type down arrow, num key, down arrow, num key, and so on with your right hand—adding additional modifiers as necessary. with the left fingers (but left-handedness is helpful).

Two: Using formatted copy from InDesign docs

1. Paste or place the copy: In both cases, you usually have a book document set up and an insertion point in a text frame. (If you end up with an overflow situation [a little box with a red plus in it at the bottom right edge of the

final text frame], then you click on the plus to load your cursor with the additional copy and autoflow it onto the additional pages required.) In CS6, the PTF eliminates this need.

2. Any styles with the same name will be automatically restyled: If you are placing, you will get a dialog box which enables you to decide how you want to handle this.

3. Any styles with different names will be added to your Paragraph Styles, and Character Styles panels: If you wish, you can right-click delete these newly added styles and use the resulting dialog box to convert them to any of the styles you are using in your new book.

Often copy added in this manner requires no additional formatting. For this book, as an example, I have used portions of copy from several of my earlier books. In all cases, I have slightly changed my naming conventions or used styles that I no longer consider effective. Converting them to my new vision of book design is a very simple matter and takes very little time. Your book designs will be continuously evolving but adjustments are very easy.

Three: Writing directly in InDesign

1. Put your insertion point in the first text frame: I covered the options for this on page 74.

2. Type the shortcut for your first style (usually the headline)

3. When you hit the Return key InDesign will automatically go to the next style you have chosen: usually Body Copy or Body Copy No First.

4. When you type the Return at the end of the paragraph you will go to or stay in Body Copy.

5. When you need to add a subhead, type the shortcut: The same is true for any special style: lists, quotes, tips, and so on. Many of these styles will automatically revert to body copy when you finish the paragraph.

6. Return will bring you back to body copy: if necessary type the shortcut for body copy to continue.

7. Keep writing: formatting as you go.

Everything in this book was done using these three procedures. Here I am dropping in the blog copy, then going through it and editing—expanding and clarifying the copy. In several cases, I have added copy from older books which I then edit and rewrite as necessary. I just added a bit of conversation from an email a few pages back. I regularly write in new copy which is automatically formatted as I go.

Benefits of Styles

❦ Consistency: Styles are really the only way to keep a long document consistent: throughout the document, from chapter to chapter, and from issue to issue.

❦ Global control: They are the effortless way to make changes to the overall look of an entire document.

❦ Production speed: Once implemented they greatly increase production speed. Formatting submitted secretarial copy becomes a breeze.

❦ Fluidity: Page layout becomes a malleable art form flowing to fit your need.

❦ Reflow: Documents that are a little too long or a little too short can be fixed by changing a style—among other things.

❦ Instinctual formatting: Styles will enable you to format copy habitually, without conscious thought. You think headline—and the paragraph is formatted to the headline style. Like in martial arts, you practice and practice until you react instinctively to an attack. With a good set of styles you can format in this manner.

❦ Pre-formatting: A good set of styles will allow you to set up the look of a document before you add the first word of copy. You can simply import style sets from a book you like.

Setting up Styles

Formatting of text is done on two levels: by paragraph and by character. This paragraph, for example, is in my normal body copy style—the one with no first line indent, used after a chapter headline. **However,** I can emphasize certain words a character at a time by simply selecting and applying a character style with the shortcut I define. I can simply type the shortcut and apply the character style as I write. But then the style must be manually turned off by clicking the **[None]** style in the Character Styles panel at present (there is no shortcut possible to apply **[None]**).

Paragraph styles format entire paragraphs. Character styles format characters within a paragraph.

Paragraph Styles & Character Styles panels

These two styles panels are the enabling concept for typographic fluidity and production speed. Styles panels are a collection of specialized typographic defaults that can be accessed at the click of a mouse or stroke of a key. You can set up styles for headlines, subheads, body copy, hanging indents, bylines, captions, tabular matter, or whatever your heart desires or imagines. Just keep your style list as simple as possible (so you can remember it).

You can also set up very complex styles for graphic objects and most parts of a table. Basically, you can globally control the look of your entire document with a little practice. I'll spend some time on Object Styles and anchored graph-

For most beginning designers, styles seem too complex to use; but believe me, they are not!

This frame is formatted by an object style that automatically formats the copy with two paragraph styles, and makes the round-cornered frame with specified insets to contain them.

It also makes this frame into an anchored object which can simply be dragged into position (in this case, after "possible" in the paragraph above), & it simply pops out here into the proper position automatically with an automatic text wrap as necessary.

ics later in the book. I'll also have a section on tables. But first let's learn the concepts on paragraphs like you see in front of you. Every paragraph in this book is formatted with styles—a set of styles I have been using for many years now.

Let's start with Paragraph Styles

These basic comments on paragraph styles also apply to the other different types of styles also, in most cases.

You get global control of the entire document
if it is all formatted in styles

If you decide that you just don't like Baskerville for this project and want to use Caslon, simply change the relevant styles and the entire document changes. If you decide that your lists need 3 points before paragraph to help the spacing—*just change the style.*

There are many other global fixes like this that are an amazing help. You get consistent indents and alignments, automatic paragraph rules and leaders for building forms and the like, automatic anchored graphics, automatic drop caps—plus much more at a speed which is phenomenal. In truth, this consistency is what makes a book look like a professionally designed book.

Based On (Building Style Classifications)

To make a good thing better, any style can be based on any other style. This means that when you change the first style, all the styles based on that style change also. The only things that do not change are the specific changes in the derivative styles.

In most books, all the headlines and subheads are tied together (based on a single style) and all the body copy, hanging indents, bulleted lists, bylines, captions are tied together (based on a single style). In complex documents, there is often a third set of styles for the sidebar materials used to entertain the good readers. I usually base my sidebar styles on my headers for easier control.

If all the heads are based on Headline and all the copy is based on Body Copy, then an entire document can be reflowed by simply changing those two styles. If you do use the third sidebar set, you may have a third style to change—but this is barely a burden. This saves an amazing amount of time in books like this that can easily be three hundred pages. In addition, I picked up the styles themselves from a previous book (see loading styles on the next page). In this way my styles evolve as my taste changes.

Next style (auto-formatting your writing) ■

As mentioned, any style can be set up to change to another when the Return key is struck. Again, this sounds like a little thing, but think about it. Every head, subhead, and specialized style in this book automatically returns to Body Text when the return is struck at the end of the header. This happens, on average, three times a page. It takes 3 seconds to pick up the mouse and click on the Style panel. This is the eighty first page of the book and 50-100 heads so far. So I've saved 3–7 minutes so far with this simple setup. For 300 hundred pages, this next style option would save a total of maybe 2700 seconds, or forty-five minutes. That much saved time really builds up quickly. And this is but one simple example of savings. Once you begin using styles habitually you will find that you save many minutes or even hours per day. Over the course of a single book, you can save nearly an entire day or more.

If you analyze the styles used in this book, you will see how much variety can be built into a style [I apologize for overdoing it upon occasion just to show you more options]. You can genuinely make writing, or importing and formatting, a semiautomatic procedure.

This entire book is formatted with the five styles panels. You will discover that this is essential when you want to convert to an ePUB, for example. Much of the type styling is virtually automatic. All I have to do is remember the shortcuts when I have to start back with one of the heads or a list. Using a well set up styles panel, I can write fully formatted as fast as I can type. Using the styles for everything I do means the shortcuts and style characteristics are firmly memorized and used habitually.

Copying (Loading Styles from other documents) ∎

This is another powerful use of the style panels. When I start a new book or booklet, I set up the size, columns, and margins. Then I load the styles from an appropriate document; and all the styles I need are dropped into place. All it takes is opening the Paragraph Styles panel's Options menu, choosing the Load All Text Styles... command, navigating the folders and files in my hard drives to locate the source document, and click choose. I get the dialog below.

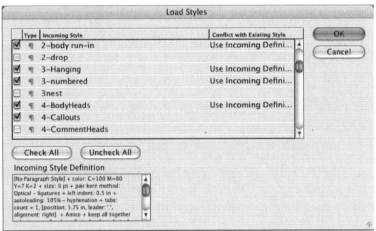

I even get a choice of whether I use formatting from the current document and rename the incoming style to avoid conflict or use the incoming definition for a given style name to convert the formatting to the newly imported styles.

Another powerful capability I already mentioned. Once the styles are added I can get rid of a style by simply deleting the bad style and using the dialog box to replace it with the style of my choice—and let InDesign reformat all affected paragraphs in the entire document automatically. This enables very fast cleanup of imported copy.

Because of their ability to reformat documents globally, Paragraph & Character Styles are indispensable. You should always use them from the very start of document creation.

Styles enable consistency. They enable exportation to ePUB. Once you make their use into a habit, you will wonder how you ever managed without the control you get from styles.

Setting up a style—easily!

Capturing a style: The new Paragraph Style dialog box is complex. But once you understand that any paragraph setting can be captured, it gets easier. In most cases it is easier to set up a paragraph the way you want it. Then, with an insertion point in the paragraph choose the New Paragraph Style… from the Option menu of Paragraph Styles panel or the Paragraph Control panel (or you can just click on the new style button at the bottom of the Paragraph Styles panel). All the settings for that paragraph will be captured in your new style.

 For detailed descriptions of all the options available, go to Appendix B: In there, I talk about all the possibilities (well, at least as many as I could remember) available to a paragraph style or character style.

Controlling local formatting

Building A Set Of Character Styles

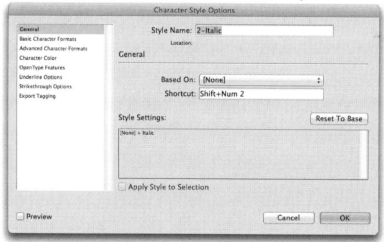

As you may have noticed: and will certainly see as I move on through this brief overview of Styles, is that character styles are a crucial part of Paragraph, Object, Table, and Cell styles. They give us the ability to format a portion of type within a paragraph. They are the solution to many problems you don't even know you have at this point in your book design development. The nested style you see at the beginning of this paragraph (where it says **As you may have noticed:**) is only one small instance.

As you saw on the previous page, the New Character Style box has many of the options of the New Paragraph Style box. The options do not change, but all fields are left blank except the specific changes you want to make. You can see in that capture, the only change is picking the Italic style. *As you can see here where the 2-Italic style is applied,* the style alters nothing else in the paragraph.

Local formatting

Local formatting is the major problem hindering professional production: One of the biggest temptations to new designers is to attempt to fix small problems, or create specialized paragraphs, by going directly to the Character or Paragraph panels and the formatting options found there. This is called local formatting because it only affects the paragraph(s), word(s), and/or letter(s) selected at the time.

The problem is that locally formatted type is not reformatted when the Styles panels are adjusted. In other words, local formatting removes that portion of the copy from the global control of the styles. This can be a real problem if you have a large document and can't remember any local formatting until you find errors after it is printed.

So, the rule is this:

Use local formatting only for final cleanup.

All local formatting should be done last, if possible. Its appropriate function is massaging the copy into its final configuration. Even then it should be done very sparingly because reformatting the book for another version will not change this local formatting. This adds a lot of time and aggravation to your necessary formatting conversions.

Extensive local adjustments can make simple reflow a nightmare costing an amazing amount of extra time and aggravation. Plus, it really messes up your ebooks. That might not mean much to you now. But imagine making changes to a book like this if there were a lot of local formatting. It would take me many unplanned hours. I have just completely reformatted the book up to this point. I made many changes to styles and added (and subtracted) a lot of the original copy. So far, it has taken me about 12 hours to rewrite the first 70 pages. There are not more than a couple paragraphs so far that have any local formatting (and they are all simple paragraph spacing adjustments to paragraphs following graphics.

Let's rephrase the concept

The solution to local formatting—Character Styles

This panel enables you to format selected text. It is meant as an addition to the other Styles panels. One of the main reasons it is so nice is that you can change only what needs to be changed.

The main thing made possible by the Character Styles panel is global control of local formatting. If you edit the Character style, everything formatted with that style is changed also. I am using nine character styles for this booklet. I have found I always use several basic character styles—when I need to temporarily go to a different font, type color, or point size for some purpose. By doing all of my local formatting with the Character Styles I retain global control over the formatting.

Before character styles, all local formatting resulted in removing the type that was custom formatted from style panel control. Then, if a global change was made to any individual style, I would need to go back and find every locally formatted piece to change it to the new settings. Now all I have to do is change the Paragraph Styles and then change the Character Styles. In fact, it has gotten to the place where any local formatting usually means I just add another style (so I can use the same solution elsewhere).

Character styles also used for the table of contents

Tables of Contents are made by collecting the paragraph styles of your choice and adding page numbers if you desire. As you can see below, there is a lot of power available. For each paragraph style added to the TOC in the setup dialog box (found under the Layout menu), a separate TOC paragraph style should be made and each can add two special character styles for the leader (or other spacing characters) and the page number. This means that you can have the leaders and page numbers look the same for all styles in your table of contents.

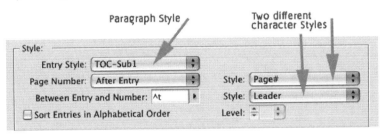

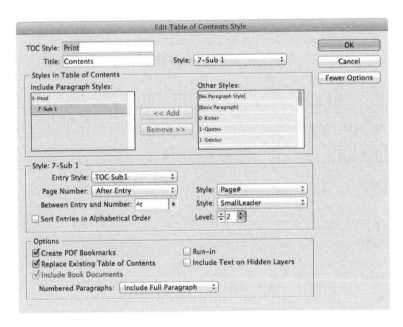

You can also do nice things like making your leaders smaller and grey so they are not so obnoxious. In this way, you can help guide the readers' eyes to the page numbers without the overt busyness of "normal" leaders.

You'll continuously develop new uses

I find new uses for both paragraph and character styles all the time, and I've been using styles heavily for almost twenty years now. Keep your creative mind open. Consider that a style might be the solution to your problem. Then solve the problem with a style.

Updating your styles as your designs grow and evolve

I received this question a while back from a friend:

I made some mistakes when I set the original paragraph styles and they have become some sort of default that has to be corrected for every new project. Do I have to delete the whole thing and start over again? I can do it, but I hope I can do it an easier way.

Resetting your paragraph defaults is very easy.

To do it globally (for InDesign as a whole)

Close all your documents. Go to your Paragraph Styles panel. Delete all styles listed. Delete all the character styles in your Character Styles panel also. Choose Load All Text Styles… from either panel menu (it's the button in the upper right corner of panel). Navigate to the document which has the styles you wish to use for your default. Choose it and click OK. That will load all the paragraph and character styles into your two styles panels. They will now be the default for every new document you open.

You can do the same with Object styles for graphics and sidebars. There are also Table and Cell styles you can load to format your tables.

To update your styles in an existing document.

Open the new document. Make sure you have nothing selected and no active insertion point. **Do not delete the currently used styles** (or all of your paragraphs will become unstyled). Then load those styles you wish to use (from the source document you choose) into your document. This process is not quite as clean. It will overwrite any styles with the same name, but it will not delete styles with a different name.

For example, I commonly get something like 7-Sub 1 in addition to the list I am already using which contains 7-Sub. In this example, I simply right-click on 7-Sub 1 and choose Delete Style. This gives me a dialog box where I can choose the style which I want to use (7-Sub) in a popup list of all styles. When I click OK all paragraphs formatted with 7-Sub 1 become styled with 7-Sub and the 7-Sub 1 style is deleted.

This deletion option also works with Character, Object, Table and Cell styles. So you can see that keeping up with your evolving sense of style is not burdensome.

Building a basic set of default styles

Before I get specific, let's review what the expected result will be. To give a personal example, I started using the shortcut Command+Num6 for headlines in PageMaker 4.2 almost 20 years ago. I developed a small, but complete, set of standard styles by 1993. I've been using this continuously evolving set of styles ever since. At this point, when I think I need a headline, my fingers automatically type the shortcut and the copy is formatted in the headline style. When I hit the return, it automatically changes to the body copy style with no first line indent, and then to normal body copy.

I no longer have to remember the styles I use or the shortcuts for them. All I do is think that I need the second level of subhead and my fingers just type Command+Num8 and the formatting is applied to the copy I am working on.

Formatting becomes extremely fast, and automated. I can simply format focusing on the type of style needed and my fingers habitually apply the styles as needed. Conscious thought is not needed to format the paragraphs or to add most of the character styles.

My current basic set of styles

At the bottom of the next page I will give you the standard set I teach. I'll also show you what I am using for this book—if you promise not to get scared. The naming/numbering conventions you use is up to you, but the concept is important. Notice that many of my style names are abbreviated. In truth, by now I could simply use numbers for the names in many cases (they have become that automatic for me in my daily use).

When you use a standard palette like this, looking for these styles is simple—because they are always in the same place. For more graphic non-fiction (like this book, for example) you will probably need a full set to add sidebar styles and so forth. In fact, at this point, this book is using 31 paragraph styles so far. There'll be three more for the index. In a book that teaches the use of styles, this is not surprising. Normally a basic default set of a dozen or so is sufficient. Take a look at a set of basic styles you can start with next.

An abbreviated suggested set for you

You will need a place to start your setup. I have developed a starter set for this (see Appendix B2). The instructions are also found linked off any of the InDesign pages on the Radiqx Press site using the Default Styles link.

I number my styles to help me remember the shortcuts and to aid in sorting the styles: All of my body copy styles are numbered 2. All of my lists are numbered 3. All of my sidebar styles are numbered 1. Headline is 6. Subhead is 7. Subhead 2 is 8. And so on. These numbers really help me manage my styles.

❦	[Basic Paragraph]	none
❦	0 Kicker	Command+Num0
❦	1 Inline Dropped	Command+Num1
❦	2 Body copy	Command+Num2
❦	2 Body Run-in	Command+Option+Num2
❦	2 No first	Command+Option+Shift+Num2
❦	3 Bullets	Command+Num3
❦	3 Numbers	Command+Option+Num3
❦	4 Body Heads	Command+Num4
❦	5 Quote	Command+Num5
❦	6 Headline	Command+Num6
❦	7 Subhead 1	Command+Num7
❦	8 Subhead 2	Command+Num8
❦	9 Callout	Command+Num9

Setting up shortcuts: One slightly irritating limitation of shortcuts for styles is that you can only use the three modifier keys, Command, Option, and Shift—plus the numerical keypad. On the PC it is much worse and you can normally only use the Control & Shift plus numericals.

The important thing to remember, when setting up your styles, is naming consistency: In our case, for example, Command+Num6 always gets us Headline; Command+Num3 always gets us some type of list; Command+Num7 always produces a second level subhead; and Command+Num9 always supplies a pull quote no matter what document I am working on. The key to quickly flowing production is simple—habitual formatting. I think headline and my hands hit Command+Num6 (without conscious thought).

On a PC: When I was working on a Dell box with XP Pro, I had a lot of trouble implementing this strategy. There are simply not enough shortcuts available in Windows. The Alt key was almost completely co-opted by the operating system so it was not available. So I used another automated method: Quick Apply.

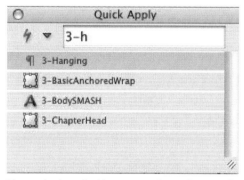

The eight-handled box icons show object styles, the paragraph glyph is for paragraph styles, & the A for character styles

Quick Apply: I have not found this to be really useful on a Mac because I usually have enough shortcuts and they are faster. But on a PC, or any laptop with a limited keyboard it may well be the only way to organize things. Remember, Ctrl+Enter (Command+Return) opens a list of the styles being used. Then just start typing the first letters of the style. When you get close, use the arrow keys to go up or down until you have the style you want selected and then hit the return key to apply the style. This obviously takes much more time than simply typing a shortcut.

Styling tips for the basic set

At the top of the next page is the Paragraph Styles palette as it was for this book on the day I wrote this paragraph. It is a constantly changing thing. You also need to remember that I can effectively use so many styles because I am writing two to six hours a day. Because of the time spent, I have little difficulty remembering the styles I am using—and I am using all of these styles every hour of the day as I write and edit this book.

If you need a complete set of instructions on setting up styles, go to Appendix B: There I go through every command in the New Paragraph Style dialog box—explaining the choices and why they are necessary to excellence in typography. Because InDesign has so many options, it is basically part two of a short course in typography. Part One is Appendix A.

Hopefully it is obvious in the list of styles shared in appendix B2 that styles 1–5, and 9 are based upon 2 Body copy. Styles 7, 8, and 0 are all based on 6 Headline. On the list I am currently using, 1-Quotes through 3-numbered are based on 2-body (except for the two sidebar styles); 4-Body Heads through 8-sub plus 0-Kicker and the two sidebar styles are based on 6-Head. With the B2 starter set, I can change the fonts for the entire document by simply changing 2 Body and 6 Headline—talk about global document control! On my more complicated setup there are several of the derivative styles that I have to check because I made font changes there also.

What I want to do here is give you some design tips to use when

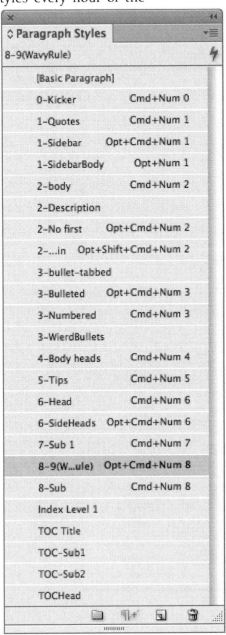

setting up your set of standard styles. I will go through the basic paragraph needs—explaining the hows and whys as I go.

Again, some of my solutions will be different from yours. In most cases, I am just talking about normal usage. You must come up with your own styles. This is the core of your layout style. If you do not work on this, you'll pay for that lapse with the extra time spent—*many extra days of time wasted*. Plus, your typography will be haphazard & ineffective. Your readers will not be pleased.

 Points: A basic reminder for those just learning. This is the basic measurement system for type. A point is now one-seventy-second of an inch. It is the minimum size that is easily visible to the naked eye.

Body copy styles

The first formatting decisions I will be talking about are for the body copy. This is the main content of your book. This is the copy that needs to be comfortable to read. This is the background against which the contrasting heads and subheads stand out. You really need to focus on making this as comfortably readable as possible

 Font choices influence these decisions: The x-height and width of your fonts have great influence. Readability has to do with the number of words per line, the legibility of the font used, the size of the letters, and a lot more. The fonts I am using in the print versions of this booklet is Contenu. It has a very small x-height. So, to maintain the optimal 10-12 words per line I am setting the type in 12-point which is quite large for print.

2 Body copy: Command+Num2

I should be able to assume that you have this under control. These are the normal paragraphs of copy. The norm is 10/12 flush left or justified left. All the other alignment options are much more difficult to read. There is a very strong expectation of normal for these paragraphs by your readers. You need to know the normals.

- Serif font: This is the standard. Most people still believe that serif fonts are much easier to read. This is being argued. For the new generations, it may be true that a humanist sans font reads very well. But for those born before 1980 or so, all of our reading experience is based on the assumption that serif fonts must be used for body copy.

- Size: The standard for body copy is 10/12 (10-point type with 12-point leading). This can vary from 9 to 12 point in size. The leading will be determined by the amount of line spacing built into the font used and the x-height. The larger the x-height, the more leading is needed. The smaller the x-height the larger the point size of the type needs to be. Also condensed fonts can be a little larger and wide fonts often need to be smaller.

- Alignment: Left or Justified left. Typographers traditionally liked flush left alignment because the word spacing remains constant. However, I have read studies which seem to show that justified copy is a little more readable with adequate column width. InDesign' superior justification abilities now make this simply a stylistic choice on your part. InDesign automatically justifies copy better than any software program we have had up to this point because it justifies the entire paragraph as a whole.

- Longer line lengths require increased leading: You are shooting for 9-12 words per line on average. Many italics also need leading help because the more narrow italics have more words per line. Formality also needs extra leading—plus a lighter, more elegant typestyle.

- First line indent: Historically, you used either a first line indent or extra paragraph spacing, not both. Now, however, it is common to see a first line indent with a couple of points of space after paragraph. There is no right or wrong about the size of first line indents. The norm would be somewhere between a quarter to a half inch. (Believe it or not, this topic causes many angry exchanges of dogmatic opinion.)

2-Body No First: Command+Option+Num2

This style is used for the first paragraph after a head-line, primarily. Sometimes it is also used under column-wide rectangular graphics. Adjust it to read well with your headers, comfortably clearing any descenders in the heads.

- ❦ Based on: 2-Body

- ❦ No first line indent

- ❦ Extra space before the paragraph

- ❦ Next style: It should go to the normal 2-Body.

Obviously, if you do not use a first line indent for your body copy, you'll need to use some other device for these paragraphs. You can try a drop cap, make the first line small caps, or something like this to help the reader know the content starts here. It also helps set off the headline.

2-Body Run-in: Command+Option+Shift+Num2

This is a common way to format the fourth or fifth level of subhead. It also works well for more informal lists and word definitions. I'm sure you have noticed that I use this device a lot. I commonly use run-ins for lists which do not require the impact of a bulleted or numbered indent. As you can see below, there is far less visual impact than a bulleted list like you see above.

Based on: 2-Body

No first line indent: The style becomes too visually confusing if you are not careful. Eliminating the first line indent seems to help.

Extra space before paragraph: Because of the lack of a first line indent and the existence of a subhead, a little extra space before paragraph seems to help in the emphasis needed.

Nested style to format the subhead: I usually set mine up to apply the style until the first colon [as you see in this para-graph]. This way it happens automatically as I write.

Run-in head uses header font: Depending on the header font used, you may need to use a bold or even black version of the font to give enough contrast for legibility.

As mentioned, I also use run-in heads to help with my lists. My writing style starts a list paragraph with a pithy statement ended with a colon. That is followed by explanatory copy. It probably drives grammarians nuts, but it works well for me (and seems very readable).

Zero and One numbered styles

I have found that I commonly have more styles based on 2-body than I have available shortcuts. As a result I have three styles that (if used) are given a shortcut using the Num Zero or Num1 keystroke. This is a relatively new addition to my working style and it differs from the basic starting styles I showed you a few pages ago.

1-Quotes: Command+Num1

Quotes must be obvious. All readers need to be able to easily and intuitively identify quotes.

- ❦ Based on: 2-Body

- ❦ Indented left and right the same amount as the first line indent of 2-Body: But, this is certainly not written in stone.

- ❦ Different alignment: Quotes are also usually set justified when the body copy is flush left and often set flush left or centered when the body copy is justified.

The main thing is to make them different enough to be an obvious solution. Some make quotes in italic, but I find that often makes them too hard to read. If you do it well, quotation marks will not be needed [though you normally will still use them].

In my Bible studies, I no longer use actual quotation marks because it is so obvious where the quotes are. I do this by having my scripture references in a carefully styled paragraph. I do use quotation marks for my in-line references. Sometimes I use a character style to italicize in-line quotes within a paragraph.

1-Sidebar Body: Option+Num1

I cover sidebar design in a few pages. This two-item list really doesn't give you any indication in the complexity of the design issues that go into sidebar construction.

* Based on 2-Body

* Sans serif: I commonly make it body copy in size with the regular version of the headline font.

Bio style for articles by various authors

A bio style: You may also want to have a different paragraph style at the end of an article with an indent that allows room for a small picture and a short bio to go with the name and credits. The little bio can add a gentle warm fuzzy to help leave the reader with a good taste in his mind about the article. You can usually use the sidebar styles for this.

0-Captions: Command+Option+0

This little item has changed greatly in the years I have set type. Originally captions were commonly set small and italic. Current research suggests that the caption is more important than the headline in attracting readers. So the current norms are:

* Based on: 2-Body

* A little larger than body copy

* Flush left

* A synopsis of the points the article is making about the picture: In other words, because the picture is illustrating the article, the synopsis helps the reader decide whether or not to read the articles.

Remember: if it is not truly important content to the reader, he or she will be angry if you trick them into reading copy that has no relevance to their life. None of these formatting tips will help bad, unusable, or poorly written copy.

4-Body heads: Command+4

This one varies for me. It can have the same left indent as the first line indent of body copy and the same font family, but bold. Or, it can be the body copy sized version of the headers with a flush left alignment.

- ❦ Based on: 2-Body or 8-Sub 2, same size as body copy

- ❦ Indent: same as 1st line indent of copy or flush left

- ❦ Bold or Black: They need the contrast to make them function as subheads.

These lesser subheads are now largely made irrelevant by the run-in styles already talked about.

Lists need special care

These are extremely important areas in your copy. In terms of reading importance they rank right up there with the headline and the picture captions. Most lists about the importance readers assign to various paragraph styles put captions first, headlines second, and lists third. Some make Headlines first. Many readers look for lists and only read the rest of the copy if the lists are helpful.

- ❦ Flush left alignment: List paragraphs are usually quite short so justified copy often looks very bad. They will almost always need flush left.

- ❦ Decorative bullets: As you can see, in this book I am using an ornament. In my Bible studies I use a cross. For marketing work, miniature logos can make wonderful bullets.

Because the reader considers your lists to be so important, you need to work at making them good-looking and obvious. A little care here will go a long way in helping your readers like your book.

3 Bulleted: Command+Num3

- ❦ Left indent: the same as the first line indent of 2 Body.

This second, interior, left indent is a great help in visually organizing your copy: You can see I am using it here in this paragraph as well. It really helps make your formatted copy easy to absorb. It is a sure sign of professionalism. It also shows reader consideration by making the layout easily understood so that the content can be appropriated without the need to figure it what the priorities really are.

- Bullet location: The bullet should hang somewhere between the left column margin and halfway to the left indent—as you see to the left here.

- Custom bullets: They are certainly not necessary but they really pack a disproportionate amount of visual punch.

3 Numbered: Command+Option+Num3

1. Left indent: the same as the first line indent of 2 Body.

2. Number location: The number needs hang somewhere between the left column margin and halfway to the left indent. You need to leave room for the longest number with your indents.

 Watch your lists carefully: Often these paragraphs are so short that you have to break for sense to get rid of the large number of paragraph widows (see Appendix A) generated. Extra care needs to be taken for readability and reader comfort.

If your bulleted and numbered lists are crucial to reader understanding in your book, you may want to make them larger, bolder, and/or in a different font than your body copy. They are very important.

Heads and subheads

Ideally, especially for headlines, these need to be written to give the reader the number one benefit of reading the content. They need to give the reader a reason to read the content—or at least give them the option of making an informed decision.

Headlines and subheads are your outline. They also produce your Table of Contents as these styles are collected for the TOC.

- ❦ Short, pithy paragraphs that give a synopsis of the copy that follows: Readers depend upon them to keep track of where they are on the page.

- ❦ In non-fiction: subheads are used to demarcate sections of copy, and the next conceptual point within a chapter.

- ❦ Recapture wandering readers: If you have a section which the reader believes is already known and understood, you often lose the attention of the reader. To recapture them, a well written subhead will pull them back into reading your copy.

- ❦ Headline/subheads need a clear hierarchy: It must be visually obvious where a subhead lies in this hierarchy. If it is not clear, you often need to make the headlines larger to give you enough size variation to make things work well.

I find that with a good set of styles developed and used, I think in terms of subheads while I am writing. They are simply added automatically as I write. Of course, you can go back and add them, but IMHO this could mean that you weren't considering the reader as you wrote the copy.

6 Headline: Command+Num6

This needs a lot of contrast with the body copy—in size, color, and/or type style. Typically the heads are sans serif and the body is serif, as you well know. I've been using a large regular sans contrasted with a book weight serif (lighter than regular) for a while now and it seems to work well.

- ❦ Used once: A headline is used once per article or once per chapter. This is the indicator to the reader that the new content section starts here.

- ❦ Size: The normal size for headlines is 24 to 36 point. Large enough to allow a clear hierarchy with your subheads.

❦ Length: In general, they should be reasonably short and pithy. In other words, they need to give the reader a clear idea of what is coming in the copy following. Though they are different than billboards, the eight word maximum is not a bad guideline.

❦ Alignment: This needs to be closely watched. If the body copy is flush left, the heads need to be flush left. If they are centered over flush left copy they will typically look off center. If the body copy is justified, the heads can be either left or centered. The main concern is ease of reading and logical consistency.

 The eight word maximum: This is supposed to be the maximum number of words allowed in a billboard. Any more than that and most readers will not have time to read the copy as they fly by at 60 miles per hour.

❦ Starts on an odd (right-hand) page: This may not be essential, but the norm here is strong enough so that a headline on a left page looks bad, feels strange, and makes the reader uncomfortable. [This is automated on the Keeps page of the style dialog.] For ebooks the headline starts a new page.

7 Subhead 1: Command+Num7

This needs to be the same basic setup as the headline but about 25 to 33 percent smaller. So for this book, where the headline is 32 point, subhead one is 21 point. Mainly, you need to clearly differentiate & prioritize the headers.

For many years I made the headlines light or book in weight but extra large and then made the subheads bold or black. Sometime I made the headline and subhead-1 the same font and then reversed subhead-2 out of a colored bar. You simply need to design clear priorities for the reader—so the reader gets a sense of the importance of the content. As always, your goal is to help the reader assimilate the copy. You must keep your focus on the reader.

8 Subhead 2: Command+Num8

This is second level of subheads and it is smaller yet and almost always flush left (even if the heads and first level subheads are centered). In this book they are small—only 14 point and regular, not bold. This is why I added the little colored square to the right of the last line using a paragraph rule with a gradient stroke. There are many ways to provide this emphasis.

❧ Slightly less contrast: If the 6 and 7 styles are black, 8 subhead 2 is often bold in the same sans serif. These second level heads do not need nearly as much contrast as the larger, more important heads.

9 Callout: Command+Num9

Pull quotes or callouts are one of the more important typographic features in long non-fiction articles and books. They are type used as a graphic to recapture the reader's attention (in case it is wandering). Occasionally they get extremely graphic, but the norm would probably be 50 to 100% larger in italicized body copy. They often use paragraph rules above and/or below to set them off.

❝(Pull quotes) are type used as a graphic to recapture the reader's attention❞

❧ If they are actual quotes: it is a common device to make the quote marks extremely large (400 to 1,000% of the point size of the pull quote). The ones used above are 1000% larger. By the way, the only difference between the two names (pull quotes and callouts) is that pull quotes actually quote part of the surrounding copy.

❧ Not used in busy layouts: Actually you will see that I use them less and less because most of my non-fiction writing uses layouts which are simply too complex. Pull quotes just become more noise (as they are above). If you are going to use them, you must use almost violent contrast in these cases.

None of these paragraph styles are to be used unless they are necessary (in your judgment). The guiding principle is still the same simple concept. **Do they help the reader comfortably and easily access your content?** If they make the layout too busy, pray for a better solution.

Sidebar styles are important

There are no real rules here, but let's give it a shot. First of all, sidebars, by definition, contain peripheral information. In other words, they contain data that is interesting and nice to know; but they are often tangential to the main thoughts and concepts of the body copy. It may help you to think of them as a bonus you offer for your good and/or loyal readers—another obscure form of ministry.

- ❦ De-emphasized a little: I still want the body copy to be primary.

- ❦ Tinted background: The best way to do this is to put the sidebar in a tinted box. Contrary to common, nonprofessional thought, a tint box tends to make items less important. The tint back ground lowers contrast so the type is harder to read. To make a tint box primary, you will need to place a background image over the entire page—then the light, bright tint boxes will stand out.

 The key to remember is that the tint in the tint box will mess up your type: Even at 150 linescreen with 300 dpi tints, the tiny little dots will blur the edges of your characters. So you need to pick typestyles that will not be damaged by those dots. This is why I usually use sans serif for my sidebars. When coupled with the fact that my sidebars are usually very brief, this works well.

Contrasting type: As far as type is concerned, you commonly want a font which contrasts with the body copy. Depending upon how you intend to use the sidebars, you may wish to pick typestyles that contrast with both the main body and its heads.

Multipurpose use: In my books I commonly set up my sidebar styles so I can use them for emphasis within the main copy also. I use the same font as used in my heads, with a plain, light, or medium version of the font for my sidebar body copy.

If you are printing in color: (or for your ebooks) a pastel color background does not chop up the type nearly so much.

If your sidebars are going to be long: maybe even a parallel story alongside your main body copy, maybe you should try something like Century Schoolbook or even a strong contrast like **Rockwell** or Lucida Bright. Because of the lessened contrast you can use much blacker type than normal. In some cases, an actual Black or Display weight printed at a 70% tint works well.

> ❦ Tables: I commonly use my sidebar styles
> in my tables also. The increased legibility
> helps within the gridwork of a table.

Good formatting is a ministry (a loving service) to your reader

If you are not aware of the options, go to Appendix B ▮

In Appendix B, I go through every command in the New Paragraph Style dialog box—page by page. Simple things—like adjusting the line spacing which is produced by choosing the amount of auto leading—are found within this dialog box once you know where to look.

As mentioned, the commands and options within this dialog box are themselves a short course in typography. Making your type effortlessly readable takes a lot of basic typesetting knowledge that is simply not part of the word processing world.

Let's continue with tables

This is an area of page layout that has only been available for a decade or so. Throughout the '90s, there was no professional application with which to make tables. Many people just did them in Word and ignored the bad type, poor letterspacing, horrible controls, and so on. InDesign has excellent table production tools.

Tables are part of type and edited with the Type tool ■

A table is a grid of text frames called cells: each cell acts much like a normal InDesign text frame. You can insert inline graphics, use paragraph styles and character styles. You can save them into Table styles and Cell styles.

You can have headers and footers with multiple rows of each if you like: When the table continues on the next frame, a new set of headers and footers is generated. The point size of headers can usually be quite small as the reader can usually figure out what the headings are with minimal help.

All selections are done with the type tool, as you can see below: The Type tool changes as it moves over different parts of a table. At the edges, it changes to a small bold arrow that lets you select a row, a column, or (in the upper left corner) you can select the entire table.

Tables can go from frame to frame: column to column and page to page. They flow like text in general with the small surprise that entire rows jump to the top of the next frame even if there is just barely not enough room.

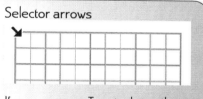

Selector arrows

If you move your Type tool over the corner of the table you are working on, this arrow appears. If you click the mouse, you'll select the entire table.

Similar directional selector arrows appear vertically at the top of columns or horizontally at the left side of rows.

Tables are separate from the rest of the text

In some ways they function like an inline graphic. In most ways they function like an interconnected group of text frames. There are a few limitations though.

- ❦ **You must make a text frame first:** you cannot have a table as a separate object. A table is inserted into an insertion point in the text.

- ❦ **Headers & footers can only be selected or edited in the first frame:** In other wards, on the first page of a table which extends across two or more frames, columns, &/or pages.

- ❦ **Page and column breaks can only happen between rows:** If you think about it, partial cells would be impossible to deal with.

- ❦ **Shortcuts are often different:** Table has its own context in the Keyboard Shortcuts dialog. You can set shortcuts that only work in tables. In fact, it can be quite disconcerting that many of your normal page navigation controls do not work from within a table.

- ❦ **Tables can extend outside the enclosing text frame:** In this way they function like an inline graphic.

 However, it can be hard to select type in the cells outside the text frame which contains the table: You'll have to put your insertion point in a cell inside the enclosing text frame and then tab through to get to the cells outside the frame. That's the only way which works reliably. This can cause printing problems also.

Table design

When setting type, there are times when rules, leaders, tabs, and columns are simply not enough. It can be argued (and Bringhurst does in his typography book) that anything more than simple tabs with no rules or leaders goes too far. That may have been true in the last century. But in this one — *He is **wrong!***

However, there is certainly a need for restraint. Too many rules, boxes, and borders imprison type and make it feel cheap. Sometimes cheap is what you need, but do it on purpose in that case. Especially in the case of tables you need to keep it light and easy to read.

Table & Cell Styles

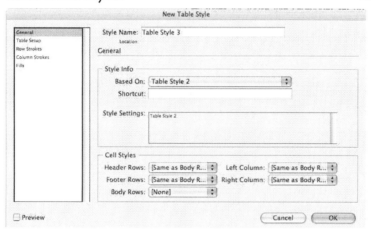

Beginning with InDesign CS3 Adobe had taken the capabilities of Paragraph, Character, and Object styles and used them to create styles for that unique text object, Tables. You can do amazing things with tables once you become comfortable with them. We offer advanced form design with tables in books sold on my Lulu Author Spotlight.

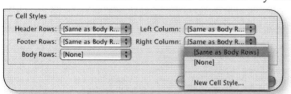

Assuming that you are familiar with how styles work, Table & Cell styles still take a little preplanning. Cell Styles come first: It is important that you set them up before you make your Table Styles—because—the first choices you make in a table style is which cell styles you are going to apply and where. Of course, it is possible to add new cells styles inline, as you see above.

Cell Styles (CHARACTER STYLES FOR TABLES)

Cell styles format selected cells in a table. You can control the paragraph style used, how the text is located within each cell, the stroke and fill of the cells, and the diagonal lines you might want to use. In the New Table Style dialog are separate choices for header rows, footer rows, the left column, the right column, and body rows

Text page

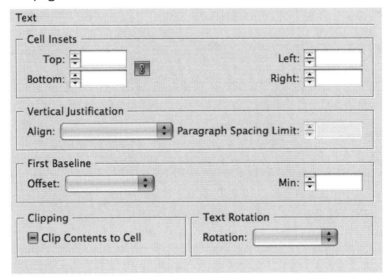

This page controls everything in the Text Frame Options dialog, plus the ability to do limited text rotation in 90° increments.

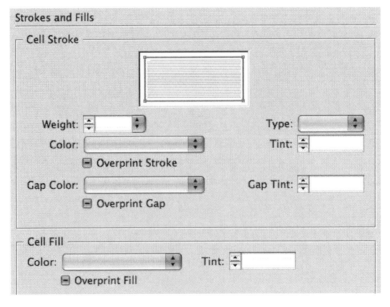

Strokes and Fills

This page allows you to set the stroke for each side of the cell with the normal choices of the Stroke panel. You click on the proxy lines to turn them on or off. Sadly, the colors you choose have to be in the Swatches panel before you start the process, or you'll have to quit and go create the new swatches necessary. Plus, if you use a gradient, you can't tint it. If you want those options like we do, go make a feature request at the Adobe site.

Diagonal lines

We assume some people somewhere use these. What else can we say?

To repeat, you need to set up all your Cell styles before you build your table styles. Actually, you don't but you'll waste a lot of time that way.

Table Styles

Table styles use all the controls for tables that you are familiar with plus you can apply cell styles to specific rows like the header rows, footer rows, left column, right column and body rows. This is where you set the overall table border and any alternating strokes or fills you might want. You can also set the space before & after the table here also.

Again the styles are very straight forward and use the same basic concepts and techniques as the text and object styles we have already covered.

Table Style: General

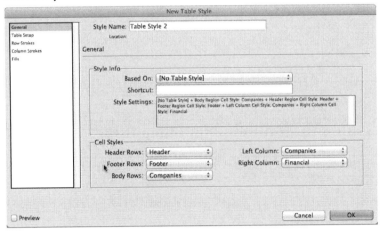

You've seen this already in Table Options

Table Style: Setup

Here you can set the border of the entire table, or that portion of the table shown in each frame, column, and page. Cell styles can override portions of this if you wish, because they are applied on top of the table style.

Table spacing: This is the only place you can control the space before and after a table. Even though a table seems to be in a paragraph, paragraph spacing will not control it.

Stroke drawing order: Best Joins is good.

Table Style: Row Strokes

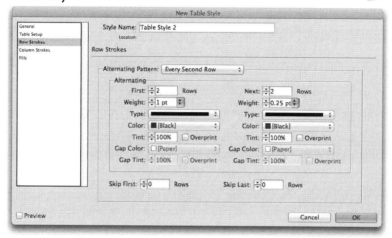

You have many options here: Every Other Row, Every Second Row, Every Third Row, or whatever Custom setup you can imagine with only two choices. Plus, you can skip x# of first rows or last rows.

Table Style: Column Strokes

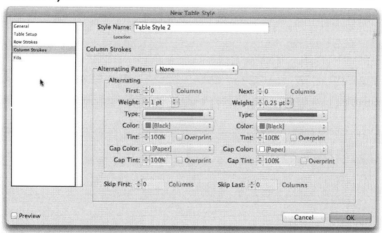

Here you have the same choices vertically.

Fills

You also have the same alternating choices for fills. The only limitation is that you have to choose whether you will use alternating rows or columns. You cannot do both. Shucks!

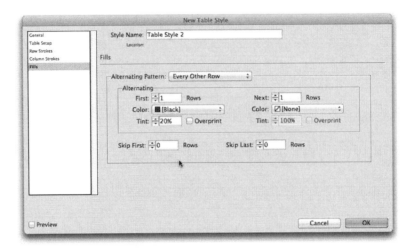

General guidance

The only real limitations are your sense of taste & style. However, remember the goal—presenting written copy in a manner that is easy to read. Each cell is like an individual text frame. So, anything you can do with text, you can do in a table. This includes things like inline graphics, drop caps, lists, and so on.

A Pictorial Guide

For this little booklet about the cities of New Mexico, I developed a form that flowed from page to page without a hitch. The only issue was making all the photos the same height.

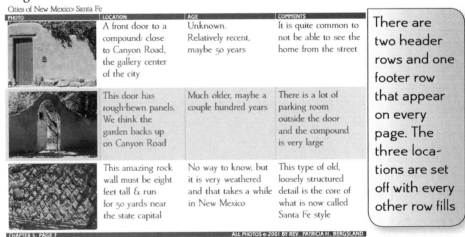

Cities of New Mexico: Santa Fe

PHOTO	LOCATION	AGE	COMMENTS
	A front door to a compound: close to Canyon Road, the gallery center of the city	Unknown. Relatively recent, maybe 50 years	It is quite common to not be able to see the home from the street
	This door has rough-hewn panels. We think the garden backs up on Canyon Road	Much older, maybe a couple hundred years	There is a lot of parking room outside the door and the compound is very large
	This amazing rock wall must be eight feet tall & run for 50 yards near the state capital	No way to know, but it is very weathered and that takes a while in New Mexico	This type of old, loosely structured detail is the core of what is now called Santa Fe style
CHAPTER 3, PAGE 7		ALL PHOTOS © 2001 BY REV. PATRICIA H. BERGSLAND	

There are two header rows and one footer row that appear on every page. The three locations are set off with every other row fills

A course calendar

This is one those horrible tables that are necessary. The challenge, of course, at a school is to make them seem non-bureaucratic. The following setup seemed to work reasonably well. It's a two-page table with a header. I tossed a lot of strange color into to the mix just to fool them into believing that this might be something relevant to their iPhone, texting, gaming world. It actually seemed to work pretty well back in 2007.

AD250: Page Layout • Summer 2007 • Submission Schedule & Deadlines				
AD250	Tuesday	Lecture	Thursday	Lecture
Week 1	7/17: Welcome!	**General Intro:** to course and page layout	7/19: **1st Class Email**	**Getting set up:** Chap#1 workspace: Defaults, preferences, workspaces, shortcuts
Week 2	7/24: 2nd Class Email **Theory 1:** Noon	**Reading:** Chap #2 Page Layout: project folder, backup, new doc, bleeds, slug,	7/26: 3rd Class Email **Tutorial 1 Due:** 3 pm	**Setting up project:** Chap #2 DEMO: booklet, pages, pages panel
Week 3	7/31: Class Email **BIO:** Noon	**Importing text:** Chap #3&4: discussion and demo	8/2: Class Email	**Text layout tools:** Chap#6: Rules and tables
Week 4	8/7 : Class Email **Theory 2:** Noon	**Graphics:** Chap #5: Pen tool, shapes, strokes, fills, gradients	8/9: Class Email **Tutorial #2:** 3 pm	**Creating outlines:** Chap#5: Pathfinder, editing paths, effects, corner effects

Building Forms

One of the secrets of this industry is that tables are the best solution to forms—old-fashioned printed forms to be filled out with a pen or pencil. You will be surprised at the number of times you need to design a form to be filled out by hand. The largest problem with forms is that so few people actually fill them out.

The stats are a little better for online forms that are submitted with a click of a button. However, for printed forms it is common to discover that only 10% to 25% of the forms printed actually get filled out by your readers. This is a similar problem to the readability issue for typography as a whole.

Some simple rules & guidelines in form design

- ❦ In a book: Is it really necessary? Remember, they are going to have to tear out a page from your book to use it. Growing up in school leaves most of us with a taboo on book damage.

- ❦ Always fill out the form yourself: If it bothers you, no one else will even try to fill it out.

- ❦ Find testers: Hopefully you can find members of the demographic you are trying to reach. But, equally important is to have a forms proofer who looks for inconsistencies, items missing, poor organization, lack of interior alignments, and so on.

- ❦ Leave enough room: Think up the longest content you think will be used.

- ❦ Use enough leading: The old hand-drawn forms used a 24-point leading as a minimum in most cases. That corresponds to a third of an inch (and often that seems cramped). If you leave too much space the writers will tend to write too large, but give them some breathing room at least.

- ❦ Organize it logically: Simple things like having the home phone, work phone, cell phone, fax, and email in the same general area are often overlooked.

- ❦ Ask for everything you need: I just finished a registration form where one of the critical pieces of data needed was the age of registrant—but they never told me that.

If you need more help on forms design

I wrote an entire book on it for CS2 called *Tables & Form Design in InDesign* that was surprisingly popular. I also included quite a bit of the forms design materials in *Adobe® InDesign® CS4: Styles & Forms*. You can find either of these books in my Lulu Author Spotlight. Just search for form.

http://www.lulu.com/spotlight/radiqxpress

Once it is written, what then?

Let's start with a brief review of the process to make sure we are on the same page. Again, this is a very complex process. It is not particularly difficult, but the procedure is certainly not simple.

The book production process

1. Get the vision: You start with your idea. You research the market and try to determine your niche. This is an area fraught with uncertainty, because you really have no idea if it will sell or who will buy it. Even free books need to be positioned to attract your readers instead of people looking for firestarter.

2. Pick a size: This again is more complicated than it looks. But in another way it is no real problem. Anything you choose to start with can easily be reformatted to another size once everything is in place and completely controlled by styles. When in doubt start with a 6×9 page.

    You need to pray about this or at least seriously think about it. Many times I have been led to a specific size to use for a particular book. Remember who is going to use your book. Know the demographics of your future (and commonly unknown to you as yet) group of readers—your niche. Often it will surprise you once you actually begin selling your book.

    For CS6, you need to plan things out a bit: Alternate layouts work well but it is a whole new type of workflow. Alternate layouts are meant to solve the problem of sending an ebook to various tablets and smartphones. I am still just using a Primary Text Frame and doing my additional formats individually. I find I usually need to write new copy or produce new graphics—especially for the ePUBs and Kindle versions where special fonts don't work well.

3. Using your set of default styles begin writing: All you do is type Command+Num6 (or what ever shortcut you use for your headline style) and start writing.

You need to keep these styles fluid in your mind. One of the real blessings of using styles is that you can develop your book style over the first few chapters.

There will be a real ebb and flow as you adjust your styles—especially your paragraph spacing—as you watch the pages come together.

4. When it is written: You need to add your front and back matter. Actually the need for these features of the book will become apparent as you are writing. In this book, for example, it became obvious that quite a bit of both the basic and advanced materials needed to be moved to appendices at the back of the book.

If I didn't do that, you (the reader) were going to be either bored by the basic stuff you already know, or worse, overwhelmed by more advanced items. I needed to separate things like editing the code of your ePUB where most of you have little, if any, knowledge or experience—and few want to learn it.

What is front and back matter?

There are several (often many) pages of materials that need to be at the front and back of your book. Many of them are optional. Several are not. Some are required for print but not used for ebooks. For example, you must have a title page and a copyright page. You almost certainly need a Table of Contents (the actual type should not be in an ebook though the setup must be done). You may or may not need an introduction, a dedication, or any of about a dozen other possibilities. You should have an index for non-fiction (again the search functions of an ebook make this unnecessary and very difficult to implement).

The following is deeply indebted to Wikipedia and the volunteer writers and editors who have spent so much time putting information like this together for us to use.

Front matter choices

- Advertising blurbs and testimonials: This would include lists of additional books by the author and quotes from reviewers. I know they are commonplace, but they are certainly gauche.

  Though this is merely my opinion, such self-aggrandizing always seems a bit desperate and is bragging at best (be it on your head).

- Half Title: This page just has the title—no subtitle, author name, or anything else. It is the first page inside the cover. You normally use the title font and style from the cover, but smaller.

- Frontispiece: This is an illustration on the page facing the title page. As you can see below, this can be a very stylish and elegant way to start your book. If done well, it offers comfort and tradition to your book design. You should consider this.

An old German title page with frontispiece from 1722

- Title page: This page is commonly a reduced version of your book cover, unless you use a frontispiece. Ideally the title page shows the title of the work, the person or group responsible for its intellectual content, the place & year of publication, and the name of the publisher.

- Copyright page: This is normally on the back of the title Page. Some would say that it is absolutely required to be there. It contains copyright owner name and the year, the publishing staff, edition and printing information, ISBN#, cataloging details for the Library Of Congress. The lawyers love this page in a big publishing house. Hopefully, we are more merciful than that.

- Table of contents: This is built and updated with the Table of Contents... command at the bottom of the Layout menu. It's powerful and I have a tendency to add too much. I am in the process of rethinking my TOC use. I'm moving smaller subhead content to the index.

- List of figures: This is more needed for fine art books than anything, but this would be the place it goes. It is also produced with the TOC commands. You'll need special paragraph styles for your captions which can then be collected.

- List of tables: If your book is data-driven, this might be a good service for your readers. This is also produced with the TOC commands. You'll need special paragraph styles for your table headers which can then be collected.

- Dedication: This where you name the people whose inspiration enabled you to write the book.

- Acknowledgments: These are all the people, groups, and Websites who helped you.

- Foreword: This is written by a real person, other than yourself.

- Preface: This covers the story of how the book came into being, or how the idea for the book was developed. It often includes the acknowledgments.

- ❦ Introduction: Here you can give the purpose, goals, and organization of your book. This is where you tell the reader the devices you use throughout the book [like little graphics for tips, how you will identify sources, and things like that].

- ❦ Prologue: Written by the narrator or a character in the book, this gives the setting and background details, some earlier story that ties into this book, or other relevant details. It sets the stage for the real content.

Many of these things are not necessary or even desirable for all books. You need to be careful that you don't bore the reader into tears—to the place where they simply put the book down because it is too much trouble to get to the actual content of the book. [Which is why they bought the book in the first place, remember?]

Back matter choices

There are many options here also. These are more reader services and references to help them as they read your book. Where much of the front matter helps fiction, the back matter is almost entirely for non-fiction. Of course, Tolkien loved to add back matter about Middle Earth—which further developed the reality of his fictional world.

It's all up to you. However, if you ignore all of these things, the reader might well feel the book is not complete.

- ❦ Epilogue: This is a great service to the reader in fiction. For me and my wife anyway, we often talk about books that just dump you off with many of the issues unresolved. We want completion, a sense that we know what happened and that it's all OK.

To quote from Wikipedia:

"An epilogue is a final chapter at the end of a story that often serves to reveal the fates of the characters. Some epilogues may feature scenes only tangentially related to the subject of the story. They can be used to hint at a sequel or wrap up all the loose ends. They can occur at a significant period of time after the main plot has ended. In some cases, the epilogue has been used to allow the main character a chance to 'speak freely'. An epilogue can continue in the same narrative style and perspective as the preceding story, although the form of an epilogue can occasionally be drastically different from the overall story."

- ❧ Afterword: "When the author steps in and speaks directly to the reader, that is more properly considered an afterword."

- ❧ Conclusion: This is also called a summary or a synopsis.

- ❧ Appendix/Addendum: This contains additional materials to flesh out a particular portion of the book. As mentioned, I have added six+ major appendices to this book to help keep a good reading experience in the body of the book.

  You might consider yet another option as a reader service. As Appendices they can work really well. But, they can also be released as separate booklets for readers of earlier editions and for more advanced readers who might otherwise skip your book.

- ❧ Glossary: Relevant word definitions

- ❧ Bibliography: Books used and additional readings

- ❧ Index: Word and phrase references by page

- ❧ Errata: No longer needed for on-demand publishing. We simply upload a revised version.

- ❧ Colophon: "With the development of the private press movement from around 1890, colophons became conventional in private press books, and often included a good deal of additional information on the book, including statements of limitation, data on paper, ink, type and binding, and other technical details. Some such books include a separate 'Note about the type', which will identify the names of the primary typefaces used, provide a brief description of the type's history and a brief statement about its most identifiable physical characteristics." [Wikipedia]

This is just a fun addition, especially for a book like this that is about book production. Come to think of it: I have forgotten to do this. Let me go do that now———Done!

Hopefully, you've been thinking about these things

The appropriate time to add front matter and back matter is during the writing of the book. A passage may suggest an appendix. For example, as I was editing yesterday, I noticed that it was really confusing to refer the reader to my Website to get the instructions to add the basic paragraph styles with which to start your use of them. It seemed good to add a sub-section pf appendix B to cover that—hence appendix B2.

Concern for reader confusion may lead to a prologue to ease them into the main story or content.

Mainly you need to be aware that all of these other things exist. Then you will develop them in process while you are writing. It's not good to start dealing with them after everything is written. Often you've forgotten the incidents that will trigger good reader service content like this.

Again! It's all about the reader

Continuously, you must be thinking about serving the reader. You are writing this for them and they deserve all the help you can give them. Often you need to radically shift things.

For example, in my verse by verse Bible studies it finally dawned on me that I was raising an almost impenetrable barrier to reading the book with all my front matter. I had an introduction/prologue that included doctrinal statements, a short (it grew with each book) testimony, and more. The short testimony of my spiritual walk at the front of the book finally grew to over a half dozen pages and was keeping the readers from reaching the real content. So, I changed it to a reference in the introduction and moved it to an afterword in the back matter.

In fact, I have started moving much of this material to the back of all my books in multiple appendices. I leave a brief listing of the appendixes available and then go on with the main part of the book. I did this to give the reader easier access to the real content. Try to watch yourself as you read other books to see what you find irritating.

Excessive front matter

This is especially true of ebooks. This is where I first actually noticed the problem. Front matter is really jarring there. There is really no comfortable way to flip pages and skip to the actual content in an ebook. So you want to get the reader there quickly. I have eliminated or moved all the front matter in all my ebooks except for a very brief copyright statement and the dedication.

But there is no right or wrong here. You need to determine what your reader would like. You might ask them in your blog. For sure, ask your reviewers. Make sure you have people from your target audience doing your reviews. Above all do not use these devices to "bulk up" your book. That's a subtle form of fraud. If the content is not necessary, do not add it to your book. K.I.S.S. (Keep It Simple Stupid) is the principle to follow in all design—especially book design.

Dealing with large & complex books

One of the important panels for assembling your book is the Pages panel. Adobe, in its wisdom, has made this slightly more difficult for us in CS6. Strangely, the basic issue is that the design of this panel still caters to people coming from Quark, though you are not.

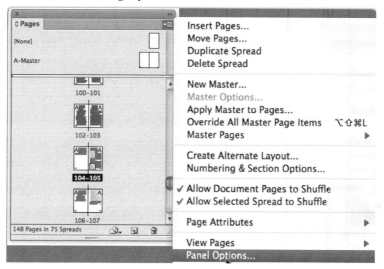

What I am talking about is that the default view of the Pages panel is very clumsy to use in a practical way. As you can see above, in the default layout, you can only see 3.5 spreads, and there is an incredible amount of wasted space in the panel. By simply opening the Pages Panel Options dialog, you can make this panel much more useful. You can rearrange things so you can see 8-20 page spreads at the same time—depending on the width of the panel. This became more difficult because CS6 chooses to hide the main horizontal/vertical control for the pages.

As you can see on the next page, there is a simple check box for Show Vertically remaining in the Masters section of the dialog. There has been one of these in the pages portion also—in every version since InDesign One first came out in 2000.

Now to change it, you need to right-click on the pages section of the actual dialog box (once you have finished setting the options) or choose the View Pages command at the bottom of the panel menu (as you can see on the previous page. This View Pages command is vertically by default. Change it to hori-

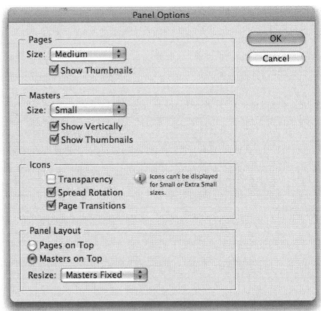

zontally. This is so important that you really need to change your application defaults by fixing the Pages Panel with no pages open.

As you can see, with these simple changes I can now see twelve spreads and probably four master spreads (if I were to use that many). The dialog box becomes much more usable. You can also see how the Show Thumbnails checkbox help you tell where you are in the book.

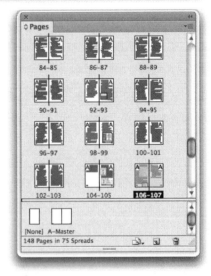

Using the Pages Panel

You can drag'n'drop pages into a new location. You can add pages or master pages by simply right-clicking on the pages or master pages portion of the panel. You can apply masters by drag'n'drop (frustrating to control, though), or by right-clicking on the appropriate page or pages in the panel. You can add sections, create an alternate layout if you are working on a DPS digital magazine project, and quite bit more with the commands in the panel menu out of the upper right corner of the panel.

Numbering the front matter pages

There is one special convention you need to follow. Front matter has a different type of page numbers. They use lowercase roman numerals whereas the body of the work uses arabic numerals. To set this up you need to add blank pages before your content and make them into a new section.

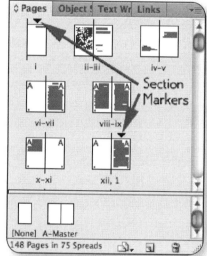
Section Markers

 In CS6, you'll also want a set of master pages which have no Primary Text Frame. Otherwise you can really snarl things up by adding things like a table of contents—making it part of the main story going throughout the book. That makes updating the table of contents almost impossible. The same is true of copyright data and so on.

Sections

Your book can have as many sections as you need. But there are always at least two: front matter and the book. To make a new section, you select a page in the Pages panel and then either right-click or use the panel menu in the upper right corner of the panel. Choose "Numbering & Section Options…". You can tell existing sections in the Pages panel by the little black triangle over the top of the page in the panel. As you can see in the capture above, this edition is currently running twelve pages for the front Matter. That will change and be adjusted as I go through the writing and production of this book. I usually only use these two sections, but I could use sections for the appendixes.

For this book, the Numbering & Section Options dialog box looks like what you see next for the first page of the actual copy. The front matter section also starts with page one, but uses the i, ii, iii, iv... (lowercase Roman numerals) style. Always check the page numbers in the Pages panel afterward to make sure they are correct.

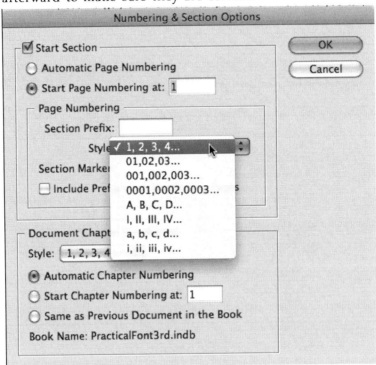

In the Book panel (talked about next) every document after the first one has Automatic Numbering checked.

The back matter usually continues the same numbering as the body content

By the way, these page numbers are the ones used for the Table of Contents and the Index. So make sure they work well for those uses. Also, Sections normally start on the odd pages (as do Parts and Chapters). These things are not major items, but not doing things in this manner proves to the readers that you do not know what you are doing.

Dealing with blank pages

Blank pages need a different master. As I briefly mentioned, applying masters to a page is most easily done by selecting the page or pages in the Pages panel. Then you can simply right-click to access the Apply Master to Pages... command. Th problem with blank pages is that there is a very strong convention in the book design business to not have anything on the blank page.

The simplest way to do this is to scroll through the Pages panel and look for empty pages. This is where the Show Thumbnails option in the Panel Options... dialog comes into its own. You'll be able to see the blank pages (though it can be slightly confusing if you use a header or footer on your master page). I usually use the default [None] master page to clear off the blanks. It cannot be deleted anyway, as you can tell by the brackets.

Full page illustrations

Many people believe that you should also clear off the pages covered with an illustration (or a full page ad). I must admit I find this convention irritating. I remember the countless times I have searched through a magazine trying to figure out where I was, because all the page numbers were gone from the advertising pages. I would make this optional, but many people insist.

The Book panel

If your books are like mine (very graphically intensive), you may find that certain operations like adding words to the User Dictionary and spell checking in general can cause InDesign to lock up after the book reaches a certain size. That happened to me with this book.

I don't like to use this option unless I have to. But once I do it solves many problems while raising new issues.

Start by opening a new book

This opens a small panel. You can add this panel to one of your side panels, but InDesign will not allow you to save it there in your workspace. It will always need to be opened separately. Actually, every time you Save As to clean up your book, it will pop off the dock. In fact, if you reset your workspace (to get your panels back to where you want them) the book panel will be removed and placed behind your documents. You'll be able to find it at the bottom of your Window menu.

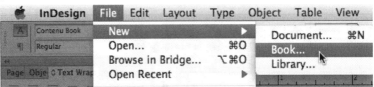

You add chapter/sections by clicking the little plus at the bottom of the panel. Add them in order, as there is no way of reordering them once you add them. Once you have them added, you need to open each one (double-click on the listing in the Book panel), and open the Pages panel. Right-click on the little section symbol above the first page of the added document. This will enable you to check Automatic Page Numbering in the Numbering and Sections dialog box. Once you have checked this the book documents will automatically continue the numbering through out the book (as you can see below). In fact, in CS6 these numbers will change as you automatically add pages while you are writing into your Primary Text Frame.

◊ WritinginInDesignWork		►►	⫶≡
WritinginInDesignWork	i-144		
WritinginInDesignWorkAppA	145-204		
WritinginInDesignWorkAppB	205-245		
WritinginInDesignWorkAppC	246-276		
WritinginInDesignWorkAppD	277-295		
WritinginInDesignWorkAppE	296-330		
WritinginInDesignWorkAppF	331-352		

There are two icon indicators you must be aware of in the dialog. First is the strange multi-shape icon in front of the first document above. The second ones are the open book icons you see after the top and second from the bottom in the list of documents. The first one indicates the Style Source. This is the document that has the styles which will be used when synchronizing the book. The open book tells you which documents are currently open in InDesign.

Synchronizing your book

This works like a champ. You simply select the command on the Options menu (or click on the little double arrow icon at the bottom of the Book panel), and all selected documents will be synchronized to the Style Source.

Of course, it is not quite that easy. What it does is add all styles to the other documents. If you have added styles to later documents they will not be added to the Source document—unless you click on front of the document where you added the style and make that your source. Then you can synchronize to add it throughout the book.

Another minor irritant is that when you synchronize, the alphabetical listing will be all snarled up. You can choose Sort By Name at the bottom of the Option menu of the panel to reorder the styles.

As you can see in the Book panel Option menu to the left, you can Preflight the book, package the entire book (if you have none selected in the panel) or the selected documents, export the entire book or selected docs to a PDF for uploading to print it, export the entire book to ePUB, synchronize, update all the numbering (if necessary), set the page numbering options and so forth. It's all very handy.

Add Document...
Replace Document...
Remove Document

Save Book
Save Book As...
Close Book

Preflight Book...
Package Selected Documents For Print...
Export Selected Documents to PDF...
Export Book to EPUB...
Print Selected Documents...

Document Information...
Reveal in Finder

Synchronize Selected Documents
Synchronize Options...
Update All Cross-References

Update Numbering   ▶
Book Page Numbering Options...
Document Numbering Options...

Automatic Document Conversion
Merge Identically Named Layers on Export

Small Panel Rows

It does take some watching. If you decide to redefine a style, you should do it in the Style Source document, and when you synchronize, you need to go through the all the documents to make sure that changes in paragraphs, anchored objects, and graphics in general have not messed up your layouts. But other than those rather obvious issues it works flawlessly.

Dealing with the supplier/distributors

SEVERAL DAYS, WEEKS, MONTHS, OR YEARS HAVE TRANSPIRED NOW as you have written your book. The front matter, body, and back matter is now complete. You have the cover designed and you've written the description. You've researched keywords to help searchers find your book. As far as you know, you're ready to go.

So, you need to get the book proofed and published. My assumption is that you are an author with very limited capital and few personnel resources. Once I accept this focus, there are relatively few suppliers. [If you hear of another one, please let me know and I'll add it to the book.] In early 2012, I am going to share techniques that work for Lulu, Createspace, Scribd, Amazon, Kindle, Smashwords, and Zazzle.

Yes, there are more showing up all the time. But most of them have up front fees—and often those fees are substantial. The best one I have heard of is BookBuddy which requires an upfront payment of $99.00 or more to upload a new book. But these techniques will almost certainly work for the new startups we will see in the next decade.

ISBN Numbers

To be a publisher, this is required. One of the major hassles in getting books published in the old paradigm was the ISBN number required to sell your book on Amazon, Barnes & Noble, and all the rest. Both Lulu and Createspace offer free ISBN numbers. You can also use ones you have purchased yourself. These are essential for distribution. If you use the free ISBN they supply, they will be listed as the publisher of record—though you put your own name (publishing house) on the copyright page.

 Who's the publisher? You are: Even though you might decide to use the free ISBN#s supplied by Lulu and Createspace, you are still the publisher. Although they are listed as publisher of record (because they own the ISBN#), they are actually your printer. Createspace, for example, will flag your book if you say they are the publisher and make you change the copy.

If you want to supply your own ISBN#: you need to register as a publisher and buy a block of them. ISBN number costs are complex and ridiculous. You can buy them in blocks of 1, 10, 100, or 1000 for $125, $250, $575, or $1000 from Bowker in the US. At the time I wrote this, you also needed to translate them into EAN-13 codes at $20-$25 per code depending on the quantity (but there are quite a few free barcode sources online). It seems obvious that Lulu and Createspace have purchased them at a large enough quantity to make their costs virtually negligible for them. The free ISBN option is a wonderful thing for us.

If you want to purchase your own single ISBN: so that you are listed as the publisher, Lulu and Createspace charge a hair under $100 for that service (a little cheaper than Bowker). That is better than the $125 single number price mentioned above (cut from $275 at the end of last year). Yes, that's steep, but it is still much cheaper than the smallest publishing package from a vanity press. They tend to start somewhere between $1000 and $2000 and go up from there (plus you are left with boxes of books in your garage to dispose of eventually).

> The main reason I'll start buying my own ISBN#s is distribution options For example, Christian books really need to be in the Christian Book Distributors [CBD] catalog and on the CBD Website. There is no access to CBD unless you are an "official" publisher. This means you need your own ISBN#s so you can register your publishing company with Bowker.
>
> Once you are registered you can use a printer like Snowfall Press. If you have your own ISBN#s they will distribute and print your books for free just like Lulu and Createspace do. CBD requires this "official" status to stock your ebooks also.

Consider the size of your niche

For example, my niche [people who write in InDesign] is very small. The total size may be only a few hundred people. For me to pay $125 for an ISBN# from Bowker would eat up much of my profits. However, if you have a larger niche, buying your own ISBN is a very good investment because you can use it for a number of different printers and it keeps your options open. Plus, many distributors will not distribute your books unless you are a listed publisher with your own ISBN#s at Bowker. You see one example in the sidebar above.

You can always upgrade later

Because of the way this works, you can always buy a block or purchase a single ISBN later if one of your books starts selling well and you want wider distribution. All you need to do is publish a new edition with few (if any) content changes. You are really in control in the new publishing paradigm. ***Don't spend money that's not required.***

I do want to briefly cover the companies I use and share their basic capabilities. You can find the step by step procedures in Appendix D

Lulu

On a practical level, these are the people who started this whole thing in 2002. Their concept was to offer on-demand publishing services for free. Their profit comes from a very reasonable royalty of 20% per sale (plus they almost certainly make a little with their production charges). In other words—you, as the creator, get 80% of the money received after the production costs are subtracted [unless you are offering the book at retail. Retail distribution requires a full 100% markup. So you get about 40% royalty there, but you still get the 80% if the book is sold through Lulu's Website]. For their ebooks you get the full 80% minus $.99.

They have a huge number of options in many sizes and many bindery options—plus, they offer the best printing quality and the best ePUB access to iBooks of the free suppliers (they are one of Apple's official aggregators).

One of the unique things they offer (& very profitably for me) are high quality, printable PDF downloads. But they recently moved the downloadable PDFs to their own page which cut those sales significantly. For my niche, many readers are aware of the typographic messes which are currently called ebooks [whether ePUB or Kindle]. My PDF sales have dropped off radically in recent months—though they were over 50% for the past two years. Right now most of my sales through Lulu are the ePUBs.

Paperbacks

They offer paperbacks that can be perfect bound [square spine], saddle-stitched [stapled spine], or coil bound [plastic spiral wire spine]. The contents can be black & white or full color. The covers are always in color. They can handle projects from one to 800 pages. The minimum and maximum number of pages depends on the size picked and the distribution plan chosen.

Hard cover

They offer both casewrap and dust cover versions from 24 to 800 pages, depending on the options selected. Plus, they offer two large premium hard cover options: 12" x 12" and 12.75" x 10.75" landscape with premium smooth finish paper in full color for coffee table books.

Specialty books

They offer cookbooks, calendars, yearbooks, wedding books, portfolios, poetry books, and photobooks. These specialty books use Lulu templates so I do not use them much. But I find that I am using the spiral-bound binding option more and more for a workbook edition. Workbooks are a work in process for me, but I really like them..

Ebooks

Any of the books can be made available as a downloadable PDF. They also offer ePUB distribution to iBookstore with a free ISBN [they are an official iPad aggregator]—as long as you charge for the book. The design of ePUBs is covered in Appendix E.

 Lulu options change: As they develop new deals they change names and offers. They have many more options now than they did in 2003 when I started. However, sometimes these have negative effects like the separation of the printed books from the downloadable PDF recently.

ISBN#s & Distribution

If you get a free ISBN# number from Lulu (currently called ExtendedReach™), it includes a listing on Amazon. If you provide an ISBN# or purchase a single ISBN#, you have to buy the GlobalReach™ distribution package (but you can still use the free one Lulu provides if you wish). This gets you wider distribution and costs a minimal $75. You do have to buy a proof copy and approve it.

With no ISBN#

Nothing is required. They used to offer what they named MarketReach™ for $25 to get you listed with Lulu's Amazon Marketplace and eBay.com with a possibility of more to come. At this point, Amazon has cut off that option. This is necessary with coil-bound books, for example, or the more unusual sizes [including the premium coffee table books]. You do not even have to buy a proof here (though it is normally still a good idea to do so).

Payments

Lulu pays directly to your PayPal account, monthly—around the fifteenth for the previous month. You do need a PayPal business account, but it is free and can be set up in a couple days.

Createspace (by Amazon)

To quote them from their original press release, "Createspace books sold on amazon.com are printed on demand, display "in stock" availability on amazon.com and can be shipped within 24 hours from when they are ordered. The books are automatically eligible for Search Inside!™, Amazon Prime™, Super Saver Shipping™ and other amazon.com programs as well."

Because Amazon is now the 500# gorilla this is the best source for selling printed books. Your only required cost is the cost of a proof. Lately Amazon has been making many in the industry angry because of their strong-arm tactics. But the fact remains, they sell more printed books online and Kindle ebooks than anyone else, by far.

The printing quality of Createspace is not quite as good

> Createspace has recently developed an online digital proofer
> It works well. But if you're not an experienced proofer and copy editor, you'll need to be very careful. The new proofer also provides a downloadable PDF.

on the occasions when I printed virtually identical versions on the two sites. It seems like the RIP is limited. For example, they require a rasterized cover at 300 dpi which really compromises the quality of the typography on the cover. Their quality control sometimes slacks off. But you cannot deny they sell books.

 Amazon pushes Createspace books harder: they offer more marketing options and better listings (which they obviously consider in-house offerings). As mentioned, recently they have cut off many of the books offered through Lulu and Lightning Source (the on-demand publishing standard for "real" publishers with their own ISBN#s and distribution). For printed books, Createspace books have been outselling Lulu's offerings by quite a bit. On the other hand, Lulu seems to do a better job selling the more unusual titles in unique niches. Plus, Lulu has the downloadable PDF option which sold as well as Createspace's printed option with higher royalties (because there are no production costs) until very recently. Additionally, Lulu ePUBs do well in iBookstore, at no cost to you. **Both companies are needed to market your books.**

Paperbacks

Createspace sells only paperbacks in a slightly reduced variety of sizes (compared to Lulu) and only perfect-bound. They offer black & white (color cover) or full color books. With the B&W books you can make a custom trim size (but with limited distribution).

 Standard sizes: for the best distribution you need to pick from the traditional, industry standard sizes. Both Createspace and Lulu tell you what those sizes are. We covered the current offerings earlier in the Page Layout Basics chapter (see page 56). In most cases, you'll need a 6x9—trade paperback version. Do not hesitate to try several sizes [no extra cost].

ISBN#s

They provide four ISBN options: a free Createspace-assigned ISBN, a $10 Custom ISBN where you can name your imprint, a $99 Custom Universal ISBN where you name your imprint and supply distribution, or you can use your own ISBN. Both custom ISBN options are offered through an agreement with Bowker®. Always check because these options change.

The Expanded Distribution Channels

Createspace has a great deal for expanded distribution. For only $25 you get larger distribution. It includes Createspace Direct which provides wholesale books to independent bookstores and book resellers. It also makes the book available to libraries, schools, and academic institutions. Finally, "you can make your book available to thousands of major online and offline bookstores and retailers, and expand the size of the potential audience for your books". They move quite a few distributed books at about half the royalty. It's an excellent deal for the $25 charge.

Payments

They do direct deposit to your banking account every thirty days (with a 45-60 day delay)—with a minimum of $25 in accrued royalties.

Scribd

Downloadable PDF distribution doesn't get much better than this. It was founded in 2007 and is designed for free booklets, but it does give you the option to sell your works. The site shows off your works well. It's a social networking site. I've sold little here, but my free offerings have been downloaded hundreds of times and I'm over 28,000 reads for my total.

I do find that I really need to be careful of my PDFs. Scribd apparently cannot handle transparency or gradient strokes. It also has trouble with really large PDFs.

I look at it as a marketing opportunity that may grow into something. It is built easily from my printing PDF, so it's a no pain, possible gain type of thing. Because it is viewed on the screen, you can do it in full RGB color and have some fun with the design.

My InDesign book has had nearly 1300 people read the preview and it may be generating the sales of the printed versions at Lulu. For some reason I am convinced that this will be an increasingly good resource in the future. But that remains to be seen.

In addition, you can get some idea of interest. When I began publishing free chapters of my possible proposal for a New Publisher book (some of which I am using here), the designing ePUB chapter generated a lot more interest than anything else I have ever offered, for example. This is also the version I send to reviewers and people who have helped me with the book.

Payments

Scribd pays directly to your PayPal account (I don't know if there is a minimum). You do need a PayPal business account, but they are free and can be set up in a couple days.

ePUBs (the ebook standard)

Lulu

Lulu uploads validated ePUBs, adds a free ISBN, and gets them in iBookstore—all for free. It does take a while for Apple to approve the ePUBs and they regularly change the rules. But Lulu keeps you apprised of the changes and the process is very transparent. The sales are good.

They have gotten very restrictive about some things. For example, your title and subtitle must be exactly as shown on your cover. Plus, they must be in initial caps with only a few carefully specified words allowed to be all lowercase. No URLs or links are allowed in the book. On the page at Lulu which talks about these requirements there are now 59 very specific rules you must follow [before they'll accept your book.] From hints I have read, they are absolutely swamped by ePUB uploads.

Publt (Barnes & Noble)

The same ePUB can be uploaded into NookBooks. It does need a different cover and rewritten verbiage for marketing. Sales are not as good as the iPad, but now that the color Nook is Web-capable with Android 2 (making it a small tablet), that will probably change for the better. You cannot use the Lulu ISBN#. But PubIt does not require an ISBN so it is really not an issue.

Smashwords

Mark Coker brought out Smashwords in 2008. He is a man driven to succeed. In a short time he has developed very high visibility and sales through his service are growing quickly. I mention Smashwords only because it is turning out to be a good resource—even though it requires a Word document and minimal graphics. The final file cannot be over 5 MB. However, Smashwords' distribution is the widest of the ebook suppliers going to Sony, iPad, Kobo, Barnes & Noble, Amazon, Diesel ebookstore and the Smashwords site. Mark is pushing the envelope in on-demand publishing. But it really only works for books which are all text like fiction.

Payments

Smashwords pays directly to your PayPal account, quarterly. You do need a PayPal business account.

Kindle

Amazon just came out with a new Kindle plug-in that lets me export a kindle book in the new KF8 format for the Kindle Fire CS5.5 or CS6. It works as advertised, assuming you have the file set up well.

- ❧ The Kindle plug-in for InDesign is only useful if you are using a document designed with the single purpose of exporting that file to Mobi for use on the Kindle (both e-ink and Fire): You'll get a snarled mess if you try to export your print book directly to Kindle.

- ❧ It only recognizes the most basic text formatting and anchored images: one of the reasons I don't use anchored images at all for ebooks.

- ❧ It does do a good job of creating working hyperlinks, the TOC, and footnotes.

- ❧ It embeds fonts well: Assuming that you have the proper licensing to use those fonts.

- 🦃 Section breaks are based on separate InDesign files in a book (you cannot break at a specified Paragraph style): Obviously this can be pretty laborious.

- 🦃 The plug-in will only recognize content order based on a single text thread with inline images: It does not recognize the use of the Articles Panel. (One reason I don't even mention this panel in this book).

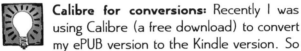 **Calibre for conversions:** Recently I was using Calibre (a free download) to convert my ePUB version to the Kindle version. So far, things look pretty good. It's very fast, and Kindle books are so limited typographically anyway—it really doesn't matter.

But now that KF8 accepts embedded fonts I am using the Kindle export plug-in. In my most recent release, the plug-in worked flawlessly from CS5.5. The plug-in for CS6 has not been released yet. I expect it to come quickly.

There is no real WYSIWYG tool to prepare fancy KF8 books for the Kindle Fire. So far, Kindle remains straight, single-column HTML with no lists or divs or anything that will really help the typography. Format 8 adds HTML5 and CSS3 to the mix. Hopefully, by the next version of InDesign, we'll have some better tools, both from Adobe and from Amazon's Kindle Direct Publishing.

Payments

They do direct deposit to your banking account every thirty days (plus a 30day delay)—with a minimum of $25 in accrued royalties.

Zazzle

This is a giftware supplier using the same basic model as Lulu and the rest. They sell a large variety of items (they claim 250+ as I am writing today). Here's the spring 2011 list:

- 🦃 **Clothing:** Custom T-Shirts; Hoodies; Embroidered Polos; Embroidered Jackets; Shoes

- 🦃 **Accessories:** Bags; Buttons; Hats; Keychains; Necklaces; Ties

- 🐘 **Cards and Postage:** Envelopes; Greeting Cards; Invitations; Labels; Note Cards; Photo Cards; Postage; Postcards

- 🐘 **Home and Pets:** Ornaments; Aprons; Calendars; Coasters; Mugs; Steins; Magnets; Pet Clothing; Photo Sculptures

- 🐘 **Office Products:** Round Stickers; Stationery; 3 Ring Binders; Business Cards; Flyers; Letterhead; Mousepads; Travel Mugs; Rack Cards

- 🐘 **Art and Posters:** Canvas Prints; Posters; Framed Prints; Photo Prints; Photo Enlargements; **Cases;** iPhone and iPad Cases

- 🐘 **More:** Skateboards; Bumper Stickers

- 🐘 They are constantly adding items: speakers, wood gift boxes with magnetic lids, and much more. They are really pushing the envelope constantly.

They print from 300 dpi PNGs made in Photoshop. All reports are that the quality is good. What I have seen were excellent. The prices are not cheap, but then they are on-demand. You set your royalties, as an add-on to their production costs.

Payments

Zazzle pays directly to your PayPal account, monthly (with a $25 minimum)—around the fifteenth for the previous month once the minimum is met. You do need a PayPal business account.

What else is needed?

Time, practice, and perseverance is required. As is the necessity of studying observing, and working on your skill sets. Plus, there is a whole new world emerging.

Designing your ePUBs

Ebooks are becoming a major force in our digital world. If you want to learn how to reformat your book into an ePUB {an ebook on iPad or Nook] read Appendix E on ePUB design and Appendix F on fixing the CSS InDesign produces with InDesign CS5.5.

Designing your Kindle books

Use the ePUB document you built and the Amazon Kindle Export plugin. Just export to Kindle. As mentioned I have started using my own fonts (which solves the licensing problem). In fact, I have started doing my Kindle book first using the fonts used in the printed books. I then convert the Kindle file to an ePUB version by eliminating the font usage and converting to the iPad possibilities.

These Kindle books export and upload flawlessly. The only problem I have seen is that the Mac Kindle app and the iPad app do not support these embedded fonts yet.

Have fun! It's a whole new world!

Dealing with the social realities

I probably should have covered this earlier, but I need to mention it for sure. Actually you should begin this process as soon as you have the basic idea for your new book finalized. Even if you have an agent and a contract with a traditional publishing house, you need an active social presence online.

Your own Website

Probably. But not certainly.

In this day and age, you may do well to focus on your blog and make it your Website. This is what I have done with my main domain bergsland.org where I have The Skilled Workman, my spiritual blog. The reasons for this are many.

1. **Website design is ridiculously complex:** This is getting worse rather than better. Because much content on the Web is interactively delivered from your server, providing custom content according to your needs [in the best cases], you need to be able to understand and write complex code. For most of us, this means hiring a pro. This costs thousands of dollars

2. **Website marketing is a specialized skill:** Usually we are talking about what is called SEO here [Search Engine Optimization]. You can learn the basics of SEO fairly quickly, but if you have major marketing needs, you will do better to hire a pro for this as well. However, both Blogger and WordPress do an adequate job of SEO.

3. **Websites need to updated constantly:** Common wisdom tells us that your home page needs to be updated weekly or better, if possible. If your reader comes back to your site and it looks like it did the last time, they'll quickly quit coming

by to look. Annual updates are the absolute minimum—no matter what kind of site you have.

4. **You have to learn how to code regardless:** At a minimum, you'll need to learn HTML and CSS. There really is no good method of putting up a Website without understanding HTML and CSS. Adobe has come out with Muse [but the coders complain it is overly complex code]. iWeb looked good, but you have to use iPhoto.

The bottom line is that a Website might be good, but it is very hard to monetize. Plus, it is very difficult to develop a site that people actually use.

A blog or two

Blogging has become the de facto minimum within the social Web. You actually do need a blog. After all, it is meant for people like us. We write. We like to write. And we are supposedly good writers. But there are some issues here also.

1. **It takes a solid commitment:** Like your Website, your blog is not going to be instantly popular (barring a miracle). As a result, you must start with a real dedication to your craft and a willingness to keep writing even when you see very few outward results.

2. **It takes consistency:** You really need a schedule. It is possible that you will be one of those people who cannot help yourself and post new things all the time. But, even if you are, you need to make sure that you are consistent. Followers are difficult to find, and you need to keep your commitment in front of you at all times. You're in for the long haul.

3. **It takes frequency:** You do not need to be crazy about this. But you need at least a posting per week, at the same time & day, which your followers can rely upon.

4. **It takes a new writing style:** Blog posts require shorter paragraphs, pithy statements, frequent lists, exceptional headlines, and more.

Blogging is very different from writing a book. People often do not read any further than the bottom of the page. They will not scroll up to see the rest of your amazing prose. Think excitement, joy, helpful, entertaining!

Blogs have a hard time getting traction if they are too diverse. You may want a personal expression blog and a book specific blog. You want one to your niche. You want to include everything interesting to those in your niche without going beyond your competency. Maybe two blogs?

FaceBook for fiction & niche building

We can add MySpace here—for musicians, especially. This is a place to be more personal with your friends. However, you need to stay focused on your writing and the content of your writing. If you write about restoring classic tractors, it is unlikely your friends will be too excited about your latest find in French wine. But then, maybe you're writing about French tractors used by vintners in Bordeaux.

Because FaceBook is so focused on friends, it is not easy to use it for building readership and an audience. It can certainly be done, but it will take a skillful writer with a vastly entertaining wit and style.

However, you can have your blogs post to your FaceBook page. You can certainly post links to new finds in your field. You can post about where you are speaking, signing books, leading tours, and all of that. Of course, Clive Cussler has nearly a quarter million followers and Tom Clancy is running almost 500,000 likes. Check out your favorite authors and see how they do it.

Twitter for your niches

If you have a good non-fiction book and it is selling well, Twitter is the perfect place to develop a feed as a resource for the readers and people of your niche. If you have genuine knowledge, you can make yourself into an indispensable expert quite quickly.

The main thing is to keep tightly focused. A twitter feed is a great resource for the reader, but a very irritating waste of time if most of the tweets do not meet your need.

You are not limited in the number of feeds you can have. Practicality limits how many you can realistically keep track of. The main thing is to keep your tweets useful and meaningful to your readers and your niche.

Linked-In Groups

This network seems to be more about employment and careers. As I work for myself now, I have very little use for this part of it. However, the groups can be very good sources of information and a way to make yourself known. I am using the groups increasingly. It's a good way to meet people in your niche. You'll be surprised. There is probably a group for your niche, maybe several of them.

Find your own way

You need to budget your time and not waste it. There are ways to keep your time expenditures under control. Try things. If they become intrusive cut back. Follow the lead of success and effectiveness. If it doesn't work, drop it. However, this is a long-time commitment to your life as an author. Your readers and fans want and need a way to be in touch with you. Increasingly, it is expected. It's up to you to provide that for them.

You can do this!

Once you get over the hurdle of buying InDesign and learning the basics covered in this book, you will be excited by how much more easily the writing process proceeds for your books. It is truly amazing for someone like me who began with the laborious traditional process that took many months to get a book ready for sale—after it was written.

I began the first edition of this book after an email I received on June 30, 2011. By July 5, I'd basically finished all the body copy—building out of pieces of earlier books and adding new copy as necessary to make it all coherent. It was done as a lark just to see if there was any audience. The first version of the book was published by July 8th, 2011 at 7x10 inches on Createspace. The Lulu 6x9 version (which I have rewritten extensively) was done within a week or so. The ebooks were out shortly thereafter.

I was really surprised at the positive response and the size of the readership. It quickly became obvious that it was worth fleshing it out to include everything I could think of to help people in my new-found niche. This revised and updated 2nd Edition is being written at the beginning of 2012. Hopefully, I will attain that goal and develop a much more useful resource for those of you who love InDesign—especially as a tool with which to write fully formatted books. It will be released as soon as possible after the release of CS6. So far I have added over 150 pages of new content. It's a much better book.

It will take you a while to get that fast, but it'll change your life. Be prepared for surprises. Many of the books I have done had little response. The ones which succeeded surprised me. Over the years a large body of work has emerged. I'm truly amazed at where this all ended up. You will be also.

Have fun with it!

A: Typography

Type has nothing to do with typing.

It is obvious that even the terminology is different. However, we have hardly begun. Much more significant than the new language are the actual mechanics of typesetting. The rules have changed! In fact, one of the difficulties in teaching publishing classes today involves a paradox. Writing classes are secretarial.

1. Classes all teach writing using Word: but Word cannot produce professional typography or the formatting services required by the reader.

2. Writing groups assume Word: if you give them a PDF many will freak out.

3. Learning to type in a keyboarding or word processing class teaches students so many bad habits that you wonder if it is worth it: you'll need to train yourself how to write fully formatted.

As an author, typing skills obviously help. However, you are wasting your time and confusing the entire process if you do not learn to type, format, and edit professionally. To do that you need InDesign.

As my reader, I have no idea what you know

Your background can vary so much that I can't begin to guess what you know and what you do not know. This first appendix covers materials that you probably do not know unless you have studied typography a little and used a page layout program like InDesign for awhile. It is for Office users, primarily. However, I am fully aware that many users of InDesign do not have any typographic training. So, this stuff may be a revelation to you also.

Most of you will find, to your dismay, that many of the things you thought you knew about typing and word processing are simply wrong: Professional type is a whole new world. Things you were taught as necessary now become typographical errors. Your readers can give your books a bad review because of one typo (or typographic error). Many typos are taught as correct writing by people who do not know how to design a book. Type is where the rubber meets the road.

At this point, we're going to talk about some major differences. By the time we finish this chapter, I hope, you will be into the new paradigm enough to notice the rest as you read the materials you come across in daily living. It is very important to realize that these differences are not minor quibbles. They have a major effect on your ability to communicate with type. They are absolutely necessary for professional document construction and career advancement.

Type is not typed!

One of the major concepts of book design (often lost by traditional graphic designers) is the centrality of the copy. Our entire idea is to provide the reader with content which meets his or her need. More than 95% of this communication will take place through the words you place on the document. In fact, most of the books you design will have few graphics—unless you specialize in non-fiction skill training as I do.

This is why this book emphasizes type so strongly. Without type knowledge you will have a hard time communicating. Type is typeset, and that is one of the major skills you'll need in your career.

The old proverb is that a picture is worth a thousand words: This is true, but it takes an exceptional picture to express exactly the thousand words necessary to produce the desired action on the part of the reader. These pictures can be produced. However, they will take you lots of time and money plus the services of an exceptional illustrator or photographer. Even exceptional designers can rarely pull it off without needing additional explanatory verbiage. As wonderful as the mutt below

1,000 word pictures

Here's a picture:
I wish you could tell me what the 1,000 words are. In nonprofessional work, graphics are often just dumped in place with no reason at all — just like the sad mutt above.

right is, explanation is needed. So, in the real world, you will be dealing with words, but we are talking about typeset copy, not typewritten words.

So, who really cares?

Actually, you do. One of the things of which most beginning designers are not aware is the extreme (but usually subconscious) distinctions between what I call secretarial type and professional typeset copy. You are very aware of the differences—just not on a conscious level.

You have been making decisions about companies, products, and services for years that are based, at least part, upon their perceived honesty, integrity, trustworthiness, and so on as seen in their advertising and marketing efforts.

This is true in books also. Many of your readers' perceptions about your concept and content will come from reactions to type used not only inside the book, but on the cover. It is likely you cannot explain the difference at this point. However, you can tell at a glance whether something is bureaucratic, cheap, top quality, and so on by the typography.

The democratization of typography

The problem, of course, is that everyone now believes that they have the capability to produce writing—whatever that means. It is possible (to a very limited extent) in Word, and that covers almost everyone. It is very difficult to generate professional typography in a word processor though. All of this is confused by the fact that everyone has access to the same fonts, and the same basic capabilities. Most people simply do not have any idea how far typography goes beyond word processing.

Before we can get into this, though, we have to start with terminology. Typography requires a new language. Much of this is based on historical printing usage and the font design process. Without at least a few of these terms you will be lost. This has been complicated now that all of the digital terms have been added to the mix.

So, we really need to start with a little of font design. Not only the different fonts, but the internal measurements of each font, the pieces which make up those fonts, and the various characters which are necessary—particularly in our field of book design.

People often start with font design

But this brings us to the first major confusion in typography. Many believe that typography is font choices. They spend a huge amount of time on which fonts to choose, how fonts developed historically, and the reader reactions to these fonts.

This indeed is a good portion of typography, but this pursuit misses the entire point. The point of typography is to use words to communicate. Font choices can help—but this is really a small portion of what we need to be concerned with as typographers and book designers.

Fonts are not typography — fonts are used to create typography.

I am not minimizing the importance of choosing fonts which are easy to read and comfortable for your target audience. But we mustn't confuse the tools and materials with the techniques for using those tools. In addition, we cannot focus on these two areas without maintaining the end product as our primary goal.

For example, let's first consider woodworking for furniture.

- ❦ The type and species of wood chosen (as well as the fabric and hardware)

- ❦ The saws, chisels, planes, and power tools used

- ❦ The smoothing, fitting, and joinery skills employed

- ❦ And the finishing techniques of shaping, adjusting, polishing, and coating

- ❦ Are all subservient: **to the beauty and comfort of the chair being built.**

All the pieces of the process are part of the whole, but they only serve the end goal: comfort and beauty. Plus, of course, how the chair fits the decorating style used.

In this book, I'm focused on typography for books.

- ❦ The fonts chosen (as well as the words and images)

- ❦ The drawing, image manipulation, and layout tools used

- ❦ The paragraphs, columns, pages, graphics,
  and formatting skills employed

- ❦ And the final adjustments necessary to
  make the type beautiful and polished

- ❦ Are all subservient: **to the beauty, clarity, and
  comfort experienced reading the book.**

A book is all about the author (& illustrator) communicating easily and comfortably with the readers. The readers should not even notice the book, but be drawn into the content unavoidably. If the book is noticed, it needs to be a pleasurable complement to the content.

Let's begin with the language of type

To begin with, most typographic terminology comes from the dominant printing technology used from 1460 to 1970—now called letterpress. This is changing somewhat, but most of the present terms will remain. Before you can set type, you must be able to speak the language and understand the concepts.

You can tell how severe this is as we begin by learning a new measurement system. Type is not measured in inches or millimeters. It is measured in points. This is not going to change for many reasons.

Today all type is sized in points.

Points were an excellent sizing tool, becoming dominant and standardized in the 19th century. At approximately 72 points per inch, the smaller sizes of body copy could be clearly differentiated. Type that is one point larger or smaller is almost the smallest increment of size that can be distinguished easily with the naked eye. We can see the differences between 9 and 10-point, 12 and 13-point. Normally, we cannot see the difference between 11 and 11.5-point type except for certain copyeditor geeks (you know who you are).

Picas (12 pts per pica) and points became the standard. Today all type is sized in points. The old distinctions between European and American points have disappeared, but all use points (and will for the foreseeable future).

The computer has helped

One of the developments in type sizing that eased things a bit was brought about by Apple's Macintosh. When Apple came out with the Mac and its GUI, they set the screen resolution at 72 pixels per inch. In the years since 1984, the 72-point-per-inch standard has become universal on desktop computers. This is true even though high-resolution monitors make this measurement meaningless.

The nice thing, for us Americans, is that this is exactly 72 points per inch. At this time the pica [6 picas per inch] is disappearing. In fact, we can safely say it is gone in most cases. But points may never go away. Some software (including InDesign) still make picas their default measurement, but few use it any more except illustrators. One of the first things you do when you install InDesign is fix your preferences. The main preference to change is switching from Picas and Points to whichever measurement system you are really going to use: inches, pixels, or millimeters. As far as I know, the only industry still using picas is newspapers, and they only use it for column widths. So, if your New Document dialog says that your letter size page is 51p0 (51 picas and zero points) by 66p0, you'll know what you need to fix.

Letterpress terminology

As you would suspect, much of our type terminology comes from letterpress printing. After all, this printing technology was dominant until a few decades ago. I could give you dozens of letterpress terms that would be of historical interest only. However, it is enough that you recognize the source of many of the terms we use.

A typical example is leading (pronounced like the metal). It would be better (or at least more accurate) to change the term to line spacing. For a number of reasons, that probably won't happen. Leading came from the letterpress practice of increasing the space between lines of type by adding strips of lead between the rows. These strips came in standard thicknesses: 1/2-point, 1-point, and so on. In

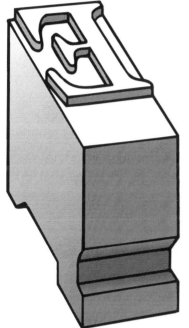

letterpress usage, you could only increase leading and could never have line spacing that was less than the type size. That is no longer true with digital type, but the term remains.

Let's remind ourselves how letterpress type was sized and assembled. Just getting a visual in your mind will straighten out a lot of this. The major fact to remember is that letterpress type is cast metal. The letters are cut into dies and cast into blocks of metal. They all have to be the same height, thickness, hardness, and so on. You have to be able to fit them together into blocks that can be locked into place in the chase (the holding frame for the type). If any letter is a lower height, it won't ink up as you roll the brayer across the surface of the type. If it stands too tall, it will be smashed by the printing pressures of the steel rollers. Much of our present type usage comes from factors that were determined by the physical nature of letterpress.

A *slug* of type was always .918 inches high and left enough room vertically on the top surface for all the characters in a font of type. This was because all type had to fit into evenly sized rectangles to line up properly on the composing stick. Often, these terms no longer mean the same things. A slug

157

is now what we call the black bar highlighted when you select type [which indicates the leading].

Face, for example, used to mean the actual printing surface of the letter. Now, in common usage, face often means a type style such as Helvetica or Times—although in that case the word typeface is often used. As is lamented by grammarians, American English is a living language under constant change.

The same is true of the word *counter*. A counter was the recessed area around the letter above which the face of the character protruded. Now it is usually used (if at all) as a term for the open areas inside a *P* or *e* or *g* or even an *s*, for example. I will give you a diagram in a little bit that covers some of the old terms which remain relevant.

 Many of you are probably grumbling to yourselves at this point: You say in your twenty-first-century superiority, "Who cares?" Actually, you care or you will care. Most of you will find that the longer you design documents, especially books, the more you will fall in love with type. Type will become a very important graphic tool for most of you. This importance will increase throughout your career. Often the shape of the letters is the only graphic element in your designs.

The stick controlled a lot

We need to remember how type was set. All the slugs had to be placed in rows on the composing stick — one letter at a time. This is where the rectangles of letterpress were built, and they had to be precise. If anything was out of size, the slugs would move or fall out as they were printed.

There are hundreds of specialized terms used for all this equipment. If you are curious, read almost any book written on printing up to the end of the twentieth century.

As a result, many terms in your software are from letterpress and font design. For example, the sizing of type remains the same — from top of *ascender* to bottom of *descender*, with the capital letters being slightly shorter than the ascenders and all characters fitting within that height. This was determined by the necessities of the composing stick. But there are more words to define.

Type parts: the vertical metrics

The **baseline** is the imaginary line that all the letters and numbers sit on. The **x-height** is the height of the low-ercase *x* (the *x* is the only lowercase letter that is normally flat both top and bottom). However, I saw it called a *mean line* in a diagram on a typography Web site a few years back [although I have never actually heard anyone use that term]. **Ascenders** are the portions of lowercase letters that rise above the x-height as in *b, d, f, h, k,* and *l.* A *t* doesn't ascend far enough to be called an ascender, usually. **Descenders** are the portions that sink below the baseline as in *g, j, p, q,* and *y.* The **cap height** is the height of the uppercase letters [usually a bit shorter than the ascender].

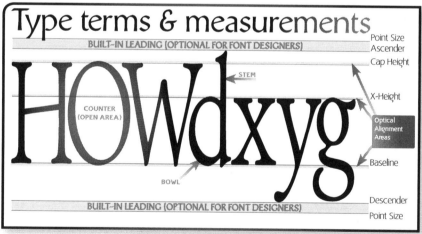

The reason that *x* is specified is that it is normally the only lowercase letter with a flat top and bottom. Curves have to extend over the lines to look the proper height. Yes, it is an optical illusion. The same is true of letters such as *A* or *V* that have points. If the point does not protrude past the guidelines, the letter looks obviously too short. Even people who know nothing about type will know that something is wrong. Type design has many of these understandings that have become rules.

You will discover that this optical alignment is crucial to excellence in type. You need to even align the sides of the columns optically to make them seem straight, clean, and perfect.

 TERMS: Some of you may have noticed that a few paragraphs back we used two old letterpress terms. Most of you didn't. Those two terms are uppercase and lowercase. The original terms were majuscules for large letters and minuscules for handwriting using small letters. Majuscules came to be called capital letters. Minuscules remained a mouthful. Uppercase and lowercase come from common typesetting practice where two wooden cases of letters were used in a standard setup. The upper case contained all the capital letters. The lower case contained all the minuscules. In other words, the common phrase caps and lower case (or C&lc) is just one of those things we do in English {though more properly, it is U&lc—upper and lower case].

The upper case
THIS HELD THE CAPITAL LETTERS
The lower case
this held the miniscule letters
Each font and each point size had its own set of cases.
Grandin Building: moveable type cases on 3rd floor [where Book of Mormon was published for first time in 1830].

The major point to remember is that all letters of a given typeface and a given size fit into rectangles that are the same height.

AaBbGgQ
Everything has to fit in the same height!

We've spent a lot of time on this because it is an important concept to understand. Often paragraphs or lines of type look very different in size, but in fact they are the same point size. This is primarily due to variations in x-height and built-in leading in the specific font chosen. Any letter that goes exceptionally high or low changes the size of the entire typeface.

dpdpdpdp**dp**dp

DIACONIA   FUTURA   BERNHARD BODONI   BERNHARD TREBUCHET
MODERN

These fonts are all the same point size.

For example, examine the graphic above very carefully. As you can see, there are huge differences in x-height between Diaconia and Bernhard Modern. Bernhard Modern has a lot of built-in leading also. Even though Diaconia and Futura have very similar x-heights, you can see that Futura has no extra leading built into the font, whereas Diaconia has some. The result is that 10-point Futura will look as large as 11-point Diaconia (and maybe 15- or 16-point Bernhard Modern). These things must be taken into account when you pick your fonts for your projects.

This will be confusing for a little while. However, if you remember these few ideas, you'll be able to understand much better how type works in your software. The options will begin to make sense.

Type (or font) measurements

❧ **Type size:** Type size is measured from top of ascender to bottom of descender in points (plus

161

the built-in leading). Capital letters are usually approximately two-thirds of the point size, but a little shorter than the ascender. The x-height is normally around one-third. The most important factor in visual or comparative size is the x-height. Sans serif faces, covered in a bit, commonly have larger x-heights. Many fonts have some amount of line spacing built in above and below the characters that is included in the point size.

🍎 **Leading:** Sometimes called line spacing, leading was traditionally measured from baseline to baseline. In other words, leading was the distance advanced to leave room for the next line, measured from the baseline of the original line to the baseline of the following line. **To use typewriter imagery:** when you hit the carriage return, the roller advanced the distance necessary to allow the next row of type to be typed without overlap. It was simple to calculate leading in traditional typesetting by using a pica gauge. Now, it is a visual process you watch on your screen in InDesign. You can see the leading by highlighting your copy. Adjusting it up or down is done by watching what happens on the screen.

 Type speak: Point size and leading are often written as a fraction. The point size becomes the numerator and the leading the denominator. It is written 10/12. This would be spoken ten on twelve, meaning ten-point type with twelve points of leading.

As mentioned, many fonts already have built-in leading. You need to be aware of things like this when you pick a font, as mentioned. A font like Futura has almost no built-in spacing and therefore needs to be set with extra leading for readability (as if you could read Futura anyway). A font like Bernhard Modern has so much built-in leading you might be tempted to use negative leading as in 14/13.

A more extreme leading problem comes with type set in all caps (or small caps). If you are using a font that is all capital letters, you may want to set the type as 24/18 or so. Visually, there is far too much space between the lines with the bottom third of the point size blank [because there are no descenders].

The leading slug

I mentioned that the meaning of the word slug has changed. While you are getting used to your software, it is helpful to highlight your type and examine the result. The height and vertical location of the black box containing the reversed-out type shows the leading. After a short while, you will understand how InDesign handles leading. For example, it is radically changed if you add an inline graphic with auto leading turned on. This is also the easiest way to see how your font fits the leading.

 The main thing about leading is that it greatly affects readability: Normally, the longer the line length, the more leading is required. We will talk about workable line lengths in as we proceed (in Appendix B).

Fonts and font design

There are many more things you need to know about typefaces. We covered this briefly on pages 34–39. I have a short history in a little bit in this appendix. I cover it in quite a bit more detail in my *Practical Font Design* books. First, as you have surely noticed, this book uses the terms typefaces, type styles, and fonts interchangeably. This is common practice; but it is not entirely accurate. My goal is to give you the common language spoken by your peers — not to be a grammatical Gestapo.

A font, for example, is a very specific thing. A font is the entire set of characters for a given type style. In the days of letterpress, a font was all the characters in a given point size. You had Times 12-point, Times 14-point, Garamond 18-point, and so on. In some old fonts, this was hundreds of characters.

When phototype became available in the 1950s, a font came in several sizes. The common machines charged you about the same for a font as was paid in the 1800s (several hundred dollars). But these film strips could be enlarged through various lenses to give you a dozen or more sizes for your money. A common setup, using twelve lenses in a turret, was 6, 7, 8, 9, 10, 11, 12, 14, 18, 24, 30, and 36 point. Zoom lenses were the most exciting. For example, one phototypesetting machine went from 6-point to 72-point in half-point increments and 72-point to 144-point in one-point increments.

Today, in the digital arena, a font is simply a complete set of characters for a given style. It is available in any size from a tenth of a point to 1296 points in InDesign. Below I am showing you the font used for this book named Contenu (which I designed), showing some of the 563 characters available in it. Notice the three styles of numbers (among other things).

Contenu Book

ABCDEFGHIJKLMNOPQRSTUVWXYZ1234567

abcdefghijklmnopqrstuvwxyz1234567890

ABCDEFGHIJKLMNOPQRSTUVWXYZ1234567890

!@#$%^&*()!@#$%^&*()_+{}|:"<>?,./;'[]\=-¡

½ ¼ ¹ ¾ ³ ² ¦ - × ~ Ä Å Ç É Ñ Ö Ü á à â ä ã å ç é è ê ë

í " " ï ñ ó ò ô ö õ ú ù û ü † ° ¢ £ □ • ¶ ß ® © ™ ´ ¨ Æ Ø ∞

±¥µªºæø¿¡¬ƒ≈∆«»…ÀÃÕŒœ–—""''÷ ÿ Ÿ/ ‹›ﬁ ‡·‚„‰

Â Ê Á Ë È Í " Ï " Ó Ô Ò Ú Û Ù ı ˆ ˜ ¯ ˘ ˙ ˚ ¸ ˝ ˛ ˇ

Hundreds of characters

However, hundreds just barely begins to cover the characters needed for typesetting. Typewriters were limited to about 88 characters, although that varied a little. We had the QWERTY keyboard and then those same keys with the shift key held down. The shift key was called that because it physically shifted the entire set of letters—lifting them high enough to use the second set available on all the metal keys.

QWERTY keyboard

The story I have always heard was that our current QWERTY keyboard was originally designed to be difficult to use because they had to slow down typists. They had to type slow enough so that the keys didn't hit each other and lock up the machine. This was evidently a major problem when typewriters were first invented.

Many of you still think that these are all the letters we need. This is not true. This is not even close to being correct. In fact, we need access to several hundred characters, as professional typesetters. Even in English we are really limited. But first, we need to mention one of the major differences between PC and Mac.

7-bit ASCII: the PC limitation

When Bill (Gates) and the crew designed DOS, they knew nothing about typesetting. As a result, they were very pleased to offer 7-bit ASCII. ASCII is just an acronym for a regulating group setting a standard numbering order for letter characters, but the key here is 7-bit. Remembering your digital code, 7-bit is 128 choices. So, with 7-bit ASCII, PCs had 128 characters.

Good, you say. That is much more than the 88 found on a typewriter. And, in fact, these machines were used only as glorified typewriters. In truth, there wasn't much glory there, but that's another story.

8-bit ASCII: the Mac limitation

When the Mac came out, it supported 8-bit ASCII. We Macophiles have used this for years to lord it over our poor restricted buddies using PCs. However, even the 256 characters of 8-bit ASCII do not even come close to what is needed for typesetting. It does enable us to set type professionally in most European languages—sorta.

Upper ASCII

8-bit ASCII is essential for desktop publishing. Without all 256 characters, there are many things that are a real pain. As a PC user, you will run into that pain very quickly. There are many special characters that you will need to use all the time. On a PC, these characters are called upper ASCII characters and are only available by holding down the Alt key and typing four numbers on the numerical keypad. The chart on the next page shows all 128 upper-ASCII characters. Those from 129 and up require the Alt+four-number routine. The number is in the gray bar to the right of the character the character. The code in the middle column is for the Mac keystroke: O = Option, S = Shift.

Keystrokes for the upper 128 of the ASCII set
Mac & Windows shortcuts for the standard characters in most fonts

Glyph	Mac	Pc:Alt+
0129		
,	SO-0	0130
ƒ	O-f	0131
„	SO-w	0132
…	O-;	0133
†	O-t	0134
‡	SO-7	0135
ˆ	SO-i	0136
‰	SO-r	0137
Š		0138
‹	SO-3	0139
Œ	SO-q	0140
0141–0144		
'	O-]	0145
'	SO-]	0146
"	O-[	0147
"	SO-[	0148
•	O-8	0149
–	O--	0150
—	OS--	0151
~	SO-n	0152
™	O-2	0153
š		0154
›	SO-4	0155
œ	O-q	0156
0157–0158		
Ÿ	Ou-Sy	0159
0160		
¡	O-1	0161
¢	O-4	0162
£	O-3	0163

Glyph	Mac	Pc:Alt+
€	SO-2	0164
¥	O-y	0165
¦		0166
□	O-6	0167
¨	SO-u	0168
©	O-g	0169
ª		0170
«	O-\	0171
¬	O-l	0172
0173		
®	O-r	0174
¯	SO-,	0175
°	SO-8	0176
±	SO-=	0177
²		0178
³		0179
´	SO-e	0180
µ	O-m	0181
¶	O-7	0182
·	SO-9	0183
¸	SO-z	0184
¹		0185
º	O-0	0186
»	SO-\	0187
¼		0188
½		0189
¾		0190
¿	SO-?	0191
À	O-A	0192
Á	Oe-A	0193
Â	Oi-A	0194

Glyph	Mac	Pc:Alt+
Ã	On-A	0195
Ä	Ou-A	0196
Å	SO-a	0197
Æ	SO-'	0198
Ç	SO-c	0199
È	O`-E	0200
É	Oe-E	0201
Ê	Oi-E	0202
Ë	Ou-E	0203
Ì	O`-I	0204
Í	Oe-I	0205
Î	Oi-I	0206
Ï	Ou-I	0207
Ð		0208
Ñ	On-N	0209
Ò	O`-O	0210
Ó	Oe-O	0211
Ô	Oi-O	0212
Õ	On-O	0213
Ö	Ou-O	0214
×		0215
Ø	SO-o	0216
Ù	Ou-U	0217
Ú	Oe-U	0218
Û	Oi-U	0219
Ü	Ou-U	0220
Ý		0221
Þ		0222
ß	Os	0223
à	O`-a	0224
á	Oe-a	0225

Glyph	Mac	Pc:Alt+
â	Oi-a	0226
ã	On-a	0227
ä	Ou-a	0228
å	Oa	0229
æ	O'	0230
ç	Oc	0231
è	O`-e	0232
é	Oe-e	0233
ê	Oi-e	0234
ë	Ou-e	0235
ì	O`-i	0236
í	Oe-i	0237
î	Oi-i	0238
ï	Ou-i	0239
ð		0240
ñ	On-n	0241
ò	O`-o	0242
ó	Oe-o	0243
ô	Oi-i	0244
õ	On-n	0245
ö	Ou-o	0246
÷	O/	0247
ø	Oo	0248
ù	O`-u	0249
ú	Oe-u	0250
û	Oi-u	0251
ü	Ou-u	0252
ý		0253
þ		0254
ÿ	Ou-y	0255
0256		

≤ ≥ Ω ◊ = π ∏ ß ∑ √ ∫ ≠ These Option characters are not available on a PC. On a PC, hold down the Alt key and type the ASCII number on the numerical keypad. The blank Mac keys are Control characters not normally available. For a Mac, S = Shift and O = Option. For Mac composite characters like Ô [Option+U then the O], you type the combination to access the accent (which remains invisible) and then type the letter you want the character to appear over — at which point the accented character will be typed.

This is not to say the Mac is much better. However, all these extra characters are available with the Option key. You do have to memorize the shortcuts. But, Option-8 for a bullet is much easier to remember than Alt+0149. And, Option+Shift+8 for the degree symbol makes visual sense, at least. Many Mac keystrokes are easier to memorize.

Plus, once you learn the double-stroke combinations to add accents, they are simple to remember: Option-n, then n gives you ñ [ntilde], for example. Option-e, then any vowel will add the accent éáó [eacute, aacute, oacute]; Option-u adds the umlaut (or diaresis) ü [udiaresis]; and so on. In fact, if you have a strange letter that looks like another letter, try it with the Option key. For example, the ø [oslash] is just Option-o.

The cross-platform issues

In early desktop publishing this was a major issue. Not only were PCs 7-bit and Macs 8-bit, but PCs could not read Mac fonts and Macs could not read PC fonts. InDesign solved this problem. However, as we will see in the next couple of pages, the problem is so huge that a solution had to be found, and it has been. We'll discuss this OpenType solution after we look at some special characters.

Additional characters

Small caps

One of the typesetting options in most professional software (and many word processors) has been the use of small caps. Most of you are probably familiar with this from tutorials of any of the professional publishing programs. Small caps are capital letters that have been reduced to the x-height and used in place of lower case letters.

The problem is that you may have never seen true small caps. What we normally get is proportionally reduced caps. THIS MAKES SMALL CAPS LOOK MUCH THINNER AND LIGHTER THAN THE CAPITALS THEY ARE WITH. WITH TRUE SMALL CAPS, THE STROKE

WEIGHTS OF THE SMALL CAPS ARE THE SAME AS FOR THE CAPS AND lowercase OF THE NORMAL FONT. There are quite a few specialized fonts that have no lowercase — just caps and small caps. There isn't room to fit true small caps into an 8-bit (256 character) font that already has lowercase letters.

Old style figures

Some of you may have noticed that the numbers used in the body copy of this book seem to flow with the type a little better than usual. That is because the font I am using has old style figures. Most of you probably think that numbers always look like this: 1234567890 These are called lining figures. Actually, I tend to call them bookkeepers' numbers, because I think that is the only place to use them. But that is another story. For Contenu Book, the font used here, the numbers look like this: 1234567890 — instead of the lining figures. In fact, because it is one of my Open-Type fonts I have the choice of Lining 1234567890, Oldstyle 1234567890, and Small Cap 1234567890 figures.

Lining figures are appropriate for use with capital letters, but nothing else. In fact, they look like capitalized characters in the flow of regular C&lc copy. Oldstyle figures are far less intrusive and flow much better when reading. Small Cap figures are used with small caps. They flow so much better that it is likely that many of you didn't even notice that I was using them until I just mentioned it. There isn't room to fit oldstyle figures into an 8-bit font that already has lining figures [& certainly not Small Cap figures].

Ligatures

In some cases, letters simply do not fit very well. The typographic solution has been to make special composite characters where two or more letters are made into one character that looks better. In Gutenberg's 42-line Bible, since justification hadn't been invented yet, he used over 3,000 ligatures to help justify his copy. However, in many fonts, through the years, ligatures have been essential to the beauty of the type. Again, the problem has been the 256-character limit. Usually there are only eight ligatures in most fonts: fi, fl, ffi, ffl, Æ. æ, Œ, and œ. Contenu Book has many more: ME, NE, NN, LR, Th, Wh, ch, ck, ct, ffy, gg, ry, sp, st, sh, sk, ty, bb, ft, and a few more.

Swashes

The Lord is my shepherd;
I shall not want.
He maketh me to lie down
in green pastures:
He leadeth me
beside the still waters.
He restoreth my soul:
He leadeth me in
the paths of righteousness
for His name's sake.
Yea, though I walk
through the valley
of the shadow of death,
I will fear no evil:
for Thou art with me;
Thy rod and thy staff
they comfort me.
Thou preparest a table
before me in the presence
of mine enemies:
Thou anointest my head
with oil;
my cup runneth over.
Surely goodness and mercy
shall follow me
all the days of my life:
and I will dwell
in the house of the Lord
for ever.   PSALM 23

With some of the old fonts, especially those that mimicked handwriting, specialized character variants were created to add grace and style to the type. These swashes also were lost when we went to the 256-character limit.

In the sidebar to the left, you see the twenty-third psalm set in Caflisch Script Pro from Adobe. This font has many dozens of swashes and ligatures added automatically. Especially notice the k in the word walk in "Yea, though I walk through the valley" in the middle of the psalm when compared to the k in maketh (the third line). This swash at the end of the word was added automatically by the font. Also notice the d in goodness compared to the d in days (the 6th and 4th lines from the bottom of the psalm).

Fractions, numerators, denominators, superiors, and inferiors

To typesetters, fractions are a real problem. Most PC fonts have ½, ¼, ¾ plus ^{123}. But, what do you do about 61/64 or something like that? In reality, that should look more like this $^{61}/_{64}$. But again that only works when you have an OpenType font with Numerators and Denominators.

169

There isn't room to fit fractions, numerators, denominators, superiors, and inferiors into an 8-bit font—or any of the options individually for that matter.

Superscript and subscript

These are conceptually the same as superiors and inferiors except that they apply to all the caps, lower case, and numbers. The most common place you see them is in mathematical and chemical formulas.

An algebraic expression might be something like this: a^3+b^4. A chemical formula might look like this: $N\,O$. This type of thing obviously does not work very well with oldstyle figures. It's a little better with lining figures [a^3+b^4 & N_2O_3] though they still need fixing by moving figures up and down. The problem with this is the same as with true small caps: these characters need to be designed smaller but with the same stroke weight so they look like they fit. Plus, by now you know there simply isn't room to fit all the superscript and subscript characters into an 8-bit, 256 character font.

Expert sets

The only solution, before OpenType, has been what are called Expert set fonts which have all of the oldstyle figures, true small caps, ligatures, swashes, and so on for the normal font. These are a pain to use and they are very rare. If you find one, you are faced with constantly changing fonts. There is certainly no automatic substitution. They do add additional 256 characters to the mix, but even that is not really enough. Plus, as you have probably guessed, it would take several Expert sets to give us the characters really needed.

The OpenType solution

This relatively new font format solves most of these problems. InDesign was the first professional application to use the format. The Creative Suite is about the only place where they are in constant use. They do not work in word processors. OpenType is completely cross-platform. For the first time you can use the same fonts on a Mac and on a PC. But the new format goes far beyond that.

So, what does it do?

First, it completely solves the number of characters limitation. OpenType fonts can have over 65,000 characters. Few do, but they can, if needed. What this means on a practical level is that almost all of the options we have talked about are available (or can be made available) automatically in InDesign as you write: oldstyle figures, optical scaling, true small caps, inferior and superior characters, automatic building of true fractions, ligatures, swashes, plus Greek and Cyrillic alphabets. All of these are optional settings in InDesign.

Font families

Kabel Book
Kabel Medium
Kabel Demi
Kabel Bold
Kabel Ultra

Bodoni Book
Bodoni Roman
Bodoni Bold
Bodoni Bold Condensed
Bodoni Poster
Bodoni Poster Compressed

Over the years, font design has developed groups of fonts that are obviously variants of the same basic font. They are called font families. These families can have differences in weight and width. Commonly, they have also have italic variants; but that is really a special case, as we will see in a bit.

Font weight

Weight is the thickness of the stroke. Here are the common weights arranged in order from thin to thick: Extra Light, Thin, Fine, Light, Book, Regular or Medium or Plain or Roman, Semi Bold or Demi Bold or Halbfett, Bold, Heavy, Extra Bold, Ultra Bold or Ultra Heavy, Fat, Display, and Ad. Book is usually the most elegant. It is designed for use in books. It is a little lighter than regular (medium) and a little narrower. This makes it possible to get more words on a page.

These radical weight variations are relatively new to font design where most of our standard fonts are four to five hundred years old. The first to appear was Bold, and that did not show up until the eighteenth century.

As advertising became a major force in graphic design, many specialized fonts were developed for the ads. Because these ads were commonly called display ads (as opposed to classified ads), these fonts became known as display fonts. Many of these display fonts showed extreme weight variations, but they were not linked to normal fonts. As far as I have ever been able to tell, extended font families are primarily a late twentieth-century phenomenon.

Font width

There also used to be separate, usually individual, fonts with different apparent widths, as in the following:

There are narrow, extra-condensed, condensed, expanded, wide, extra-wide, and so on. At this point, the demand for fonts with these variations has diminished because any decent publishing software can do what was done to that poor *O* above (to the horror of traditionalists). However, this is certainly one of the descriptive characteristics of a font.

You can see the difference between **Bodoni Bold** and **Bodoni Bold Condensed**. The **Bodoni Poster Compressed** is quite a bit narrower. Whereas **Bodoni Poster** is very wide.

Heed a few words of caution, however: A font in which the horizontal strokes are thicker than the vertical ones looks very strange. When you make a font narrower by choosing horizontal scaling, the vertical strokes get narrower and the horizontal ones remain unchanged. This can happen very easily if you make extreme adjustments to the horizontal and/or vertical scale. Many purists are horrified at any width adjustments. However, if you keep it to plus or minus 5%, no one (except for a very few nit-picking copyeditors) will be able to see it. Wide set-widths are not so much of a problem, but discretion is always in good taste. Deformed type is not usually an indication of sophistication, but of immaturity.

Italics and Obliques

One standard for type is the carved type in Roman columns honoring emperors' great deeds. They are still the classic standard. You should check out fonts like Trajan, Augustinian, and their ilk. To our eyes, they look extremely elegant, and they are. The name has remained in the fact that many people call vertical type roman, to this day.

The problem with these carved letters was that they were all caps. What we now call lowercase letters crept in as people wrote the words. As they wrote faster and faster, monks and scribes developed minuscules. These forms were roughly codified by the scribes and officially adopted by Emperor Charlemagne in the late 900s. Called Carolingian minuscules, he made them the standard for education. They are definitely recognizable as what we now call normal lowercase letter shapes.

The second time this happened was in Italy in the early Renaissance. In Venice, a man named Aldus Manutius developed a font based on the handwriting of his day, which he called *Italic*. It became very popular, but because of the narrowness and tight fit of the letters, it was not as legible – and still isn't. Italics were completely separate fonts and they were not used on the same page as roman fonts until the pomp and ebullience of the Baroque.

In this day and age, every normal vertical style has a matching italic – Bergsland Pro Roman, *Bergsland Pro Italic*. As you can clearly see in these four words, italic is a very different font. The *a, n, r,* and *d* show the most obvious differences. With some fonts, the matching of these two type styles is done very well and elegantly. In other cases, the two fonts are seemingly just forced into the same bed.

One of the aberrations of the digital age is a new phenomenon of fake italics called *oblique*. These are not true italics, but merely slanted roman characters – for example, **NuevoLitho** and **NuevoLitho Italic**. This is not a true italic. Obliques have been known to drive type purists nuts (but for most of them it's just a short putt anyway)!

I tend to think they should get a life and simply not use the fonts they don't like, but then that's just me. In some cases, obliques are a good solution. For the radical geometric sans serif fonts of the 1930s, a true italic would be foolish. This should be the choice of the type designer. What you definitely do not want are the faux italics produced by software (like Office) that simply skews the letters. Thankfully, current versions make this optional in most cases.

Some font terminology

Before we get into specifics, I want to define a few descriptive terms to help me explain to you some of the differences between the fonts. The terms are a little esoteric, but I think you will find them helpful to categorize things in your own mind.

- **Stems:** the vertical strokes in letters like *h*, *k*, *l*, *r* and so on.

- **Bowls:** the rounded parts of letters like *b*, *d*, *g*, *o*, *p*, and even *c* and *s*, according to some.

- **Crossbars:** the horizontal strokes on *A*, *H*, *e*, and so on.

- **Head and foot serifs:** the serifs at the top and bottom of a stem as in *h*, *l*, *k*, and *d*.

- **Adnate or bracketed serifs:** serifs that flow smoothly out of the stems.

- **Abrupt serifs:** cross strokes at the end of stems with no bracketing.

- **Terminals:** the endings of the curved portions of letters like a, c, r, C, G, and so on. Lachrymal terminals are tear-drop shaped.

- **Axis:** the angle the pen was held at to produce the modulated stroke of calligraphers.

- **Stroke:** the lines that make up the characters from the old assumption that letters are calligraphic and drawn with separate strokes of a pen or brush.

- **Modulated stroke:** a stroke that varies in width as it proceeds around the letter form.

- 𝄞 **Humanist axis:** the axis for normal right-handed calligraphic penmanship.

- 𝄞 **Contrast:** how much the stroke is modulated.

- 𝄞 **Aperture:** the openings of curves on letters like *a*, *c*, *e*, *s*, and so on.

- 𝄞 **Slope:** how far italic and oblique letters slant in degrees.

There are more, but this will be enough for our purposes. As you can see, type can get very technical—and I have barely scratched the surface. The differences will seem insignificant to you now, as you start. But they are really very important. Aperture, for example, tends to control the friendliness and readability. Axis changes from a humanist slant of -12° to mechanical vertical [0°] strongly influence our reaction to the warmness or coolness of a font. But we'll discuss these things as we go, giving you examples so you can see the differences.

Old Style serif fonts: readable and beautiful

Garamond 3

ABCDEFGHIJKLMNOPQRSTU
VWXYZ1234567890abcdefghijk
lmnopqrstuvwxyz

This Linotype version of Garamond from 1936 is based on the American Type Founders design by Morris Fuller Benton and Thomas Maitland Cleland, who based their work, in turn, on seventeenth-century copies of Claude Garamond's types by Jean Jannon. *Myfonts*

Garamond 3 Therefore they say
& italic: Therefore they say unto God

The fonts we are most comfortable reading are those based on Old Style forms (I'm including all fonts from 1450 to 1775). These original serif fonts are exemplified by the work of Claude Garamond in Paris in the early to mid-1500s. This type of font is the standard to which all other fonts are compared. They are full of smooth sensuous curves. They are light, and open — beautiful, comfortable, and elegant. The stems are vertical. The bowls are nearly circular. The cross-bars often rise to the right. The axis is always humanist. The aperture is comfortably open. They are direct descendants of the incredible calligraphic work of the fourteenth and fifteenth centuries.

Through the 1500s and 1600s, these old style letter forms went through gradual changes. Designers began playing with the forms. Sloped capitals were added to the italics. Paired roman and italic fonts appeared. As Europe was caught up in the extravagance and luxury of the Baroque and Rococo, those lavish curves and flourishes made their way into type design as well, as we see in Galliard below. The very open aperture makes this font very accessible.

ITC Galliard

ABCDEFGHIJKLMNOPQ
RSTUVWXYZ1234567890
abcdefghijklmnopqrstuvwxyz

ITC Galliard is an adaptation of Matthew Carter's 1978 phototype design for Mergenthaler. Galliard was modeled on the work of Robert Granjon, a sixteenth-century letter cutter, whose typefaces are renowned for their beauty and legibility. *MyFonts*

Type design gradually became drawn as opposed to written. Eventually characters were constructed and lost the connection to the written forms. This period was extravagant, but tightly based on classical old styles. Even the finishing portion of this entire period we are calling Old Style was merely filled with rigidly defined, carefully drawn forms. By the middle 1700s, fonts like Baskerville appeared with a rigidly vertical axis (usually called a rational axis).

Throughout this period, careful adjustments were tried with axis, aperture, serif style, and so on. However, to our eye in the twenty-first century, all of these fonts are minor variations on a common theme. Old style fonts are still the normal choice for body copy. Your personal style will determine which you choose. The variations definitely have their own character and leave their feel in the documents that use them. Beyond that, they are all Old Style letters.

Baskerville

ABCDEFGHIJKLMNOPQ RSTUVWXYZ1234567890
abcdefghijklmnopqrstuvwxyz

John Baskerville had John Handy cut from his own brilliant designs, based on a lifetime of calligraphy and stonecutting. *MyFonts*

There are type styles of the late 1700s and early 1800s, which are used occasionally for books. These are hard, tightly structured letterforms which push out the emotional, warm, comfortable type of the Old Style fonts, replacing it with spiky, carved, structured forms. Serifs lose all bracketing, becoming thin, horizontal lines. The aperture is shut down quite a bit. The axis is rigidly vertical and accented with often extreme stroke modulation. Fonts like Bodoni can be very beautiful, but they are never comfortable.

Bodoni Book

ABCDEFGHIJKLMNOPQ RSTUVWXYZ1234567890
abcdefghijklmnopqrstuvwxyz

In the mid-1800s, a type design movement began making type for the workers, the common man, the non-educated. They were never really popular with designers, but they have had a lot of influence. They are based on fonts like Bodoni or Didot but they have an even stroke weight with virtually no modulation. The aperture is nearly closed. Serifs are close to being unbracketed slabs with the same stroke thickness as the rest of the letterform. There are no small caps, old style figures, ligatures, or any of the other graceful tools of typography. For all of this they can be surprisingly readable.

One of these fonts, Century Schoolbook, is the font most of us used when we learned to read in the first few grades of school. It may be the most elegant of the bunch. In general, heavy, clunky, and old-fashioned are the terms associated with fonts like these. Typical would be Bookman, Cheltenham, or Clarendon.

Clarendon

ABCDEFGHIJKLMNOPQ RSTUVWXYZ1234567890 abcdefghijklmnopqrstuvwxyz

Slab serif type, when the serif is bracketed, is sometimes referred to as a Clarendon. This font originated in England in 1845 and is named for the Clarendon Press in Oxford. Clarendon was intended to be a heavier complement to ordinary serif designs.

The only other traditional style grew out of the modernist movement of the early twentieth century. Here letter forms are constructed geometrically, with purely circular bowls, no modulation, slab serifs, closed aperture, and so on. Intellectually, they could almost be considered the scientific extension of the socialist expression found in the Bookman, Cheltenham, Clarendon school of thought. Typical fonts of this type are Memphis, Rockwell, and City. The readability is usually very low.

Memphis

ABCDEFGHIJKLMNOPQR STUVWXYZ1234567890 abcdefghijklmnopqrstuvwxyz

Many recent serif faces play with attributes of any and all historical styles. Often they experiment with distinctive serif stylings, sharp angular features, fanciful modulations. However, these more playful aspects are often very restrained and elegant. They take pieces from all over and show a wide variety from Times New Roman to Palatino to Veljovic. Often, like in Usherwood, the x-heights are very large and the letterspacing very tight — strictly a fashion statement from the 1980s. They tend to have limited use for specific groups of people in identifiable niches. But they can be very pretty. Some of the best are interpretations of old fonts into a newer, more contemporary look. A good example of that would be Adobe Caslon.

Adobe Caslon

ABCDEFGHIJKLMNOPQ
RSTUVWXYZ1234567890
abcdefghijklmnopqrstuvwxyz

For her Caslon revival, designer Carol Twombly studied specimen pages printed by William Caslon between 1734 and 1770. *MyFonts*

Modern sans serif font choices

There are not nearly as many options in sans serif type. Of these choices, very few are useful for body copy. Until recently sans serif fonts were not designed for body copy use. For example, one of the most grotesque fashions (currently common in my area) involves using geometric sans fonts for everything. The resulting marketing pieces look "modern", but they are virtually unreadable.

Futura

ABCDEFGHIJKLMNOPQ
RSTUVWXYZ1234567890
abcdefghijklmnopqrstuvwxyz

Designed by Paul Renner in 1927, Futura is the classic example of a geometric sans serif type based on the Bauhaus design philosophy. *MyFonts*

Like the geometric slab serifs, these sans serif fonts are largely absolute geometric constructs. The real problem with geometric fonts is the readability problem. They can work fairly well in headlines, but using them for body copy is a serious mistake.

The things you need to do to make these fonts even vaguely readable do not work in the reading environment of a book. Typical fonts of this type are: Futura, Kabel, Avant Garde, and Bauhaus.

Sans serif typefaces started in the early 19th century with a single line mention of a monoline font in Caslon's last catalog. The original fonts were all caps. In Europe these are called grotesques. Around the turn of the 20th century, these fonts were very popular. The original fonts in this category are commonly called Gothics in the United States, and include fonts like Franklin Gothic.

Franklin Gothic

ABCDEFGHIJKLMNOPQ RSTUVWXYZ1234567890 abcdefghijklmnopqrstuvwxyz

Franklin Gothic was designed by Morris Fuller Benton in 1902 as his version of the heavy sans serifs first made popular by Vincent Figgins in 1830. *MyFonts*

I've already talked about the bad reader reactions to fonts like Helvetica, Univers, and Arial. They are a new form of a large group of fonts which are very popular but have no real place in book design.

There are some very pretty sans serifs which are relatively warm and friendly, even though there is no modulation of the stroke. Many of these fonts make relatively good body copy in short bursts. They have been used for books, but it is rarely a good reader experience. They all have a distinctively warm feel — relative to other sans serif faces. Common faces in this genre would be Gill Sans, Frutiger, Corinthian, Skia, and Trebuchet — among many others.

Gill Sans

ABCDEFGHIJKLMNOPQ RSTUVWXYZ1234567890 abcdefghijklmnopqrstuvwxyz

Designed by Eric Gill and based on the typeface Edward Johnston designed in 1916 for the London Underground signage. *MyFonts*

The sans serifs which really work for body copy are actually neither fish nor fowl. Instead of serifs they tend to have slight flares, They have a modulated stroke and a humanist axis. They are the most elegant of the sans serifs. Most commonly available would be Optima, Poppl Laudatio, and Zapf Humanist.

Optima
ABCDEFGHIJKLMNOPQ
RSTUVWXYZ1234567890
abcdefghijklmnopqrstuvwxyz
Hermann Zapf created this one in 1958 for Stempel. This humanist sans combines features of both serif and sans serif design.

Humanist sans serifs are growing in popularity. They are quite readable. They may well become the fashion for body copy in the near future. Stylized and Humanist sans serif typefaces are very clean, neat, and unobtrusive. You should give them a try.

Use a companion font for the heads & subheads ▮

This font family needs to be carefully chosen. It needs to have enough contrast to the body copy font to make the heads stand out. But it must have the same, or a very similar, x-height. This way you can use it comfortably for things like run-in heads, where the first few words in a paragraph are used as a contrasting low-level subhead. Your family choice should probably have a similar width. It should emphasize your stylistic decisions which were made to appeal to your readership. These choices are the main determinant for the basic historical and decorative style which is used in the niche with whom you are trying to speak.

Type color

Finally, we need to discuss one of the most important attributes of copy set with excellent font choices—the smoothness of the color of the type. What is called the *type color* is created by the design of the font character shapes and the spacing of those characters as well as the spacing of the words, the leading between the lines of type, and the paragraph spacing.

This is one of those places where you want an excellent font. In quality fonts, the characters fit very evenly and smoothly. This character fit is called letterspacing. Beyond that is a very careful use of spacing throughout your documents, in general. This is your responsibility. This is the core of typography. This is one of the major places where word processors are left in the dust. Even excellent fonts will not help a word processor.

The professional page layout programs, like InDesign, have very precise letterspacing and word spacing controls. Leading can be controlled to a ten-thousandth of a point. Baseline shifts up or down of individual words and even entire lines of type can be adjusted very precisely.

Paragraph spacing is controlled to a ten-thousandth of a whatever (inch, millimeter, point, kyu, cicero, pica) by the space before and space after fields in the paragraph formatting dialog box or palette. In addition are the margin and column gutter controls, plus the ability to make optical margin adjustments so the edges of the columns appear cleaner. The level of control needed by typographers goes far beyond word processor abilities.

Professional type should have an even color. When your book is seen from far enough away so that the body copy can no longer be read, it must blend into smooth gray shapes. You will come to see that this even type color is imperative. It is what allows the control of the reader's eye which you need for clear and comfortable communication. You will learn to keep your type as smooth as possible, stepping outside of that only to make important points that the reader really needs and wants to know.

Smooth type color needs to become one of your major concerns.

This smoothness is what makes headlines, subheads, and our specialized paragraph styles work. The white space surrounding specialized paragraphs stands out from smooth type color. This white space attracts the eye and leads it to that statement. Without smooth type color, you are forced to make your headers much stronger and the reader often feels like you are shouting at him or her. That is definitely not a comfortable reading experience. Smooth type color needs to become one of your major concerns.

Typography determines reader reactions

It goes far beyond your font choices—important as they are. This is the first and most important thing you must understand. You are not only trying to control or at least predict the reaction of your typical reader to your content. You are also working you make your book a comfortable, friendly, and familiar part of the life of a typical reader within your specialty.

Now we are going to talk about basic things that you must add to your writing style. Many of these things run contrary to what you were taught when you learned to type. This is especially true if you ever took a typing course. You will find you have many things to unlearn.

I.   No double spacing   ▓

Typing classes teach that one should always double-space after punctuation. This was made necessary by the typewriter characters themselves. All characters on a typewriter are the same width. This is called a monospaced typeface. The result is that punctuation becomes hard to see. The double space emphasizes sentence construction and makes it visible. When you are using monospaced fonts, this type of extra spacing is necessary.

You can see an example of the horrors of monospaced type on the next page.

Typesetting, in contrast, is done with proportional type. This means that every character has its own width that is designed to fit with the other characters. Typeset words form units characterized by even spacing between every letter. In fact, professional typesetting is judged by this smooth type color, as we just discussed. Double-spacing is not needed because the better-fitting words make punctuation a major break. In addition, there is extra white space built into the typeset punctuation characters themselves. Double-spacing after punctuation puts little white holes in the type color. These speckled paragraphs are not nearly so elegant, beautiful, or clear.

```
If you look at this paragraph
closely,  you will see that the
spacing looks far different from the
paragraphs above and below.  It is
set in Courier,  which is a
monospaced font.  As you can see,
the spacing is horrible.  Much of
this is because of the letter shapes
themselves.  But the main problem is
that all characters have the same
width — including spaces and
punctuation. As a result, everything
lines up vertically. This is what
monospacing means.
```

In the sample above, the paragraph in Courier was a real pain to typeset: There are so many automatic controls in InDesign that the monospaced characters would not line up correctly. I had to make a separate text block and turn off all the controls to make this demo. Even yet, the monospacing has been modified a little to make it work like typewriter type.

This double-spacing typing rule is taught even though most people using word processors have not used monospaced type for years. The rule is just taught because "We have always done it that way."

2.   No double returns

No multiple text blocks, if possible

Keeping your type in cohesive text blocks: One of the major difficulties you will have as you begin setting type is keeping your copy in coherent blocks of text. Ideally, all of the copy on a book page (except for the sidebars and possibly the captions) needs to be in a single text block. In some layouts, it may be a single frame per column, but the concept is clear. If you use multiple text blocks, you lose any easy alignment control. This is where you should really use multi-column text frames (but I never do that).

Paragraph spacing

Spacing between the paragraphs is not done with the Return key: It is done with the Space Before and Space After fields in your Paragraph panel or dialog box. The extra space between paragraphs helps the lines of type in the paragraph hold together in a unit. It is especially important to do this in bulleted lists where the paragraphs are short — two or three lines.

The reason for this is that spacing in typography uses adjustments that are so small, you cannot control them by eye. Although you can clearly see the relationships, hand-adjusted consistency is impossible on a 72 dpi monitor because most of the adjustments are less than a point—or smaller than a pixel. You can only adjust type relative to itself in increments of small portions of a point.

The first place you will run across this dilemma in our current discussion is with paragraph spacing. Space between paragraphs is controlled with the space before paragraph and space after paragraph options—not with multiple returns.

 Opinion: Here we come to a place where there is major disagreement between typographers. You will have to decide. Your decision on most of these matters will help determine your personal sense of style. Just remember, please:

Spacing helps to communicate, it doesn't just make a pretty page.

Some of the more anal typographers demand that you put no space between paragraphs, and that all vertical spacing be a direct multiple of the leading. This is to produce that prime virtue, in their minds, of text blocks that are lined up horizontally top and bottom. Beyond that, they want all lines of type in parallel columns to be lined up. Type should fit a tightly defined grid.

IMHO, that type of rigid structure is deadly to clear communication. I do not want all of the lines of type to line up horizontally. That is one of the ways that my readers can easily stray from the column they are trying to read. This type of symmetrical rigidity contributes to the boredom of many layouts. Yes, we must have spacing in control. Yes, we must maintain consistency in our layouts. But rigid grids are as stifling as prison bars.

Double return problems

With these concepts in mind, how should we set up our paragraph spacing? First, be aware that double returns add huge, horizontal white bars that run across your pages—disrupting type color. When cleaning up secretarial copy, you will regularly come across multiple returns—maybe a dozen or more. This is because most secretaries have no clue about the flow of copy. These things are not taught in word processing classes. So they simply type multiple returns to get to the next page.

You want to establish a rhythm to your pages that makes the paragraphs easy to see without being obvious. A couple of points before or after each paragraph is enough. If you do not use a first-line indent, you will probably need to use four to seven points before or after your paragraphs. Try to use as little extra spacing as possible while still making your structure easy to follow while reading. To keep it consistent, this spacing needs to be built into your paragraph styles. Then you can control it globally as your sense of style develops through the writing of your book.

For headlines and subheads, their positioning is controlled to a large degree by the space before and the space after a paragraph. You want more space before a header and less after so the header is tied to the copy that follows. For this reason, I usually use a couple of points after my body copy paragraphs to help with the lead-in space to the next paragraph style—especially headers.

3. Space, space and a half, or double space? ▪

None of the above! This is why we use leading instead of spacing. Spacing is old typewriter terminology. The three options listed above were the only ones available for typewriters. In almost every case (unless you are trying to mimic a typewriter) a single space is too close, a space and a half is too far, and a double space is ridiculous. Again, the focus has to be on readability.

 Before we go on, another review of type speak is required: Point size and leading is expressed as 10/12 or 21/21.5 plus the alignment. This is pronounced ten on twelve or twenty-one on twenty-one and a half. In these cases, 10 and 21 are the point size and 12 and 21.5 are the leading in points.

So, a common statement would be something like this: body copy is normally 10/12 justified left. This would be a paragraph with 10-point type and 12-point leading set justified with the last line flush left—like this paragraph and all the body copy in this book. When the point size and leading are the same, as in 16/16, it is referred to as being set solid. If the leading is less than the point size it is negative leading.

Leading is determined by font design, point size, line length, and reading distance. All fonts have differing built-in line spacing. If you recall the graphic seen on page 145, it proved that Futura had none and Bernhard Modern had a lot. Bernhard Modern also had a very small x-height. As a result, if we accept that normal body copy is 10/12 (and it is), then Futura should probably be set at 10/13 and Bernhard Modern at 12/12.

Some leading norms for normal reading distance:

- 🐭 **Tiny type:** Type smaller than 7 point is usually set solid. With type set that small, you usually don't want people reading it. It is used for the small type used to produce legalese [which no one reads anyway].

- 🐭 **Body copy:** This is the normal reading copy in your documents. It is rigidly required to be 10/12 by traditional publishers, as mentioned. However, when you have the control, those figures should be adjusted by x-height and built-in line spacing. Larger x-heights require smaller point sizes. A large amount of built-in spacing between the top of the ascenders and the bottoms of the descenders in the line above takes less leading. Long line lengths require more leading. In general, bold, sans serif, or condensed fonts need more leading. *This is your job:* to figure out what reads best.

❦ **Headers:** Headlines and subheads are commonly set solid. The larger the point size used, the less leading is needed.

❦ **All caps:** Setting type in all caps often requires negative leading. This means that the leading is less than the point size. If you think about it, the reasoning should be clear. All caps have no descenders. Descenders are about a third of the point size. So headlines in all caps might well be set 36/28 or so.

This header is set with negative leading: 24/20

Autoleading: One of the things you need to get under control is autoleading. The factory default is 120%. This means the leading will be 120% of the point size. This sounds good, and works well for body copy (10/12). However, it is disastrous for headers. I usually have the autoleading set at 105% (or less) for them. This is something you control in styles (as we cover in Appendix B).

 Even worse is when you drop in an inline or anchored graphic as a character in your paragraph: The autoleading adjusts to give room for the graphic. In these paragraphs, you will need to turn autoleading off. This also happens if you make a letter, a word, or words larger in a paragraph.

4.   Tabs and fixed spaces   ▓

Spaces cause many other problems for people trained in typewriting. On a typewriter, the spacebar is a known quantity. This is because every character in monospaced type is the same width—even the space. This is definitely not true for type. In fact, in type, the space band is often a different size than it was the last time you hit the key.

This is caused by several factors. First, the word space character in various fonts varies in width. There is no standard. This space also changes with point size, of course. This is not a problem with typewriters because they only have one size and one font. Because of typewriter-based training, most people accustomed to word processors do most of their horizontal spacing with multiple spaces. This is one reason why the first thing you usually have to do with secretarial copy is eliminate the double spaces.

More than this, word spacing is one of the defaults that should be set to your standards. Page layout programs give you very precise control over word spacing. Finally, word spacing varies with every line when setting justified copy. The way this works is as follows.

Justification

Here are several sample rows of type to demonstrate how justification works in your paragraphs.

Leftover space at the end of a line is divided by the number of spaces and added to each space. Fixed spaces are not adjusted by this.

Here are several sample rows of type to demonstrate how justification works in your paragraphs.

When you are setting a line of justified type, you determine a justification zone. When the last word that fits in a line ends in this justification zone, any remaining space in the column width is evenly divided and added to the word spaces in the line. If the last word does not reach the zone, the length of the zone is divided and added to the spaces in the line (any additional space is divided and added as letterspacing between every letter in the line).

What this means is that the spaces on every line are a different width in justified copy. Look at the gray boxes on the first and third line above. InDesign works hard to minimize this on a paragraph basis, justifying the whole paragraph at a time. More than that, the word spaces are different from paragraph to paragraph whenever size, font, or defaults change. As a result, you never really know how wide a spacebar character will be.

The problem of predictable spaces has been solved by using some more letterpress solutions. When type was composed, it was brought out to a rectangle no matter what the alignment was—right, left, centered, or justified. The characters used to do this were blank slugs, called quads, that were a little lower than type-height so they would not print accidentally. These quads came in three widths: em, en, and el, plus what were called hair spaces. The el space is long gone; it is now usually called a thin space. InDesign has all four types. The recent versions have added several more that typographers deem essential. A quarter space, third space, and sixth space have been added and more.

Originally these characters were blanks the width of an *m*, *n*, and *l*, respectively. Of course, they were standardized. These spaces are now defined as follows: an em space is the square of the point size; an en space is the same height, of course, but half as wide; and a thin space varies. InDesign's hair space is one-twenty-fourth of an em.

These fixed spaces are used a lot. For example, they should always be used for custom hand-spacing, because the spacebar can vary proportionally if you change the point size. Fixed spaces remain proportionally consistent. Another fact to bear in mind is that lining numbers are normally an

190

en space wide. This means that an en should be used as a blank when lining up numbers (an em for two numbers) for accountants and bookkeepers.

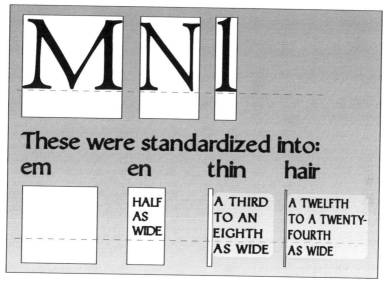

Tabular construction

Custom spacing should normally be done with tabs. Typesetting tabs are much more powerful than typewriting tabs. They come in four kinds: left, right, centered, and decimal. Actually these decimal tabs can be aligned on any character you choose like the x in 2x4. All tabs can be set up with leaders. These leaders can be lines, dotted lines, or any repeating character you need. Again this has been extended radically so that you can now make leaders out of a repeating set of up to 8 characters. You're only limited by your imagination.

There is no legitimate use of the double space.

Secretarial tab use

One of the additional problems you will have with word processing copy done by others is poor tab use. A single tab is often used for the first-line indent. You will have to delete that. Because many word processor users do

191

not know how to set tabs, they just use the default tabs that come every half inch. As a result, you will often find several tabs in a row—used like multiple spaces. They will all have to be changed to a single tab. In addition, because most do not know how to do bulleted or numbered lists, every line is commonly returned manually using multiple tabs. I'm certainly glad you never do anything like that. You will have to get rid of all of them. You will get very fast with Find & Change.

In general, get used to the idea that the spacebar should only be hit once. It cannot be used to line up portions of different lines. They will constantly be out of alignment. In fact, you need to be a little careful. On a computer keyboard, any key that is held down will automatically repeat, including the spacebar. In typesetting there is no legitimate use of the double space. The same is almost true of the tab, but there are exceptions with tabs.

5.   En and em dashes

The next major change we need to discuss is dashes. Typewriters only have one—the hyphen. Type has three—the hyphen, the en dash, and the em dash. All three have very specific usage rules.

HYPHEN   EN DASH   EM DASH

Hyphen: This is the character used to hyphenate words at the end of a line and to create compound words. For example, 10-point is the normal point size for book publishers' body copy. In fact, hyphenation is used no other place. So, you have a couple keystrokes to learn.

En dash: This dash is an en long. It is used with numbers, spans, or ranges. For example, pages 24–39 or 6:00–9:00 or May 7–12. It is a typo to use a hyphen in these cases. The keystroke for an en-dash is Option+Hyphen.

A special case: In rare cases, hyphens and en dashes need to be mixed for clarity. I used one a few paragraphs back when presenting the width of a hair space for InDesign. It seemed to me to be easier to read and understand one–twenty-fourth of an em with the en dash between the one and twenty-fourth. This is the typographer's decision to make.

Em dash: This dash is an em long. It is a punctuation mark. The keystroke for an em-dash is Option+Shift+Hyphen. Grammatically it is stronger than a comma but weaker than a period. Other than that, there is no standard anymore.

American English is a living language in constant flux. These changes have accelerated in recent years. In many cases, there are no rules anymore. Em dashes are used more every year. In many ways they are very helpful—but traditionalists tend to have knee-jerk reactions to anything outside the grammar books (written decades ago).

Typewriters use a double hyphen for the em dash. This is an embarrassing error to professionals. In fact, it is one of the sure signs of amateurism.

Finally, do not think you will not be caught. Hyphens are about a thin space wide. They are higher above the baseline than en or em dashes. Also, they are commonly slanted up with little swashes on the ends (although you see swashes for all three in Contenu).

6.   Real quotes and apostrophes

Here is another place where typewriters are limited by the lack of characters. All typewriters have is inch and foot marks. Quotation marks and apostrophes look very different. This is another typographical embarrassment when used incorrectly. There are more keystrokes you need to learn, though you can solve most of the problems by turning on Use Typographer's Quotes in Type page of Preferences. The shortcut is Command+Option+Shift+' by default.

Feet' Inches" Quotes "double" & 'single'

Again it is important to use the right characters. An apostrophe is a single close quote.

Character	Mac	PC
Open single	Option+]	Alt+[
Close single	Option+Shift+]	Alt+]
Apostrophe	Option+Shift+]	Alt+]
Open double	Option+[	Alt+Shift+[
Close double	Option+Shift+[	Alt+Shift+]

Dumb quotes

The typewriter inch/foot marks in almost all fonts are actually wrong. They are the mathematical marks used for prime and double-prime. True inch and foot marks are slanted a couple of degrees. Some typographers italicize them. Typographers often call prime and double-prime marks dumb quotes from their use by typists.

Language differences

One of the more disconcerting things to keep track of in this increasingly global society is usage differences in the languages. For example, in America, we are taught to use double quotes for a quote and single quotes for quotes within a quote. British usage is the opposite.

Other languages use completely different characters or changes like open double quotes which look like close double quotes on the baseline—to our American eyes.

Increasingly, we are designing documents set in multiple languages. It is important to keep track of these things. Consider, for instance, the Spanish practice for questions, ¿Que pasa? or expletives, ¡Vámonos!

Guillemots: ‹ › « »

Single and double guillemots are used by several European languages in place of curly quotes. For French and Italian, they point out like «thus». In German they often point in, according to Bringhurst, using »this style«. But then I am not a linguist so I don't know the ins and outs. The point is to be careful.

Bringhurst's work, *The Elements of Typographic Style*, has a great deal of information on specific typographic usage in other languages for those of you doing a lot of this work. It is important to do it right so the reader is not offended.

7. No underlines

The next difference has to do with the physical nature of typewriters. Because they only have one size of type, there is no way to emphasize words except for all caps and underlining. Underlining is necessary for these antiques. In typesetting, underlining ruins the carefully crafted descenders. In addition, the underlines that come with the type are usually too heavy and poorly placed. They also compromise readability and type color by messing with the white space between lines.

If you decide that an underline is an appropriate solution, please adjust the color and location with your Underline Options dialog to avoid compromising the readability of the type.

The goal of typesetting is to make clean, elegant type that is read without distraction. Underlining is almost as bad as outlines and shadows, as far as professionals are concerned. They ruin the unique characteristics of the font. At times they serve a useful design function, but this kind of modification should be used very discreetly.

How to deal with underlines typographically—change them

When receiving copy typed by others, you will usually find body copy littered with underlines. Our job, as typesetters, is to convert those underlines to the proper usage. **Proper Names** should be set in a bold version of the font. Periodic names like *National Geographic* or *People* magazines must be in italics. Words that are simple *emphasis* should also be set in italic. *For strong emphasis*, you may want to change fonts.

8. No ALL CAPS

As mentioned in the underline section, setting letters in all caps is the other way to emphasize words on a typewriter. Typesetting has many more options. There are many more options like *italic*, **bold**, ***bold italic***, SMALL CAPS. PLUS WE CAN USE A larger size, and more.

There is something else, however. Studies have shown that type in all caps is around 40 percent less legible than caps and lowercase, or just lowercase. All caps is also much longer than the same word set C&lc.

Because our major purpose is to get the reader to read our piece and act on the message, you should never use all caps (unless you have a good reason). For example, all caps is often used to make a piece of type less legible and therefore to de-emphasize it. Some people say that all-cap headlines are fine, but I would disagree unless you are careful.

Readability

Readability is an interesting and complicated phenomenon. Everyone has theories. What most agree on is that people recognize letters by the distinctive outlines on the top of the letter shapes.

This is the major reason why setting type in all caps is so counter-productive. Because uppercase letters tend to be in rectangular boxes the tops of characters tend to look very similar.

ATTRACTIVE WOMAN

is not nearly as easy to decipher as

cowardly lion

and the bottom halves almost never work, as in

intellectual snob

(intellectual snob)

As you can see, the straight line formed by the tops of the caps and the bottoms of the lowercase (even the descenders do not help) are not distinct enough to recognize easily. Please, remember that difficulty is not a good attribute of reading material.

 By the way, all caps reversed is even less legible: In fact, text set that way (light on a dark background) will not be read unless you force the reader graphically with size, color, or some other such ploy. The worst, for reading, is type that goes back and forth from positive to negative. You will loose a surprisingly large percentage of your readers by doing that.

On the Web and for presentations, it is true that light, glowing letters on a dark background can be easier to read: This is true for any type used as a light source or backlit. However, you need to remember that on the Web the backgrounds often do not print. White type on white paper doesn't read well at all.

These readability issues are primary to typesetting. You really need to keep track. Remember, you can read it because you set it. Your readers do not have that benefit.

9. Letterspacing, kerning, and tracking

Here is another typesetting capability that cannot even be considered by word processors. We mentioned letterspacing earlier. Letterspacing is the built-in spacing between characters in a font. The basic idea is that the white space between letters should be identical for all letter pairs. Obviously, this is not simple or easy. AT, OOPS, and silly have very different spacing problems—especially the ill. The better the font, the better the letterspacing. In very cheap fonts, individual letters may be far to the left or right. I bought one once where the lowercase *r* was always at least 9 points to the left.

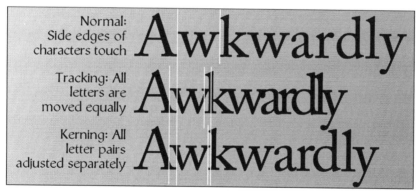

Normal: Side edges of characters touch — Awkwardly

Tracking: All letters are moved equally — Awkwardly

Kerning: All letter pairs adjusted separately — Awkwardly

Tracking
Tracking is the official term used to replace letterspacing in digital typesetting now that we can move letters either closer together or farther apart. In reality, either term can be used and understood. The actual procedure for tracking

simply inserts or removes an equal amount of space around every letter selected or affected.

Although tracking is used all the time by typographic novices, it is despicable to traditional professionals. Quality typefaces have the letterspacing carefully designed into the font. Changing the tracking for stylistic reasons or fashion changes the color of the type at the very least. A paragraph tracked tighter looks darker. At worst, it can make the type color of the page look splotchy.

Tracking suffers from the vagaries of fashion. In the 1980s, it was very common to see extremely tight tracking in everything. I was guilty of it myself. May it never be among you. Tight tracking severely compromises readability by obscuring lettershapes.

Global tracking changes: If you are using a display font for your body copy, it will commonly be set too tight. In this case you may want to increase the tracking, globally, for the entire document. The same is true when using a text font for heads. Here you want to move the letters closer. These global changes work fine.

Kerning

Kerning is a different thing altogether. Here the problem is with letter pairs. There are thousands of different letter pairs. I guess the total would be around 20,000 or 40,000 pairs. There is no way to set up the spacing around letters to cover all situations: AR is a very different situation than AV; To than Th; AT than AW.

Literally thousands of different kerned pairs are needed to make a perfectly kerned font. Some kern together and some kern apart. Most of them can only be seen at the larger point sizes. Here again we see the difference between excellent and cheap fonts. Professional fonts have around 1,000 kerning pairs built into the font metrics. Cheap fonts commonly have a couple dozen or none at all.

As mentioned, quality fonts have kerning designed into about a thousand letter pairs. In addition, all professional publishing programs allow you to adjust kerning for individual pairs. InDesign give you keyboard shortcuts (most often

198

Option+Left Arrow and Option+Right Arrow). Adding the Command key multiples the amount moved.

InDesign offers Optical kerning which automatically checks the letterspacing and adjusts it for you. It does a remarkable job. Some years ago, I put a font up on MyFonts.com to sell that was unusable outside of InDesign. I had forgotten that I had purposely made uneven and bad letterspacing for the headers in my first book on InDesign to show how well optical kerning worked. Then I used it in another application. Needless to say, I had to take it off the market until I fixed it.

We are always expected to check the kerning on all type larger than about 18-point: Yes, you really are required to hand kern all headlines if necessary. It's the only way, in most cases. Unkerned type looks cheap and unprofessional. In body copy sizes, a quality font will cover the kerning necessities.

10.   Be careful with hyphens.

Because typeset line endings are automatic, so is the hyphenation. You can turn it on or off. Hyphenation is done by dictionary. You can set up the hyphens when you add new words to the user dictionary (see help).

Another problem is that automatic hyphenation can create hyphens for many consecutive lines. Here there is sharp debate. Most of us agree that two hyphens in a row should be the maximum (a three-hyphen "stack" looks odd). Page layout software allows you to set that limit. Many set the limit at one.

Yet another problem comes when you run into something like two hyphens in a row; then a normal line; then two more hyphens. The final problem comes when the program hyphenates part of a compound word. **Be careful with hyphens!**

Finally, never hyphenate a word in a headline or subhead. It just isn't done. In fact, almost all headers should be carefully examined if they go to two lines or more. Normally they need to be broken for sense with soft-returns

[Shift+Return]. In your header paragraph styles, simply turn hyphenation off. I originally turned hyphenation off for this entire book. I later turned it back on for the body copy—simply because the type color was no longer smooth.

11. Eliminate widows and orphans ▪

As Roger Black states in his pioneering work, *Desktop Design Power* (Random House, 1990, out of print) "Widows are the surest sign of sloppy typesetting." The problems arise as soon as we start trying to simply define the words. See the subsection below on orphans.

I am using the most common definitions (also the ones used by Black). A widow is a short line at the end of a paragraph that is much too short. What is too short? Again, there is sharp debate. The best answer is that the last line must have at least two complete words and those two words must be at least eight characters total. Bringhurst says at least four characters. (But then his typography is filled with short sentence fragments at the end of paragraphs that look horrible, as far as I am concerned.) You need to eliminate all of them like the word "above" which follows: a-bove.

Orphans (paragraph fragments in columns)

The software will really mess you up here, if you are not careful. Programmers usually have no idea what a widow is. Often they confuse widows with orphans. InDesign uses Bringhurst's definitions. I do not know any traditional type-setter who uses these conventions, but then I only know a few hundred or so. I agree with people like Sandee Cohen, Roger Black, Robin Williams, and many others. Actually, everyone agrees what excellent type should look like. There are only semantic differences—word definitions.

An orphan is a short paragraph or paragraph fragment left by itself at the top or bottom of a column. In Bring-hurst-speak (and he is marvelously witty), a widow is an orphan at the bottom of a column. An orphan is one left at the top of a column. A classic example is a subhead left at the bottom of one column with the body copy starting at the top of the next column.

InDesign allows you to control both of these problems fairly well with their *keeps controls*. A keeps control, in the option menu of the paragraph dialog or panel, allows you to determine if a paragraph must stay with the following paragraph (in the case of the subhead, for example). It also allows you to set the minimum paragraph fragment allowed at either end of a paragraph. This is normally a two-line minimum, top or bottom, beginning or end. Be careful—all existing software considers a widow to be an orphan at the bottom of a column and an orphan comes only at the top (they are both orphans).

Fixing widows (last lines of paragraphs)

Bad paragraph widows mess up the type color. They allow a blank white area to appear between paragraphs which stands out like a sore thumb. There is no way to eliminate them except by hand. The best way is editorially. In other words, rewrite the paragraph!

Occasionally that is not possible. In that case, you must carefully adjust the hyphenation, horizontal scale, point size, or word spacing (in that order).

Here we get into local formatting. However, a difficult widow can often be eliminated no other way.

1. **Hyphenation:** Often you can eliminate a widow by simply adding a hyphenation point to a word with a *discretionary hyphen*. A discretionary hyphen is a character that places a breaking point in a word that is invisible unless a hyphen is needed. The shortcut varies. The InDesign default is Command+Shift+Hyphen. Sadly, this character is often not available on the PC.

2. **Horizontal scale:** Here we get into another of those typographic purist fracases. Using horizontal scaling to condense or expand letterforms makes these guys and gals freak. However, plus or minus 5% is invisible. This is the easiest way to pull back a widow. Even most typographers can't see the changes.

3. **Point size:** Make the point size a half-point smaller. As you recall, a point is about the

smallest difference the human eye can see. An entire paragraph with type that is a half-point smaller is an invisible change.

4. **Word spacing:** In justified copy, the word space is elastic. You'll need to customize this setting because the defaults are terrible. Let's say your software is set at 80% minimum, 100% normal, and 115% maximum. If you change the normal to 95%, you move the words a little closer and might eliminate a widow. [I talk about this option more in Appendix B]

    You must be gentle or your corrections will stand out worse than the widow: The point size should never be changed more than a half point, for example. Always make your changes to the entire paragraph. Extremely short paragraphs often cannot be fixed, except to "break for sense." This means placing soft returns so that each short line makes sense by itself (as much as possible). Remember, the best method is rewriting the paragraph to add or subtract a word or two to get rid of the widow.

The absolute worst orphan is a widow at the top of a new page—especially if it is the hyphenated back half of the last word. Other horrible typos are: widow at the top of a column; subhead at the bottom, as mentioned; a kicker separated from its headline; and a subhead with one line of body copy at the bottom of a column.

These errors must be eliminated at the proofing stage. This is what we mean by massaging a document into shape. Corrections like these are among the primary factors that cause people to react to a design. If they are missing, your design will be classed with amateur productions like school and bureaucrat output.

12. Use bulleted lists.

The use of bullets and dingbats is unknown to typists. Bulleted lists are an extremely effective means of attracting the reader's attention. In fact, there has been a lot of study to find out what readers see and respond to. These are the paragraphs you use to attract the reader's eye or to re-attract it if it is wandering in boredom. The readership order goes like this:

- First, **picture captions**—everyone looks at the pictures first. Photos are checked out before drawings, unless the illustrations are exceptional. The caption should be the synopsis of the major benefit in the story to the reader.

- Second, **headlines**—primarily because of size and placement. The headline should also be the synopsis of the major benefit in the story to the reader. No reader reads everything. You need to tell them why this story is important to them.

- Third, **callouts or pull quotes**—these are quotes pulled from the copy or statements about the copy that are enlarged to the point where they become interesting graphics in their own right. They are exceptionally valuable in pages of nothing but body copy to capture the wandering eye. Care must be taken. An improperly pulled quote can change the editorial focus of the article.

- Fourth, **bulleted or numbered lists**—like this one. Bulleted lists are read by scanning readers before subheads, drop caps, or any of the other graphic leads commonly used. The assumption is that lists are synopses of the surrounding copy. Readers use them to determine if the rest of the story is worth reading.

Dingbats

Dingbats

There are hundreds of dingbat fonts. Many of them are excellent sources of fashionable clip art. Here are a few samples from three fonts called MiniPics -Confetti, MiniPics -LilDinos, & MiniPics -LilFaces.

With typesetting we have even more options than simple bullets. Dingbats are fonts made up of graphics. Every keystroke is a different graphic. Zapf Dingbats is a font that almost everyone has on a Mac. The ones to the left are from Wingdings, which has a similar function on a PC. Almost everyone has several dingbat fonts, even if they don't know it.

Font creation programs allow you to use a logo in a font. Top-quality dingbat fonts are a good way to pick up a collection of clip art that can be used as you type. For a time, dingbat fonts became one of the best sources of fashionable art. Using dingbats for bullets increases the attraction of the list. Just be careful that the reader is led to read the copy and not simply be amused by your graphic.

Often dingbats are graphic enough to make excellent starts and/or pieces of logo design: You may want to buy several of these resources. MyFonts.com has a huge collection. Several type designers specialize in dingbat font design.

13.   Use small caps.

Small caps are a specialized letterform. Correctly speaking, they are a smaller set of capital letters (often a bit larger than the x-height), used in place of the lowercase letters, which are designed so they have the same color as the rest of the font. Here is where you have to be careful, again. PAGE LAYOUT SOFTWARE CREATES SMALL CAPS BY PROPORTIONALLY SHRINKING CAPITAL LETTERS. This makes them appear to be too light. THE BEST METHOD IS TO USE FONTS THAT HAVE CUSTOM-DESIGNED SMALL CAPS. There were few font families like this prior to this millennium. But now, many of the OpenType font families have real small caps.

There are only a few places where small caps are required. However, I strongly agree with Bringhurst here. He has many other places where he recommends small caps. What we are basically saying is that strings of caps within body copy should be SMALL CAPS. Otherwise these acronyms and abbreviations appear to be shouting.

There are several things attached to this position. First of all, this use of small caps is coupled with the use of old style numbers (or if you use my fonts, small cap figures). Second, small caps are often, but not necessarily, used only in body copy. Your task, should you accept this venture, will be to convince your copy editor that this is correct procedure. Most of them are using old, newspaper-based, manuals of style. Basing typographic style on newspapers is like basing fashionable dress on Wally World.

Nevertheless, there are a few places where you use small caps even if you do not have true small caps. For times and dates, the proper use is not A.M. or AM or a.m. but AM. The same is true of PM, AD, BC, BCE, and CE. In these cases, you always use small caps with no periods.

But what about statements like USA 1776? Here the determining factor is whether or not you have oldstyle or small cap numbers in your font. In general, you should always use oldstyle numbers in body copy, at least. So, all strings of caps like this should be small caps: ASCII, USA, UN, USSR, CIA, NASCAR, and so on.

Adding letter space for readability

To increase readability, you will need to add letter space to the small cap strings (though a good font will have this built in). This should be designed into the font you use. You should also do this if you are using all caps for headlines. Seriously, any time you are using words made up of capital letters you need to add space between the letters until they become readable. The guiding principle is to add as much as you can without causing the letters to separate into individual characters instead of a unified word.

Lining numbers with all caps

Even though we have stated that lining numbers are really only appropriate for bookkeepers, accountants, and CPAS, there are other appropriate uses. One of these is in the midst of all caps.

GOD BLESS AMERICA! REMEMBER 9/11/2001 & 2008.

Yes, there are occasions you will be using all caps. You will have to letterspace to help readability. In this situation oldstyle numbers would look foolish.

Readability is crucial;
common sense is required.

14.   First-line indents

We have briefly touched on first-line indents for body copy paragraphs. This is the preferred method of telling the reader that a new topic sentence is being developed—a new thought expressed. I also mentioned my practice of adding a point or two after paragraphs to help the reader see that first-line indent on a busy page.

The amount of that first-line indent is up to you. You're the designer. The norm is somewhere between a quarter inch and a half inch. Robert says that the minimum is an en, but that is far below what I would call a minimum. An en just tends to look like a mistake. Some say the indent should equal the lead so when using 10/12 you should indent 12 points. Many specify an em, which in the 10/12 example would be 10 points. That is barely over an eighth of an inch—too small for me.

The first-line indent should equal the left indent of your lists.

Actually, I think the first line indent is more intertwined than any of those intellectually fine sounding indents of fixed spaces. One of the things to consider as you set up your paragraph styles and page layout is that second consistent interior line which is made by your first-line indents, the left indent of your lists, the left indent of your body heads, and the left indent of your quotes.

As a result, I have personally arrived at a first-line indent of .4 inch. You may want to use less or more, but IMHO anything less than a quarter inch (18 points) just looks like a mistake. It is not really visible; so it merely irritates. Anything more than a half inch makes the eye feel like it has to lunge in to find the beginning.

15.   Drop caps

One of the typographic devices used to indicate the beginning of a story or chapter is the drop cap. In this use, the first letter or letters of the first paragraph is (are) made

206

large enough to be three, four, or five lines of type tall and inset into the paragraph.

The first-lines of that paragraph are tabbed around the letter or letters. First of all, this is very easy with page layout software. InDesign's implementation allows you to drop as many letters as you want as far as you want—interactively. You can just click the buttons in the Paragraph or Control panel until you like what you see.

If I speak in the tongues of mortals and of angels, but do not have love, I am a noisy gong or a clanging cymbal. And if I have prophetic powers, and understand all mysteries and all knowledge, and if I have all faith, so as to remove mountains, but do not have love, I am nothing.

If I give all I possess to the poor and surrender my body to the flames, but have not love, I gain nothing.

Love is patient; love is kind; love is not envious or boastful or arrogant or rude. It does not insist on its own way; it is not irritable or resentful; it does not rejoice in wrongdoing, but rejoices in the truth.

Love bears all things, believes all things, hopes all things, endures all things.

Often, the drop cap is in a radically different font. It can be set very dramatically in a flowing script that hangs off in the left margin. It is often in a different color. Commonly used are the illuminated capitals of the medieval scribes.

Mainly, it needs to be dramatic.

The largest mistake with drop caps is overuse. They need to be used very sparingly. As you can see in the four paragraphs above, multiple drop caps are merely confusing. They should never be used more than once on a page. Really, they should only be used once—for the first paragraph of a story, article, or chapter.

16.   Proper accents for languages

When you are using a word or phrase from another language, always accent it properly. Some of these things are commonly missed. Words like résumé, moiré, façade, and the like have entered common usage in English. But if you are using the pine nuts from the Southwest in your cooking, they are piñon nuts. Being from New Mexico, I know the ubiquitous and unique New Mexican hot peppers are chilé. Chili is that weird stuff (to my taste inedible) with beans and/or meat from Texas.

This type of typography is only common courtesy. You need to be aware that in the old Commonwealth it is still cheque and lorry. In those countries, corporations get plural verbs—as in: Shell Oil are drilling five new off-shore wells south of Norway.

In America, you need to be very careful of local usage. I mentioned the chilé example already. In speech, what is sillier (or more annoying) than an out-sider calling the fertile valley south of Portland the Will•i-a•mette' Valley instead of the Will•**am'**•et as it is locally pronounced? You will find that all locales have local usage. You need to use it.

We have just gotten started.

I could go on for many pages with typographic nice-ties. This is just a first introduction to type. The Chinese showed their wisdom again by considering calligraphy to be the highest form of art.

Once you understand type, you will see its beauty. Well-drawn type is absolutely gorgeous. After a while, you begin to understand why some of the best graphic designs are simply type.

This goes far beyond simple beauty, though. Excellent type is much easier to read. It eases customer fears. It helps make good experiences (think about a dinner menu at a fine restaurant coupled with a marriage proposal). It is what makes your book a joy to read (assuming you can write ;-).

Typographers

As we have seen, there are three categories of people producing words on paper—typists, typesetters, and typographers. We have been discussing the first two. Typographers go beyond this to make typesetting an art. You should now have an inkling of how difficult that is. They are some of the finest artists in existence.

Becoming a typographer is a worthy goal. It will take you many years. What I want to impress on you is that a surprising number of you will head in that direction. Book design becomes so involved with type that you fall in love with it. My only request is that you remain kind and recognize that there are many opinions about type. Strange to say, almost all of them are subjectively correct.

They are simply elegant creative solutions to the communication issues of the book.

B: Typography Part 2

Building excellence into your styles

As I mentioned in the main body of the book, my intention is to go through all the options on all the pages of the New Paragraph Style dialog box. Most of these options are not understood by new book designers.

They give you immense control over your typography **IF** you know what their purpose is and how to set them up. They enable you to largely automate your formatting and provide control of the reader's eye which is amazing.

Going through the pages of
the New Paragraph Style dialog box ◼

If you look at the page list in the column on the left side of the dialog box, it might look like nothing changed for the CS5.5 & CS6 versions except for the addition of an Export Tagging page—but this is a big deal.

This is actually a vast improvement to the ePUB export process. I cover what this new capability includes and how to use it effectively in Appendix E—which is about designing your ePUBs. Basically, I do it all at once using the Edit All Export Tags dialog box. But it is really a good thing.

 Changes for CS6: As usual, the new version looks deceptively the same as CS5.5, CS5, CS4, CS3, and even CS2. The InDesign engineering team spends a great deal of time on small improvements. These improvements are often barely visible. However, the end result of all of them is a vastly improved workflow and greatly increased production speed. If you haven't looked them over for a few versions, you might find some real gems in the following discussion.

Basically, you are going to discover there are several basic settings which are very different for heads as opposed to body copy. Some you probably know, like turning off Hyphenation for heads. Some you don't...

General page

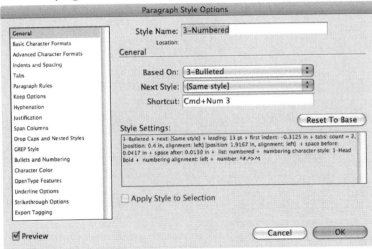

Style Name: I strongly suggest that you number all of yours using the number for used by your shortcut. It is a great aid to help you remember the shortcuts.

Based On: This will be the style you should have chosen before you opened the new style dialog box. Changing it retroactively did not always work well in earlier versions but CS4+ does a lot better [click the Reset To Base button]. The new style is an exact copy of the style it is based on. Changes made in this new style will be the only commands NOT changed if you update the style it is based on.

For example, the style of the previous paragraph is identical to the 2-body style (used in this paragraph) but without a first line indent. It does include a nested character style and it is called 2-Body Run-In. 2-Body Run-In is used for the next paragraph also.

Next Style: As mentioned, you can use the next style setups to automatically format type as you type.

Shortcut: This is about production speed. On a PC you are very limited, but the 30+ shortcuts available still help a lot. You use any of the modifier keys (Control, Alt, and Shift) plus one of the numbers on the numerical keypad. The problem is that Windows preempts many of these. Alt cannot be used alone. Several others simply aren't available.

Through CS3, a Mac had nearly a hundred shortcuts available because it has four modifier keys: Command, Option, Control, and Shift. (CS4+ lost the use of Control.) Even without the Control key there are 70 combinations or so. Almost all of these shortcuts can be used except for a few that are preempted by OSX (and you even have the option to turn off the OSX shortcuts if they interfere with your working style).

> Yes, you must use the numerical keypad for style shortcuts. This is a real issue for laptops. You may need to buy an external keyboard or learn to use Quick Apply.

Basic Character Formats

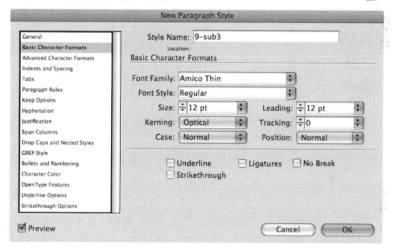

As you can see, this page contains virtually everything in the Character panel. What isn't on this page is on the Advanced Character Formats page. You can control every aspect of font selection, size, leading, letterspacing (both kerning and tracking), caps, small caps, and scaling. I was assuming you know all of this. **But I can't do that.**

Very important!

Adjusting fields with Up & Down Arrow keys: I only mention this because it dumbfounds most of my students. Any field (Font Family, Font Style, Size, Leading, and so on) can be adjusted up or down by the use of the arrow keys. It is an amazing timesaver, as you can imagine. In fact, it saves so much time I have never even learned the shortcuts for larger and smaller. The arrow keys are easier to implement and faster.

Font family: The up & down arrows work here with your installed font list. You can also hit the up arrow to go to the beginning of the word and start typing the name you need. If you are quick, you can get in three to four letters to narrow your choices.

Font Style: This is the main place where changing fonts can mess you up. Quite commonly one font will use Bold and the next will use Heavy. You have to watch this.

Size: You know this one.

Leading: If you do not like the auto leading setting you are getting, you can change it on the Justification page.

Metrics: Optical or Manual. Optical tends to be a little looser than Metrics, plus cheap fonts often have bad metric spacing (which Optical really helps).

Tracking: This is the place to compensate for font designer decisions you do not like. Fonts from the 1980s tend to be too tight, for example. Text fonts are often too loose for Display use. The change should be made here because then it is global.

Case: The choices are Normal, Small Caps, All Caps, and OpenType All Small Caps. I ask you to bug Adobe with feature requests until we can get the Title case and Sentence case options also.

Position: Superscript, subscript, OpenType Superscript, OpenType Subscript, OpenType Numerator, OpenType Denominator. I could see using it in a character style for fractions.

Advanced Character Formats

Here you see the rest of the Character panel. This is where you need to come for scaling and baseline shifts.

Baseline shift: This moves the characters affected by the style up or down. Negative numbers move them down. I have used it for Kickers, for example, to move them down into a better fit with the header underneath.

Horizontal and vertical scale sometimes help, but mainly a baseline shift is used a lot for bullets in a character style because many bullets need to be adjusted not only in size but up and down.

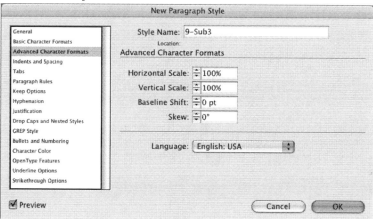

Language: More importantly, this is where you pick the language used. As we are forced more and more into multi-lingual documents, this will become more important. I can easily see separate sets of styles for English, French, and Spanish (& more than that for EU stuff).

Indents & Spacing

This page is used very often.

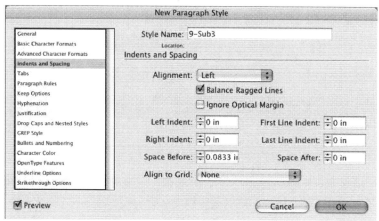

Alignment: Remember, InDesign has seven alignments: Left, Right, Centered, Justified Left, Justified Right, Justified Center, and Full justified. The last option justifies the last line also. It is necessary of you want to justify a single line paragraph. You will regularly be changing lists from Left to Left Justified or the reverse, depending on the length of the paragraphs.

Balance ragged lines: You really need to be careful of this one. This option makes line breaks based solely on line length. It does not break by phrases. The result is often heads or subheads which do not read well.

Break for sense to help readability

One of the things you need to become aware of and add to your repertoire is the practice of making sure that line breaks of flush left copy in narrow column occur between phrases. Let's use the subhead above, set large, to show you the problem. There is a huge difference in readability between these two choices.

Break for sense to help readability

The above version is much more difficult to read than the following version:

Break for sense to help readability

You are responsible to make sure your headings [those which are large enough to only have a few words per line] have line breaks to help readability. Again, this is called breaking for sense.

Indents: Left, First line, and Right indents. The first line indent can be as large negatively as the left indent is positively. This is what enables the indents necessary to make a list with the bullets or numbers hanging in the space between the left column edge and the left indent of the list.

Secondary alignments

You will find that keeping secondary indents the same as your first line indent of your body copy style is a big help.

This interior alignment aids your readers.

 It will go a long way to making your formatting more consistent

 It makes your layout much easier to comprehend

 It requires less effort on the part of the reader.

Please notice in the paragraph below with the dropped inline graphic. The left indent is the same as the first line indent of my body copy. The right indent is also that same size. It makes a nice balance. The left indent of my lists is also the same size (as you see above).

 Again the arrow keys: remember, that the quickest way to adjust things is to tab to the field you want to change, then use the up and down arrows to adjust, then tab out to execute. If you need to readjust, Shift+Tab will take you back to do it again.

This does require a larger than normal first line indent to work well. Even the default third of an inch is a little small for me. I have settled on a .4" indent. I've used it for many years now and it works really well.

Align to grid: I don't use grids, so I have no real help for you here. If you find something you think should be added to this book, email me and I'll add it.

Tabs

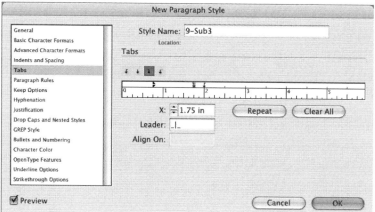

In this dialog is the complete Tabs panel: Each style can have its own set of tabs. This is where tabs really come into their own. You set tabs once per style and then apply them by style when you need them. Here is the tool you need to set forms by adding leaders throughout your Document. It's much easier and better than drawing rules and trying to line them up by hand.

Decimal Tabs (special character tabs): In InDesign the decimal tab can work with any single character. So, you can align the tab on the x for dimensional lumber, or maybe a colon for a **Short Name:** short description list.

Double stacked right-angle triangles: In the ruler, these show you the first line indent on top and the left indent on the bottom. Yes, they can be moved separately, but it's tricky.

X: here you can type in the location which really helps for Right tabs at the right edge of a column.

Leader: It can be any characters you can type (up to eight of them).

Align On: This is where you enter the character to use for the decimal tab. You get a period by default.

You need to keep tables in mind.

The only proviso in all of this is that it is often better and easier to use a table than setting up and using very complicated tabs.

The next four pages

Here is the true use of these options: the complete dialog boxes from the Paragraph Styles panel menu: Paragraph Rules, Hyphenation, Keep Options, and Justification. What you will discover as you learn to add the controls in these options is that this is really where much of the difference between amateur and pro lies. You can do a lot with these controls to make your type look good semi-automatically.

Paragraph Rules

Paragraph rules are normally used only within paragraph styles: They are too tedious to use otherwise. However, once they are set up in a paragraph style the rules are added automatically every time you use that style. If you look at the subhead in the preceding paragraph, look at the short, square paragraph rule on the right edge with a graduated stroke (a rule is a line which is colored with a stroke).

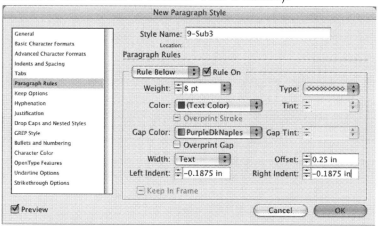

 TIP: If you understand how InDesign does rules, you see that each paragraph can have up to four rules attached to it: above paragraph, below paragraph, underline, and strikethrough. Any of these rules can use any of the stroke styles, be any color (including any color for any gaps in the stroke style), any width up to 1000 points, and any location up to 18 inches up or down. Paragraph rules can also be any length up to the width of the pasteboard so a rule in a narrow column can stretch across an entire page if that is what you need. (Of course you can use more than this with rules applied by nested character styles.)

There is a great deal of room for experimentation

This means you can use a huge variety of rules to attract attention or divert it. You can make a rule that functions as an automatic tint box in back of your type. When you need them, they are available.

Basically rules (plus underlines & strikethroughs) are only limited by your imagination. They can certainly be overdone (I do that myself quite regularly by giving myself the *demo* excuse). But, they are excellent tools for directing the reader's eye—and for controlling emphasis.

 Just be careful with type in a tint box: Doing this always reduces contrast and makes type harder to read. Be careful to compensate with font choices, point sizes, leading and the rest of the controls in my arsenal.

Keep Options

These options are used for almost every headline and subhead. The use depends on the type of paragraph. The Keep With and Together options can almost eliminate orphans (isolated lines and paragraph fragments).

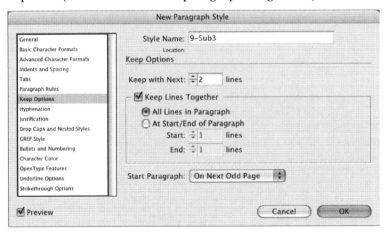

Keep With Next: with 2 or 3 lines. You certainly do not want a subhead or headline isolated by itself at the bottom of a column—one of the worst widows.

Keep Lines Together: You normally check All Lines in Paragraph for headers.

At Start/End of Paragraph: I usually use Start: 2 & End: 3 for body copy. End: 2 lines often leaves you with a line and a partial line which does not look good. However, if you regularly write four-line paragraphs, you better use Start: 2 and End: 2 to keep the software from a nervous breakdown.

Start Paragraph: This is the place where you can set styles to start new articles or chapters and have them start on the next odd page. (Remember to do that for your headlines or the style you use to start each chapter—it is virtually required that chapters and sections start on the odd [right] page). This all gives you an immense amount of automatic layout control.

Hyphenation

Again let's use headlines and subheads as an example. They should not hyphenate—ever. Often tightly written, terse lists with short paragraphs are set flush left with hyphenation turned off.

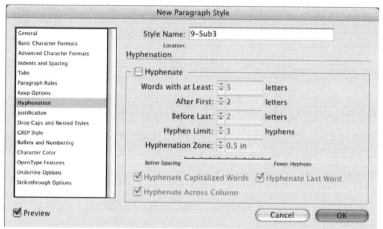

The actual hyphenation setup is something you want to determine before you even start putting together the documents. These settings are determined by grammarians and your usage. For some reason, typographers really get upset about this (even though they rarely agree with each other [which tells me there is no real standard]). Many say you cannot even have two hyphens in a row. Some say a hyphen every other row is terrible. Often you will have to make a case by case judgment as you massage the copy to fit your tidy, well-designed little boxes.

On the other hand, almost everyone agrees that agrees should not be hyphenated after the a in a-grees. Much of this is common sense. The rules are good, but readability trumps everything. For example, would you hyphenate hyphenat-ed? Most wouldn't, but it would be clearly readable. Isn't that right?

Justification

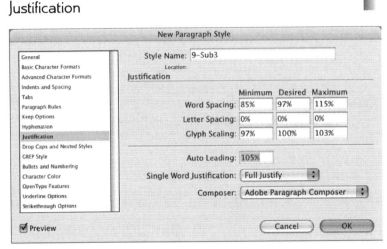

Normally these settings are only used when you make the setup for a newspaper or magazine. This is a place where the experts do not agree at all. Everyone has their own opinion. Our choice is to control the word spacing as tightly as possible to make a smooth type color. I go far beyond most recommendations.

In my experience, InDesign justifies body copy with the normal 9-12 words per line exceptionally well. I have changed my default settings to 85% Min, 97% Desired, & 115% Max with superior results. Most say that Desired should always be 100%, but some fonts simply have space characters that are too wide. But these settings are part of your personal style.

However, you will want to regularly make Auto leading changes. It is true that auto-leading for body copy in almost always 120% (or 10/12). On the other hand, headers are commonly 105% for C&lc and 80% or less for all caps and small caps (that have no descender). Gradually, you will find that careful adjustments to a style here save you a lot of grief as you actually begin to flow copy into your document.

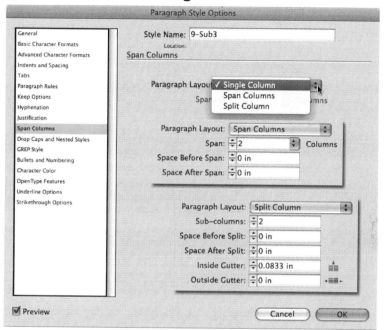

The three options are composited in the single image above. Span columns has been the most demanded feature for InDesign for about three versions now. They got what they asked for, but...

Before you get too excited, this most demanded feature only works with multiple columned text frames.

It will not span a headline across threaded frames. When you think about that it immediately becomes obvious why this is so.

My guess is that it will work really well in something like a newsletter or newspaper using a rigid multiple-column-grid structure. But even there it seems a bit tedious to work with. What I am not sure of is if it will be faster and more efficient than the current necessity of placing these multiple column headers in a separate text frame.

In general, text frames with multiple columns are really tedious to work with. In fact, they are so bad, I never use them. But then most of my work is single column work like this book. They are the norm for CS6's new Liquid Layout features for ebooks and apps.

New to CS5: Split columns

One of the nice new things in CS5 is the ability to select lists and split them into multiple columns within a single column. The easiest thing is probably to show you. You can see where the command is available in the Paragraph control panel capture below. It works really well for lists of names that you need in columns to save space. But you can do it with any selection of type.

One of the nice new things in CS5 is the ability to select lists and split them into multiple columns within a single column. The easiest thing is probably to show you. You can see where the command

is available in the Paragraph control panel at the top of the next page. It works really well for lists of names that you need in columns to save space. But you can do it with any selection of type.

However, you can see above where I used Split 2 that you really need to watch the justification issues which result. The left column above (especially) has very bad justification problems. But the right column is almost as bad because it is too tight to read easily.

Like I said, it is probably best used for lists of stuff: I just typed the list that follows. Then I selected it all and chose Split 3 from the drop-down menu in the control panel. This is a very nice feature.

☙ Books	☙ Trains	☙ Fighters
☙ Boats	☙ Bikes	☙ Bombers
☙ Planes	☙ Cars	☙ Limos

Of course, there is always a fly in the ointment. These split columns will not transfer at all into your ePUB or Kindle versions of your book. So, you need to think about how you are going to handle that issue [a table?].

Drop Caps & Nested Styles

Drop caps: You can set a Character Style to use with your drop caps. That is commonly done because drop caps are often in a different font (at least). Drop caps in InDesign are much more powerful than many designers realize.

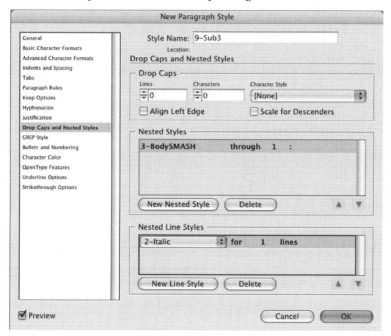

Nested styles: (Yes, these use character styles: I will cover them next.) I always used to call these run-in heads. Adobe's name indicates what they really are—because they are much more powerful than simple run-in heads. Simply put, a nested style allows you to automatically apply a character style to the start of the paragraph until a specified delimiter appears. You can have a bold style run-in until the first colon, for example—a very common addition to this book

Dropped In-Line Graphics: For example, as you can see to the left in this paragraph, I commonly place [import] a graphic at the beginning of a paragraph and then use the drop caps feature to lower the graphic 3 lines with the rest of the paragraph in a run-around. One time for a tall, narrow poster, I dropped the inline graphic 28 lines—

down through seven or eight paragraphs below the insertion point.

Headline font in regular through colon: You've seen this through out the booklet. But I can easily add a second nested style through the first em-dash. You can see something like this at the top of the next page.

Smash through colon: *Italic through the em-dash*–then back to normal copy. I could even add bold through a second colon—if I Wanted.

I started just to try and do something outrageous, but then I realized that this is actually quite practical for certain types of lists and bibliographies.

This is the set up I used for the next two paragraphs below the capture. Notice I put two colons for the third run-in (it counts the first one used also). Once the style is set up I do not have to do a thing except type the copy or apply the shortcut to apply the style to existing copy. The nested styles just appear like magic.

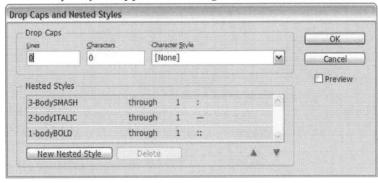

Publishing With InDesign: *by David Bergsland*–**Practical training in page layout:** What an embarrassing book that first book was (thankfully, it's out of print)!

The Bible: *by God's inspiration*–**Practical training in living:** now this is truly an excellent book!

Adding new character styles from within the new style dialog: This is one of the major additions CS4 has added. In CS3 or earlier, I was constantly having to close out a partially finished style to add a character style for a drop cap, nested style, and so on [like I still must do with Swatches].

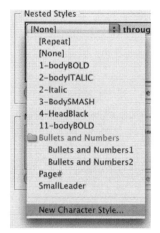

Now there is a New Character style choice in the pop-up menu.

See character styles after I finish paragraph styles.

Nested Line styles: To be honest, I haven't played much with this one. It became available in CS4, but so far in two+ years, I've never found a use. But it would seem to be a nice addition to the repertoire. It allows you to be able to apply a Character Style by line. This has never been a style I liked. One of the more common uses is small caps for the first line. The next paragraph shows another option.

Something like this could be

tried. The 1st line is in 24 point, the 2nd line in 18 point using the header font, the 3rd line in 15 **point using the body copy font, and the 4th line in** 12 point bold. I've also seen the 1st line Black, the 2nd line Bold, the 3rd line Demi, the 4th line Regular, the 5th line Light. You can do the same thing with colors—or with colors in addition to all these things.

To me, it's always seemed pretty desperate—a lack of a better idea. It draws too much attention to the type. Typography should be invisible, simply displaying the content. Too bad that's not true for this book. *Remember!*

Typography should invisibly give you the copy as almost irresistibly readable.

Bulleted & Numbered Lists

InDesign has finally reached the promise of earlier versions with its list options. At least it seems that way to me. Some still complain, but that's always the case. I suspect some software somewhere has a fancy option. Part of it is being able to add new character styles on the run (see above). But, it now does what I expect when I choose an option. Maybe I've just been trained by the earlier versions.

Bulleted lists

The bullets can be added from any font you have installed on your computer. You can use Unicode to specify a certain character that is available in any font (like a bullet) or a specific character from a specific font (like a dingbat). You can also format the bullets with a character style (a newly added one if that is necessary).

As mentioned earlier, the only real problem seems to be the common necessity of adding baseline shifts for dingbats in unusual fonts set at a larger or smaller size than the rest of the copy in the paragraph that follows the bullet. The bullet needs to look like it is vertically centered in slug of the first line of type—in most cases.

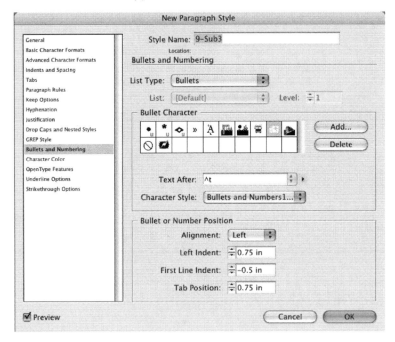

Numbered lists

The numbered list options are more extensive yet. You have any of the numbering formats available to page numbering plus 01, 02 03, etc. You can specify how you want numbers and special characters added at the beginning of a paragraph with very few limitations. [You can't put a tab before the number, for example.] Plus, you can apply a character style to the number to make it a different font, size, color, and so on. And finally under mode you have the choice of continuing from previous number or restarting at a specific number.

 Fixing numbering issues in the copy: If you choose Continue From Previous Number, you will regularly want to start over. With an insertion point in the paragraph, a simple right-click enables you to Restart Numbering.

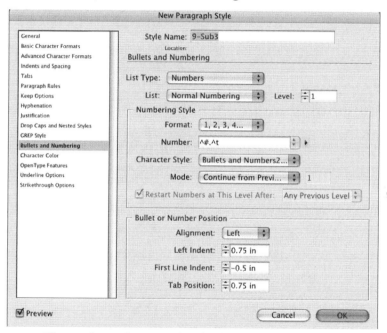

The only real issue I've had is trying to control the numbering when it gets too long. The flush right controls never quite work the way I want them to.

Character color

The key here is to remember that you can only choose from colors that have been added to the Swatches panel. This is why I insist you really need to set up your color swatches before you set up your styles.

You can apply any color, tint or gradient that is in the Swatches panel (plus make tints of the solid colors) to the stroke and/or the fill.

If you double-click on the stroke or fill icon to the left of the Swatches list, and the New Color Swatch dialog will open up. There is no way to add a gradient from within the styles dialog, however. For that you must close out the style and go back into Swatches and add your gradient—which can then be applied when you reopen your style.

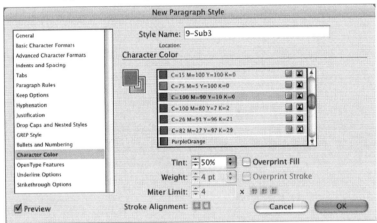

OpenType Features

Here you can add Discretionary Ligatures, Fractions, Swashes, Titling Caps, Ordinals, and many of the other advanced typographic benefits of an OpenType Pro font. The only problem is educating the readers. Sad to say, they are still freaked out by many of these typographic treats. I even gave up on using them in this book after getting reviewer complaints :-(þ

Mainly this feature is used to pick the type of numbering you want to use. You should use lining figures for copy set in all caps or for accounting copy, oldstyle figures for lowercase copy, and small cap figures for copy set in small caps. (Small cap figures are quite rare, however, so you may be forced to make a bad choice of lining or oldstyle.)

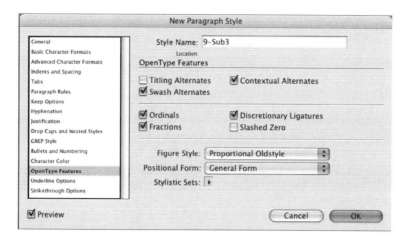

Underlines & Strikethroughs

These options have all the power of paragraph rules but they apply to the specific words. In other words, you can use these options to add rules that appear on every line of a paragraph (unlike paragraph rules that can only appear once per paragraph).

As you can see on the previous page, this is the underline page. The options are the same for strikethroughs. They aren't used often, but they are an excellent way to add highlighting, for example, if you have a full color book.

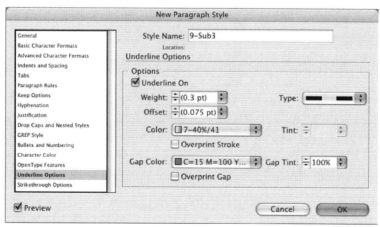

Export Tagging

I won't cover this much here. We'll go over this in depth in Appendix E, where we cover ePUB design and production. But this is really a big deal. It enables us to control the CSS produced when exporting an ePUB—which is the best control we can get over ePUB typography (without extensive coding).

As you can see, you can set the HTML tag and class you'll get when exporting to ePUB. However, I find I always miss something. So, I've gotten used to using the Edit All Export Tags command found in the panel menu. There you can see all of the tags at the same time. This helps me make a plan that works a little better. But the choice is yours. It really is a great help in making more readable ePUBs.

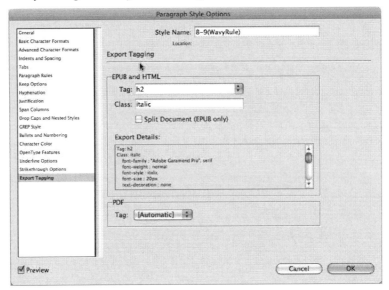

Just remember to keep your set of styles as simple as possible! [UNLIKE THIS BOOK]

I keep telling myself that I really need to show you options you may not have thought were possible. But it really gets busy—doesn't it?

Objects Anchored to Text

One of the nice things InDesign added several versions back is the ability to anchor an object to a location in the text. This makes it possible to have a graphic frame or a text frame floating next to a column of type that will move with the type. More than that, if you copy or cut the type and paste it in somewhere else the anchored object comes in along with the type in the column. If you cut the object itself, it keeps its anchored attributes.

 Very important tip: Once you have formatted an object as an anchored object, you can cut it and paste it in anywhere else in the type and it retains its anchored properties.

The good news is that you can simply turn on preview and make changes until you have what you want. The even better news is that these options are usually part of an Object style which I will cover next, and Preview works the same there.

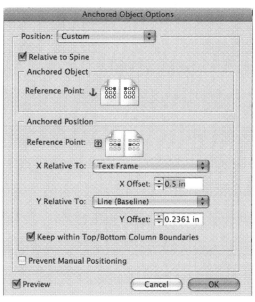

Position: Can be "Custom" or "Inline or Above Line". Custom gives you many options: a Relative to Spine checkbox, which proxy handle used to locate the position, and measured from which reference point in the text frame. I use Inline or Above Line for my conversions to ePUB because the controls for exporting anchored objects still need quite a bit of help.

Relative to spine: I am using this almost exclusively in this book and in almost all of my books. This way, if an anchored object is moved from the left page to the right page, the object changes sides. In this book, anchored objects are on the right on the left pages and on the left on the right pages. I wanted to keep the body copy to the outside edges of the book because it makes it easier to read and you do not have to break the spine of the book to do so (hopefully). This automates this choice.

Reference points: The top choice is for the handle of the object being anchored. The bottom choice is for the handle of the frame that contains the Anchored Object Character (AOC) .

X offset relative to: The horizontal offset can be measured from the anchor marker, the text frame, the column edge, the page margin, or the page edge using your chosen reference point.

The Y offset relative to: The vertical measurement can be measured from the line (baseline, cap height, or top of leading), the text frame, the column edge, the page margin, or the page edge.

 When beginning, the measurements seem to defy logic: In most cases I find I have to adjust and readjust my anchored object settings to get what I want. That is one reason why I always add my anchored objects with an Object Style (which I will cover next). On practical level, I almost always have to move the objects after they are anchored. But they retain that new location without any issues.

Keep within top/bottom of column boundaries: This moves the anchored frame up or down so it does not extend beyond the top or bottom of a column.

Prevent manual positioning: You can lock it up so the frame is exactly where you want and cannot be moved. However, I always want to massage the location—at least a little.

This does take some practice

There are at least four ways to add an anchored object to your page. The one I recommend as the best (the 4th one in this little list) will be discussed at the end of the Object Styles section that follows this section on Anchored Objects. And I didn't even mention pasting in copy that already has an anchored object attached to it.

First: Inserting an object into an insertion point

This is the method that Adobe assumes you will be using. n general, this is very inefficient method of using objects. I do not recommend it because you have to set up every anchored object separately and because it demands many locally formatted adjustments to make it work. It does add several extra options at the top of the dialog box. I.

Content: You can choose the frame type: text, graphic, or unassigned. Of course, leaving it unassigned means you can use either option.

Object style: You can pick an object style to automatically be applied to the anchored object. As you will see in the next few pages, this enables us to preset these anchored object options and save it to a style.

Paragraph style: You can pick any paragraph style to be applied (which, of course, can include a nested character style).

Size: Height & width of the frame added. You use this to make an anchored object a specific size (you must leave these fields blank if you don't want the original size of the graphic changed when you paste it into the frame).

The process is easy but a little complex. You use an insertion point in the text from which you want the object anchored. Then you choose Object>> Anchored Object>> Insert... . If you do this a lot you'll want to add a shortcut.

An Invisible Anchored Object Character (AOC) is added at that point that looks like a Yen symbol (¥) in the color of your frame ¥Anchored Object Character. An empty frame will be added that is anchored to that location. You can then add type to the newly generated frame or place a graphic into that frame.

The frame will be anchored to the insertion point and move with the type.

Second: Converting an inline graphic

This is probably the easiest to understand. You place or paste a graphic into an insertion point—thereby creating an inline graphic. Then choose Object>> Anchored Object>> Options and follow the same procedure that I talked about in the first (Adobe-style) method. The options you set up in the Anchored Object dialog are applied to the selected graphic. Again, you have to do this for every object.

Third: Convert a graphic to an anchored object with an object style

Then cut it & paste it into an insertion point. It's almost like magic as the object just pops into position from the insertion point you choose. This is the best method for many reasons.

 Text wrap limitations: There is one foible of anchored objects. If you want to put a text wrap around the anchored object, it will only wrap text starting with the line below the anchored object marker. So, you regularly need to make sure you add the AOC marker to the line above where you want the text to wrap around the object. You can copy and paste the object by copying and pasting the AOC, but because it has no width it is tricky to select and move just that character. It is far easier to just select the anchored object itself, cut it, and then place an insertion point where you want to be anchored from—and paste.

Fourth, and best: Drag from the Anchored Object Icon on the right side of the top edge of the frame to the insertion point location within the text you need then format and locate the anchored object with an object style: Most people don't use anchored objects much as they begin to design, but use them increasingly as they discover how well they work for sidebars and the like.

Here's a variant of three using
the new Anchored Object Icon on your text frame

they·work·for·sidebars·and·the·like

Anchored Object Icon

Drag into text to change anchor position.
Shift-drag to make inline object.
Option-click to open dialog.

The only real problem with anchored
objects is that InDesign does not convert
them well when exporting to ePUB—yet:
I am sure this control will come in CSNext or CSNext+1.
But we do not have it now.

Object styles

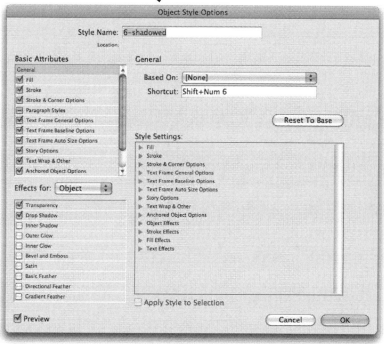

You can have styles for objects as well as text. This will enable you to more easily maintain a consistent look. In these new object styles, you can control everything found in the following panels:

- Paragraph Styles
- Text Wrap
- Swatches
- Stroke + Corners
- Frame Fitting
- Effects
- Text Frame Options
- Anchored Objects
- Story

So, you can set any of the Text Frame Options, turn on Optical Margin Alignment, Adjust the Frame Fitting options, and control the anchored object settings. You can make styles for text frames and for graphic frames.

In addition, you can make any of the saved object styles into your default text frame style or default graphic frame style for automatic text wraps and the like.

This Is One Of Those Options That Is So Complex It Takes A While To Get Used To: As you can see on the previous page, the dialog box is a bit complicated. But it will probably become one of your mainstays. Object styles may not seem to be as necessary as paragraph and character styles—but, they certainly help production speed once you have them set up—especially if you have a book like this which uses many graphics.

As in the paragraph and character styles, they give you global control of the look of your entire document. They really help with consistency of placed objects. Like with any style, if you edit a style every instance of use is changed. Of course object styles can be based on another style and all of the styles can be applied with shortcuts of your choosing.

Set up Object Styles early

Adding anchored objects is a little tedious unless you have some object styles set up. As I discussed in the page layout chapter, designing your columns and sidebar areas before you start your book saves an immense amount of time.

There is no way I can tell how you are going to use object styles and anchored objects. All I can say is that you will use them and that you need to make plans before you begin bringing in your copy and graphics if possible. As you become used to the idea, you will use it more and more in your layouts.

The goal is to develop a set of paragraph, character, object, table, and cell styles that are available by default in all new documents you create.

B2: A Set Of Default Styles

I have pulled these instructions off the Website so you are not forced to go there. Here is what you are going to end up with in your copy of InDesign.

The Designed Default Styles Set

Style	Mac Shortcut	PC Shortcut
0 Kick	Command+Num0	Ctrl+Num0
1 Inline Dropped	Command+Num1	Ctrl+Num1
2 Body	Command+Num2	Ctrl+Num2
2 No First	Command+Opt+Shift+Num2	Ctrl+Alt+Shift+Num2
2 Run-In	Command+Opt+Num2	Ctrl+Alt+Num2
3 Number	Command+Num3	Ctrl+Num3
3 Bullet	Command+Opt+Num3	Ctrl+Alt+Num3
4 B-Heads	Command+Num4	Ctrl+Num4
5 Quote	Command+Num5	Ctrl+Num5
6 Head	Command+Num6	Ctrl+Num6
7 Sub1	Command+Num7	Ctrl+Num7
8 Sub2	Command+Num8	Ctrl+Num8
9 Callout	Command+Num9	Ctrl+Num9

Setting up the set of default styles

We have to start out by setting up the Body Copy Styles

❧ 2 Body; 2 No first; 2 Run-In; 3 Number; 3 Bullet; 4 Body heads; 5 Quote; & 9 Callout

Start by opening the Paragraph Styles panel

You should have no document open. You want to be setting the Application Defaults so that these styles are available in every document from now on.

❧ START BY SELECTING ALL THE EXISTING STYLES AND DELETING THEM

You need an empty Styles Panel to start with. All that should remain is [Basic Paragraph] which cannot be deleted.

We start with the body styles

Start by making a new style: 2 Body

- ❦ Choose New Paragraph Style... In The Panel Menu, or click on the New Style bottom at the bottom of the panel

- ❦ Then On The GENERAL PAGE:
  - ✤ Style Name: 2-Body
  - ✤ Based on: [No Paragraph Style]
  - ✤ Next Style: [Same Style]
  - ✤ Shortcut: Command+Num2 (PC: Ctrl+Num2)

- ❦ BASIC CHARACTER FORMATS PAGE:
  - ✤ Font Family & Style: Serif your choice

- ❦ INDENTS AND SPACING:
  - ✤ Alignment: Left Justify
  - ✤ First Line Indent: 0.4 in

Make new style: 2 No First

- ❦ Select: 2 Body & Then Choose New Paragraph Style... In The Panel Menu

- ❦ GENERAL PAGE:
  - ✤ Style Name: 2 No first
  - ✤ Based on: [2 Body]
  - ✤ Next Style: [2 Body]
  - ✤ Shortcut: Command+Option+Shift+Num2 (PC: Ctrl+Alt+Shift+Num2)

- ❦ INDENTS AND SPACING:
  - ✤ Alignment: Left Justify
  - ✤ First Line Indent: 0 in
  - ✤ Space Before: p3

Make new style: 3 Number

- ❦ Select: 2 Body & Then Choose New Paragraph Style... In The Panel Menu

- ❦ GENERAL PAGE:
  - ✤ Style Name: 3 Number
  - ✤ Based on: [2 Body]

- ✛ Next Style: [Same Style]
- ✛ Shortcut: Command+Num3 (PC: Ctrl+Num3)

❧ INDENTS AND SPACING:

- ✛ Alignment: Left
- ✛ Check: Balance Ragged Lines
- ✛ Left Indent: 0.4 in
- ✛ First Line Indent: -0.25 in
- ✛ Space Before: p2
- ✛ Space After: 0

❧ BULLETS AND NUMBERING:

- ✛ Pick Numbered
- ✛ Set it up like you want

❧ HYPHENATION PAGE:

- ✛ It is often a good idea to turn this off for this style

Make new style: 3 Bullet

❧ SELECT: 3 Number & THEN Right-Click And Duplicate The Style

❧ Open The New Style: 3 NumberCopy

❧ GENERAL PAGE:

- ✛ Style Name: 3 Bullet
- ✛ Based on: [2 Body]
- ✛ Next Style: [Same Style]
- ✛ Shortcut: Command+Option+Num3 (PC: Ctrl+Alt+Num3)

❧ INDENTS AND SPACING:

- ✛ Alignment: Left
- ✛ Check: Balance Ragged Lines
- ✛ Left Indent: 0.4 in
- ✛ First Line Indent: -0.25 inin
- ✛ Space Before: p2
- ✛ Space After: 0

❧ BULLETS AND NUMBERING:

- ✛ Pick Bulleted
- ✛ Set it up like you want

❧ HYPHENATION PAGE:

- ✛ It is often a good idea to turn this off for this style

Make new style: 4 Body Heads

- ❦ Select: 2 Body & Then Choose New Paragraph Style... In The Panel Menu

- ❦ GENERAL PAGE:
  - ✤ Style Name: 4 Body heads
  - ✤ Next Style: [2 Body]
  - ✤ Shortcut: Command+Num4 (PC: Ctrl+Num4)

- ❦ BASIC CHARACTER FORMATS PAGE:
  - ✤ Font Style: Bold or whatever the options are for the font family you chose
  - ✤ Add small caps or whatever you think will make your small heads work

- ❦ INDENTS AND SPACING:
  - ✤ Alignment: Left
  - ✤ Check: Balance Ragged Lines
  - ✤ Left Indent: 0.4 in
  - ✤ Space Before: p5
  - ✤ Space After: p2

- ❦ HYPHENATION PAGE:
  - ✤ Turn off

- ❦ JUSTIFICATION PAGE:
  - ✤ Auto Leading: 100% or less for caps or small caps

Make new style: 5 Quote

- ❦ Select: 2 Body & Then Choose New Paragraph Style... In The Panel Menu

- ❦ GENERAL PAGE:
  - ✤ Style Name: 5 Quote
  - ✤ Next Style: [2 Body]
  - ✤ Shortcut: Command+Num5 (PC: Ctrl+Num5)

- ❦ BASIC CHARACTER FORMATS PAGE:
  - ✤ This is the same as 2 Body, unless you want to use italic

- ❦ INDENTS AND SPACING:
  - ✤ Alignment: Left Justify
  - ✤ Left Indent: 0.4 in

- ✦ First Line Indent: 0
- ✦ Right Indent: 0.4 in
- ✦ Space Before: p5
- ✦ Space After: p5

Make new style: 9 Callout

- ❦ Select: 2 Body & Then Choose New Paragraph Style... In The Panel Menu
- ❦ GENERAL PAGE:
  - ✦ Style Name: 9 Callout
  - ✦ Next Style: [2 Body]
  - ✦ Shortcut: Command+Num9 (PC: Ctrl+Num9)
- ❦ BASIC CHARACTER FORMATS PAGE:
  - ✦ Type Style: Italic
  - ✦ Size: 18 point
  - ✦ Leading: 19 point
- ❦ INDENTS AND SPACING:
  - ✦ Alignment: Left
  - ✦ Check: Balance Ragged Lines
  - ✦ Left Indent: 0.4 in
  - ✦ First Line Indent: 0
  - ✦ Right Indent: 0.4 in
  - ✦ Space Before: p5
  - ✦ Space After: p5
- ❦ PARAGRAPH RULES PAGE:
  - ✦ Turn on Rule Above &/or Below by checking Rule On
  - ✦ The size, color, type, offset, and so on are your choice, BUT they do really help set off the callout.
  - ✦ (You'll probably need to set up more space before and after paragraph to make room for the rules.)
- ❦ HYPHENATION PAGE:
  - ✦ Turn off
- ❦ JUSTIFICATION PAGE:
  - ✦ Auto Leading: 115%

Now we set up the Headers

Start by making a new style: 6 Head

- Choose New Paragraph Style... In The Panel Menu (With No Style Selected)

- GENERAL PAGE:
  - Style Name: 6 Head
  - Based on: [No Paragraph Style]
  - Next Style: [2 Body]
  - Shortcut: Command+Num6 (PC: Ctrl+Num6)

- BASIC CHARACTER FORMATS PAGE:
  - Font Family & Style: Sans or Decorative your choice
  - Size: 30 point

- INDENTS AND SPACING:
  - Alignment: Left
  - Left Indent: 0 in
  - First Line Indent: 0 in
  - Space Before: p7
  - Space After: p2

- HYPHENATION PAGE:
  - Turn off

- JUSTIFICATION PAGE:
  - Auto Leading: 100%

Make new style: 7 Subhead 1

- Select: 6 Head & Then Choose New Paragraph Style... In The Panel Menu

- GENERAL PAGE:
  - Style Name: 7 Subhead 2
  - Based on: [6 Head]
  - Next Style: [2 Body]
  - Shortcut: Command+Num7 (PC: Ctrl+Num7)

- BASIC CHARACTER FORMATS PAGE:
  - Size: 21 point

- INDENTS AND SPACING:

- ✤ Alignment: Left
- ✤ Left Indent: 0 in
- ✤ First Line Indent: 0 in
- ✤ Space Before: p7
- ✤ Space After: p2

❦ HYPHENATION PAGE:

- ✤ Turn off

❦ JUSTIFICATION PAGE:

- ✤ Auto Leading: 100% or less for caps or small caps

Make new style: 8 Subhead 2

❦ Select: 6 Head & Then Choose New Paragraph Style... In The Panel Menu

❦ GENERAL PAGE:

- ✤ Style Name: 8 Subhead 2
- ✤ Based on: [6 Head]
- ✤ Next Style: [2 Body]
- ✤ Shortcut: Command+Num8 (PC: Ctrl+Num8)

❦ BASIC CHARACTER FORMATS PAGE:

- ✤ Size: 13 point

❦ HYPHENATION PAGE:

- ✤ Turn off

❦ JUSTIFICATION PAGE:

- ✤ Auto Leading: 100% or less for caps or small caps

❦ PARAGRAPH RULES PAGE: Turn On Rule Above By Checking Rule On

- ✤ Size: 14 point
- ✤ Color: Your choice but I suggest a gradient (if it were me) and that means you have to make the gradient BEFORE you can use it here.
- ✤ Width: Text
- ✤ Offset: -0.0525 in
- ✤ Left Indent: -0.4 in (yes this is a negative indent to bring the rule back out to the left column margin)
- ✤ Right Indent: -0.1 in (negative also)

Make new style: 0 Kicker

- ❦ Select: 6 Head & Then Choose New
  Paragraph Style... In The Panel Menu
- ❦ GENERAL PAGE:
  - ✠ Style Name: 0 Kicker
  - ✠ Based On: [6 Head]
  - ✠ Next Style: [2 Body]
  - ✠ Shortcut: Command+Num0 (PC: Ctrl+Num0)
- ❦ BASIC CHARACTER FORMATS PAGE:
  - ✠ Style: Bold Or Black
  - ✠ Size: 10 Point
  - ✠ Case: Small Caps
- ❦ INDENTS AND SPACING:
  - ✠ Alignment: Left
  - ✠ Left Indent: 0 In
  - ✠ First Line Indent: 0 In
  - ✠ Space Before: P5
  - ✠ Space After: 0
- ❦ HYPHENATION PAGE:
  - ✠ Turn Off
- ❦ JUSTIFICATION PAGE:
  - ✠ Auto Leading: 100% Or Less For Caps Or Small Caps
- ❦ PARAGRAPH RULES PAGE: Turn On Rule
  Below By Checking Rule On
  - ✠ The Options Are Up To Your Sense Of Style,
    But The Underline Seems To Be Essential

Finally two special styles I use a lot

Start by making a new character style: 1-Body Bold

- ❦ Choose New Character Style... In The Character Styles Panel Menu

- ❦ GENERAL PAGE:
  - ✤ Style Name: 1 Body Bold
  - ✤ Based on: [No Character Style]
  - ✤ Shortcut: Option+Shift+Num1 (PC: Ctrl+Alt+Num1)

- ❦ BASIC CHARACTER FORMATS PAGE:
  - ✤ Font Family: Sans or Decorative your choice
  - ✤ Font Style: Bold

- ❦ CHARACTER COLOR:
  - ✤ It seems to help if you make it a strong color

Make new style: 2 Run-In

- ❦ Select: 2 Body & Then Choose New Paragraph Style... In The Panel Menu

- ❦ GENERAL PAGE:
  - ✤ Style Name: 2 Run-In
  - ✤ Based on: [2 Body]
  - ✤ Next Style: [Same Style]
  - ✤ Shortcut: Command+Option+Num2 (PC: Ctrl+Num2)

- ❦ INDENTS AND SPACING:
  - ✤ Alignment: Left
  - ✤ Check: Balance Ragged Lines
  - ✤ Left Indent: 0 in
  - ✤ First Line Indent: 0 in
  - ✤ Space Before: p2
  - ✤ Space After: 0

- ❦ DROP CAPS AND NESTED STYLES:
  - ✤ Add a nested style; choosing 1-Body Bold through 1 : (colon)

Make new style: 1 Inline Dropped

I use this to put in things like tips. I place a graphic into the first character of the line and drop it three lines with the drop cap feature. You can put a text wrap on the inline graphic, and so on.

❦ Select: 2 Body & Then Choose New Paragraph Style... In The Panel Menu

❦ GENERAL PAGE:
- ✤ Style Name: 1 Inline Graphic
- ✤ Based on: [2 Body]
- ✤ Next Style: [2 Body]
- ✤ Shortcut: Command+Option+Num1 (PC: Ctrl+Num1)

❦ BASIC CHARACTER FORMATS PAGE:
- ✤ Font Family: the light version of the header font family
- ✤ Font Style: Light
- ✤ Size: 10 point

❦ INDENTS AND SPACING:
- ✤ Alignment: Left
- ✤ Check: Balance Ragged Lines
- ✤ Left Indent: 0 in
- ✤ First Line Indent: 0 in
- ✤ Space Before: p2
- ✤ Space After: 0

❦ DROP CAPS AND NESTED STYLES:
- ✤ Add drop cap of one character and three lines
- ✤ Add a nested style; choosing 1-Body Bold through 1 : (colon)

Obviously, the variations are endless. Have fun!

C: Image production & formats

I'll discuss cover designs at the end of this section: Image production has become much more complex with the addition of the ebook formats. There are radical differences between what is needed for print and what is needed for an ePUB or Kindle book. You have many options for graphics. What I want to do is explain these options and show you how to deal with them. But first we must deal with the reality of linking images.

 The changing standards: The ebook standards are in constant flux. The good news is that ePUB and KF8 (the new format for the Kindle Fire) have become close enough so that the graphic standards are nearly identical. However, as I sit here today, I am expecting the release of the iPad3 around March 7, 2012. The rumors were true and it doubled the resolution available for ePUBs. So, the iPad is its own standard, with Nook ePUBs and Fire KF8s being the other with much lower resolution and file size requirements. Follow my professional tweets @davidbergsland for updates.

Linking graphics

This is one of the most common issues when people [in this case, authors] begin building their books in InDesign. Many people add graphics by copy/pasting. Worse yet, many want to embed their graphics. Basically, you "never" want to do either of these things.

Embedding bloats file size: This book, for example, has 33 MB of graphics at this point in the design of the print version [120 graphics listed so far]. If I embedded the graphics, InDesign would crash. It cannot use enough RAM to keep things going [as if I could afford enough anyway].

Copy/Paste and embedding makes updating almost impossible: If I make any changes to a graphic outside of InDesign, I have to re-paste or re-embed to add those changes to my document. This goes far beyond tedious.

What we need is a way to add the graphics that keeps them outside the document with a method of updating changed graphics that is simple and easy.

Links panel

This is actually one of InDesign's strong points. No one does it better. As you can see below, not only can you link to graphics with only a placeholder appearing in the actual document. But, you can also easily update any changes. You can relink to a different version [B&W to Color, for example] or a completely different graphic. You can click a button to show the graphic in it's actual location. And much more.

For example, I just had to change and update the capture of the Links panel because I decided that you needed some call-outs to show you why you will need the four buttons at the bottom of the panel & what for.

Relink: This enables you relink to any graphic you have available on your hard drive or server.

Find Link: This will change the page view, centering the graphic on the page where it is used. For example, you can see in the capture that the selected PSD is used on page 217.

Update link: Sometimes this is updated automatically.

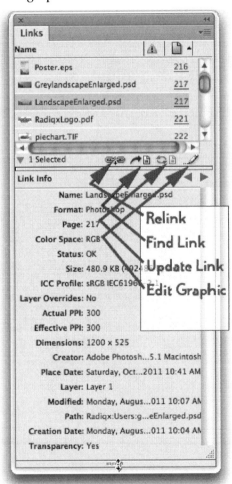

Sometimes you actually need to click on this button. You can tell which is needed by the Yellow Triangle found in the second column from the right (though it is not there because I have already done it).

Edit graphic [Edit Original]: This tries to open the original graphic and works well if you have a Photoshop graphic or an AI file. In fact, it not only opens the original graphic, but when you save it, InDesign automatically updates it. However, for PDFs it does not go to the original but tries to open the PDF instead (which is a pain in the *^%#@*&). Ah well, you can't have everything. Of course, it doesn't help at all if the original is an RGB full resolution graphic stored in originals. All my greyscale images in this book have a full color, full resolution version from which they were saved stored in the Originals folder. Of course it doesn't work when the original is a PSD, from which you saved for Web a PNG, JPEG, or GIF for your ePUB or KF8 book.

Why have a full color originals folder?

That is simple. When I go to make the color version for the color PDFs, all I have to do is drop the color images into the Links folder. All the greyscale images are replaced by the color originals (they both have identical names). Simply updating does a lot of my preparation work for the color PDFs.

When I do my ePUBs

All I have to do is save my color RGB PSDs into JPEGs of the proper size and save them into a new Links folder. Then relinking is relatively easy for that conversion also (though it is not automated).

How & why to produce your graphics

Start everything in RGB color

Because PDF, ePUB, and Kindle have no penalty for color you need to start there. You can always make a grey-scale version for print, if necessary. However, if you start with greyscale, colorizing the images is often nearly impossible.

If you are printing in color, most on-demand suppliers do better with an RGB image anyway. Those who require a CMYK image merely force you to make a color adjustment.

Start your Photoshop files in high resolution ▣

Not only do you want color (where possible), but you also want the highest resolution you will ever need in any of your printed books. Your modern ebooks (ePUBs and KF8) only support 72 dpi Web graphics at this point. But they need to be 600 pixels wide, at least. For the iPad3, I am trying 1200 pixels wide—where it matters.

Keep images in vector ▣

For an explanation of what a vector image is, keep reading. Because of all the different variations you will need for the various formats, you will do better to use vector illustrations as much as possible. These can be AIs (Illustrator files), PDFs (from InDesign or Illustrator), or EPSs (from FreeHand or Illustrator). However, you need to make sure you keep track of the original documents to allow for changes as necessary.

Why vector?

It's the most adjustable: Because vector files can be resized with no problems and rasterized at any size or resolution you need, you can have one graphic master file for all your needs in the various formats. It is also much easier to change color spaces with vector images—especially if you are using InDesign for your drawings. The Swatches panel in InDesign makes conversions like this very easy—as long as you have sense enough to have a predefined color palette.

Drawing in InDesign

Why would you ever want to draw in InDesign? Better tools and unique capabilities. While it is true that InDesign has a very limited set of Illustrator's tools, it uses them in a much better interface. InDesign works more like FreeHand used to. True, InDesign is not a true, full-featured illustration program. However, most book graphics do not require or even want the full features of blends, gradients meshes, perspective, and the rest of the fancier Illustrator capabilities. Most book illustrations are relatively simple tables, and line art info graphics. While it may be true that Illustrator can do them better, Illustrator greatly adds to your learning burden as a writer in InDesign. If you have Illustrator skills, certainly use them. But do not think they are required.

Vector versus bitmap

I do not expect all of you to immediately drop AI for InDesign. Nor do I expect you to forget about the bitmapped extravaganzas commonly developed in Photoshop. However, developing excellent type in InDesign and then rasterizing it in Photoshop will give you much better typographic control of your graphics.

InDesign creates vector graphics

Vector drawing is one of the most misunderstood tools in our arsenal. Digital drawing, sometimes known as PostScript illustration, is one of the indispensable tools of digital publishing. However, it has been lost in the hype of smart phones and digital cameras. Back in the bad ol'days (before computers), when we >gasp< had to do everything by hand, things were clearer. There was camerawork, inkwork, typesetting, and pasteup. These areas have been replaced by image manipulation, digital drawing, word processing, and page layout software. InDesign does all of these except for camerawork and image manipulation. Camerawork and image manipulation are the purpose of Photoshop.

With vector graphics, we are now talking about inkwork instead of camerawork—digital drawing instead of image manipulation. What does that mean? It means that we are looking at an entirely different type of artwork. This artwork is not focused on soft transitions and subtle effects. The purpose of this type of art is fundamentally different. These are images that are crisp, precise, and direct. This is where we leave the natural world and enter an environment with no dirt, no scratches, no broken parts, no garbage.

Let's start with an actual graphic

Scan of an ink painting   A vector conversion

It is obvious that vector drawing is very different from a painting, photograph, or any other scanned object. It's not to say that one is better than the other—they are simply different. The painting is soft, subtle, more "realistic." The vector drawing is clean, crisp, easily resizable, with a much smaller file size.

It is also extremely easy to add professional-quality, easily resizable type to a vector drawing. Any type added to the original painting must be drawn by hand. Even if you are working with a scan of the art in Photoshop, type is limited to large point sizes and fuzzy edges.

Photoshop type needs 1200 dpi to 2400 dpi to be sharp

As you can see on the page opposite, the vector landscape from above can be easily resized and have type added to it. There is no fuzziness or pixelation. The type is crisp and sharp, even though this is printed out at 150% of the original size of the drawing. If this were a Photoshop file, it would be pixelated even at this slight enlargement. By pixelated, we mean that you could see the jagged edges of the individual picture elements.

Finally, the Photoshop type would be very crude at 200 to 300 dots per inch, whereas the vector graphic has type at the typographic standard—1,200 dpi to 2,400 dpi (or whatever the resolution of the printer is). Imagine if we printed it out at two foot wide or more. The vector image would still be sharp.

Below we see the vector version enlarged 1000%. You can see some of the drawing deficiencies, but the image is still crisp. The same would be true if we enlarged it to hang as a billboard on the side of a skyscraper at 50 yards wide. There would be no pixilization.

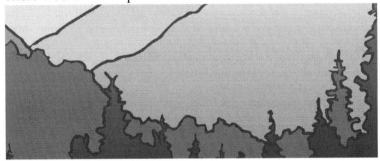

However, that sharpness is not true of scanned, more properly called bitmapped, images. The Photoshop (bit-mapped) version is ruined at two feet wide, as you can see below. When the image was enlarged to two feet wide, the pixels could not change shape. So, we now see what that bitmap really looked like.

The only reason it looked smooth was that the pixels were a three hundredth of an inch each and that is far too small to be seen. In the enlargement, the pixels are nearly an eighth of an inch square and easily visible. Also this enlarged bitmapped image was 235 MB.

The vector image remains 49 KB no matter what size you use for output. Yes, that is 235 million bytes as compared to 49 thousand bytes of data. Obviously, there are some real advantages to vector illustration.

The major advantage to vector art

🐦 It is completely resizable: Vector art is what is commonly referred to as *resolution independent*. There is no resolution to a vector file. All of the shapes, and this includes all the type, are defined by mathematical outlines that can be enlarged or reduced at will. The resolution is produced by the printer, output device, or Photoshop.

This means that I can make my original artwork for the first version of the book and then easily resize, recolor, and convert it into any file type needed for the rest of the versions. I can open it in Photoshop and convert it to 72 dpi (rasterize it) at the size needed for the JPEGs, GIFs, and PNGs needed for Kindle or ePUBs. I can enlarge the image to a poster or book cover and/or reduce the size to a dingbat used for bulleted lists all from the same original. This cannot be done with a bitmapped image.

Why you want to make graphics in InDesign

One of the little secrets in digital publishing in recent years is the fact that increasing numbers of designers are using InDesign for all of their graphic production except for photographs and scans. InDesign's drawing interface is uncluttered and works remarkably well. The primary reasons for using InDesign to draw are the six we list beginning on the next page. But the real issue goes much deeper than that. Unless you are a professional illustrator the drawing capabilities of Adobe's Illustrator are far too complex and take too much time to be used in book production.

Typographic graphics:

The core of my reasoning is simple. The graphics which are not photos are usually (at least often) type. Even the pieces built around photos are commonly made with a lot of type. You do not want to make these images in Photoshop because the type will end up rasterized at far too

259

low a resolution. As I have said, type for print is normally output at 2400 dpi or at least 1200 dpi for the cheaper technologies. Photoshop images are 300 dpi, at best. The result is that type in Photoshop images is pretty chewed up. The only way type in Photoshop works well is if it is larger than 24 point.

It is true that you can save Photoshop graphics that contain high resolution type—but our on-demand suppliers cannot handle that (at this point). For our purposes, Photoshop is a bitmap application, working in pixels that are precisely defined. Photoshop is a tool you will need to learn (at least in a minimal manner) to handle many things in on-demand publishing—it's one of the very few which can work in CMYK. Even Photoshop Elements cannot work in CMYK. The bad news is that this powerful capability to render very tiny pixels with a great deal of control is also its greatest limitation.

The good news is that InDesign has all you need to produce beautiful graphics.

In fact, it has several attributes that lead me to create most of my graphics within InDesign, because in these areas InDesign is definitely superior to either Illustrator or Photoshop. We have mentioned several of these abilities already, but they center around three basic capabilities: type, color, and PDFs.

1. Typography: Nothing else comes close. It is easier and better, in most cases, to do all your type in InDesign. Even when you are tearing type apart to make logos and graphics, InDesign is easier and faster than Illustrator in many cases. It can do many things with type that are impossible in Photoshop— simply because InDesign creates vector art.

2. Color control: No other program has the color palette control of the Swatches panel in InDesign. Nowhere is it more easy to build a

predetermined custom palette for a specific project. You can easily control the color of a large project like a book in InDesign (and keep control across all the various formats). This is much more difficult in Illustrator and almost impossible in Photoshop.

3.   Gradient strokes: This seems like a little thing, but it is huge. Many typographic decorations like rules are simply lines. Only InDesign can make gradient lines easily. Plus, these gradient lines remain editable. Any gradient in Photoshop requires rasterized art and type. *[Yes, I know that Illustrator CS6 has finally added gradient strokes. But, as usual, the implementation is so complex that it is daunting.]*

4.   Individual corner controls: Built into every frame, InDesign has corner controls that allow you to control all at once as well as each corner separately—by directly manipulating the frame.

5.   Photoshop effects: Many of the basic effects (Photoshop styles) are available in InDesign. The Effects panel is remarkable with individual controls for the entire vector object (or group of objects), only the stroke, only the fill, and any combination thereof. Drop shadows, inner shadows, inner glow, outer glow, embossing & debossing, plus transparency feathering are easy to apply and remain editable.

6.   PDF generation: InDesign simply produces the best PDFs. I use InDesign almost exclusively to make PDFs of logos, book covers, product graphics, and all the rest. This is especially true if these graphics must be rasterized into high resolution JPEGs and PNGs for our suppliers.

Createspace covers, for example, demand rasterized artwork. In fact, strange as it may seem, they require a Photoshop PDF—which is very unusual. The InDesign file is much more editable and rasterizing it into Photoshop for Createspace's (Amazon's) purposes is quick &

easy. You do not want to be doing your back cover type in Photoshop—even though Createspace requires you to do so.

Type manipulation

This is even more true with typographic art. Digital drawing goes far beyond the simple pen work seen so far. Its main power is found in type manipulation. One of InDesign's major assets is its ability to rapidly convert a word or two into a powerful graphic very quickly.

Of course, there are some major differences in InDesign. Formerly, we had to hand-draw the line to the proper width. With vector shapes, I can specify any fill with strokes (outlines) of any color or any width—virtually infinite flexibility, with a precision that was incomprehensible before the late 1980s when the first PostScript drawing programs were released: Fontographer first, followed by Illustrator and then FreeHand. Here's a simple one: the Radiqx Press logo—which is two words, a couple gradients, and a cross punched out of the modified R [using the Pathfinder panel in InDesign].

I drew this in InDesign. For color the dot over the i is a red radial gradient. For logos there is nothing better. Logos have

to be the most flexible graphics imaginable. They will be used very small, very large, and everything in between. There must be black-and-
white versions, spot color versions, process color versions, and in addition, low-resolution RGB Web versions.

Digital drawing using PostScript paths is almost specifically designed for this purpose. InDesign enables very tiny file sizes that are resolution independent. In other words, they will print at the highest resolution allowed by the imagesetter, platesetter, printer, or monitor.

The Create Outlines command converts your fonts into a collection of editable shapes. With fonts converted to paths, you can use any font and not have to worry about including it. It is still the best way to get fancy decorative fonts on the Web or into an ebook. Rasterizing your converted type into Photoshop is very easy.

Charts & graphs

Many graphics in common usage are charts and graphs. All of the common software, like spreadsheets and presentation software, produce horrible-looking work that is designed for a monitor. To translate, that means they are in the wrong color space for most color printing and far too low in resolution. Basically, every chart or graph you receive will have to be tossed completely or scanned and used as a rough template in the background while you recreate the graphic to professional standards so you can use it wherever you need it in all of your book formats.

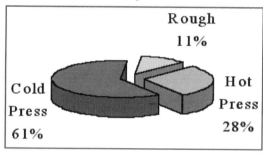

As you can see from the sample showing usage of watercolor board to the left, even the best I can do with the received graphic is terrible. I received the image as a 72 dpi, RGB TIFF generated from a PowerPoint slide. Even for this example, I have done a lot of work in Photoshop: cropping tightly; resizing the image to half size, thereby increasing the resolution to 144 dpi; and converting the image to grayscale.

The result is still hardly inspiring. The font choice is clumsy, at best—not to mention that it does not fit my Styles. The type alignment, leading, tracking, and so on are very amateurish. Worst of all, there is no explanation to help the reader determine if this knowledge is helpful, useful, or even relevant. In all ways, this graphic is useless unless it is used as part of a well-spoken, entertainingly written, enthusiastically presented oral explanation.

We have to remember, as authors and book publishers, that our explanations are found in the professional presentation of our copy. Poor font choices cannot be covered with glib jokes or even pithy commentary. Our readers are going to make choices based on the attractiveness and usefulness of our layouts.

First of all, they will decide whether they are even going to read our work. If it is not clear in concept and easy to comprehend, you have lost them. In your book, you rarely get a second chance. So, with that in mind, let us redesign this awful pie chart.

Before we can start with that, we need to know what it represents. I discover that it refers to the use of watercolor board by the art department of an architectural design firm for the past year. They are in the process of making a presentation package that they can use to show their changing focus and capabilities to prospective investors as the firm expands.

As I learn this, I also find another bar chart showing, paradoxically, that sales resulting from the use of the boards give a very different view. The rough board is used for hand-painted gouache illustrations, for which this firm is developing a real reputation. The cold press sheets are used as mounting board for client presentations to use as they seek

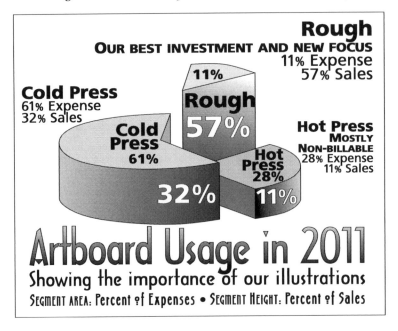

to fill the spaces of the various projects with targeted tenants. The hot press is used for quick visualizations, models, and as a mounting board for general signage.

It turns out that the expensive d'Arches 300# rough watercolor board is used for illustrations that generate 57% of all income. The cold press board used for client presentations and to present proofs to the clients for printed materials in support of their buildings represents 32% of the income. The hot press board is second as far as expense is concerned, but it only accounts for 11% of the income.

The hot press board calls for conservation measures.

With that in mind, I quickly traced the ugly PowerPoint slide (by hand, using the Pen tool); extended the height of the various slices (adjusting by eye); added more stylish type giving both sets of figures; added a title line; and colored in the shapes. It took about a half hour to fix up the graph. However, there is a much greater likelihood that it will actually be read now. More than that, the data now makes an important point which can clearly and easily be seen. I just need to double-check to make sure it is making the proper emphasis.

Ebook graphic solutions

It might seem as if the low-resolution (72 dpi) monitor graphics of the Web are a clear place for bitmap graphics. However, even here the creative freedom and flexibility of vector graphics give you a decided speed and efficiency advantage over people who are limited to Photoshop or less when it comes to graphic creation for online use.

Bitmap painting programs are extremely clumsy for quick, clear graphic production. PDF graphics from InDesign can easily be rasterized as GIFs, PNGs, or JPEGs at any size, resolution, or color space you need. By using color PDFs that can quickly be rasterized to the exact size needed, you obtain a design freedom and image control that are very difficult to accomplish in Photoshop.

The first time you try to make type fit a certain size, transform it, or simply scale type in Photoshop, you will long for the freedom of InDesign. Modified type in an InDesign PDF rasterizes clearly and sharply when compared to transformed type done in Photoshop (which cannot be transformed unless rasterized at 300 dpi or less).

The tools available

InDesign does have most of the relevant Illustrator tools, but they are laid out in a way that is instantly recognizable as page layout. Strange tools like the graphing tool, gradient mesh, blending tool, and so forth are missing, as they should be. This is a page layout program. This is not primarily a graphics creation program—vector or bitmap. Yet, the basic drawing tools are all here.

The toolbox looks comfortingly familiar. If you are used to Illustrator it seems streamlined and clean. The dizzying cacophony of dozens of tools on pop out menus from the toolbox are largely missing. What tools are left are the path manipulation tools—and they are really all you need. If you need a fancy 3D drawing with shadows and realistic textures, you belong in Illustrator.

You've been using several of these tools throughout the book already. But once you start drawing with them, their usage changes and I need to be sure you know their capabilities.

The tools

The Selection tools

The Selection [V] and Direct Selection [A] tools are very similar to Illustrator's in appearance, and they basically work the same way. The black arrow is for selecting and editing like normal. The hollow pointed or white arrow does path editing. If you need to move a frame or resize it, you need the Selection tool. If you want to modify the shape in any way, you need the Direct Selection capabilities. You also have to go to the direct selection tool to modify the wrap on the text frames (it's just another editable path.

TIP: One of the disconcerting aspects of this new page layout setup is the simple fact that you can have two separate text wraps on the same object. One for the selected frame, and another for the selected frame content. Don't confuse yourself. Be careful.

The Pen Tool [P]

InDesign's Pen tool is very definitely Illustrator's four part Pen tool, with all of its advantages and

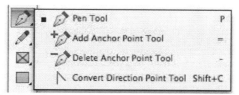

disadvantages. I have definitely found that InDesign's version works the way that I wish Illustrator's or Photoshop's did.

For those of you who are not familiar with Adobe's pen tool, it makes paths by clicking [corner] and clock-dragging [curve] in a connect-the-dots fashion. You have to closely watch the tool when producing or editing a path to find out what is happening. If you see a little plus next to the tool (over an existing path), clicking will add a point. If you see a little minus, clicking will subtract one. If you see the little open pointer, clicking will change the point type from smooth to corner or vice versa. The shortcuts are the same as Illustrator's.

The basic advice is to remember that holding down the Command (Control) key changes you back to the last selection tool you used. Holding down the Option (Alt) key switches you to the Convert Point tool. The most disconcerting aspect is that there is no way to drag out handles on a corner point. All you can do is drag out the handles with the Change Point tool creating a curve point. Then move the Change Point tool over the handles that result. This allows you to drag the handles individually converting the curve point to a corner point with visible handles. InDesign's implementation seems very elegant and obvious.

Frame generators

The next three tools are a little confusing, because Adobe has made them two separate menus: the frame tools and the shape tools. Frames have no fill or stroke. But with the x running from corner to corner, you can select and move them easily even though they are empty. Shape tools use the currently selected fill and stroke. But, it doesn't make any difference which one you are using. If you have a shape and click in it with the Type tool, it becomes a text frame. If you have a text frame with no type or insertion point in it, into which you place a graphic—it becomes a graphic frame. You can almost place anything into any frame with complete freedom. Graphics placed into a text frame insertion point become inline graphics.

The Frame Tools

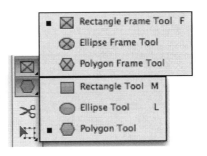

The Frame tools have no stroke or fill, yet you can move them around by clicking anywhere within the frame [they have a non-printing x though them]. The Shape tools are the normal tools where you can not select them if they have a fill of [None] assigned to them/

The Rectangle Tool [M] & the Ellipse Tool [L]

These tool are the normal drawing tools. If you hold down the Shift key; the shape is constrained to a square or circle. If you hold down the Option (Alt) key, they draw from the center out. They also draw from handle to handle like any shape tools.

The Polygon Tool

This tool is a the normal limited version of the Polygon tool available from Adobe products. As you can see from the dialog capture below, the shape of the points of the star must be

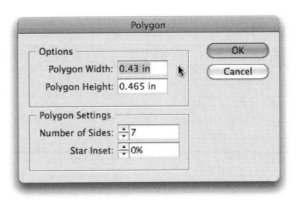

guessed. There is no preview. With an infinite variety of stars possible with every number of points, this makes this tool useless except for drawing frames for regular polygons (hence the name, I guess). Or I guess if you really want a star, you can do and redo until you get something usable.

The Pencil tool

This is a typical Illustrator triple tool: Pencil, Smoother, and Eraser. The Pencil draws freehand paths with no point control. The Smoother progressively smooths out the line

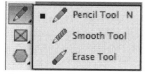

(without any real control, although it often does a nice job). You can access the Smoother tool by holding down the Option key while you draw. The Eraser does what you would like it to, most of the time. It must be hand selected.

A really nice capability is that the Smoother and Eraser work on any path you draw, with any tool. The Smoother, for example, will convert a star into a polygon with concave sides (it changes the entire shape). They even work on type converted to paths, but the effects are rather unpredictable. In general, however, these are a very elegant selection of freehand drawing tools. The main issue is the lack of control over point type or placement. I can't remember the last time I used the Pencil tool.

Converting shapes

This capability is only found at the bottom of the Object menu when you have an object selected. You can convert any shape (with corner modifications or not) into a Rectangle, Rounded Rectangle, Beveled Rectangle, Inverse Rounded Rectangle, Ellipse, Triangle, Polygon, Line, or Orthogonal Line. It works very well.

Drawing in InDesign is obviously limited

However, the transformation tools are all available as are the Photoshop effects. If you are creating a drawing or painting you will either be using fine art media or using Illustrator or Photoshop. Paint and FreeHand work well also, but you'll have a little trouble converting them to a format you can use in InDesign.

Let me cover some of the possibilities. InDesign works very well with Illustrator, for example. Of course, you can drop in native Illustrator (.ai) files. Because of the Links panel this is the best idea for AI files. What you may not realize is that you can bring in editable paths from AI. All it takes is a little set up to the application preferences.

In Illustrator you need to go to preferences ▪

In preferences you must set up the Clipboard options. If you have PDF or transparency options set up anything you copy and paste from Illustrator will come in as a non-editable object. However, if you uncheck PDF and check the option which says AICB [no transparency support] and check the button which says preserve paths, you can then copy and paste editable paths into InDesign.

Dictionary & Hyphenation	Clipboard on Quit
Plug-ins & Scratch Disks	
User Interface	Copy As: ☐ PDF
File Handling & Clipboard	☑ AICB (no transparency support)
Appearance of Black	⦿ Preserve Paths
	◯ Preserve Appearance and Overprints

The art on the next page is an ellipse painted by a brushstroke from Illustrator. Let's give you a condensed description of the basic procedure:

1. First I made a circle: I chose the Ellipse tool and held down the shift key;

2. Picked a brushstroke and applied it: These are found in the Brushes panel in AI;

3. Expanded its appearance (under the Object menu): If I do not expand it, I will have no direct access to the paths and the copy paste will bring in non-editable paths;

4. Ungrouped it: The brush shapes are attachd to the path and bent to follow it;

5. Turned off Preview [Command+Y]: so I could see the circle the brush artwork was attached to;

6. Deleted the original circle: this is what would make the brush paths difficult to edit in InDesign;

7. Copied from AI;

8. Pasted into InDesign;

9. Selected object with the Direct Selection tool and cleaned up the brush work a bit;

10. Then I made and applied a gradient fill from Swatches.

InDesign's forte is graphic assembly

This
ball of type
was added in just
a few minutes with a
brushstroke from AI
and a circle from
InDesign

The whole procedure I just described took less than a minute—real time. So, I was able to copy/paste a complex drawing into editable paths in InDesign in less than a minute. Obviously, getting editable pieces from Illustrator is quick and easy.

Using the brushstroke as a frame

To make a radical change, I modified the size of the circle to overlap the brushstroke, and pasted a picture of my home into the Circle. This took another minute—with the result you see on the next page. I added the type on top in another 20-30 seconds {the only glitch was that I had to set the new text frame to ignore text wraps as I had put a text wrap on the graphic automatically when I styled it with an object style]. Regardless, the whole thing was done in far less time than it took to write this explanation. It is dramatic if not too inspiring.

The original is in color

If I wanted a graphic I could use anywhere. All I would need to do is copy and paste the new graphic onto a new single page document, save it, and export it as a PDF. If you are looking at this in an ebook, you can see it is in glorious 300 dpi CMYK color—ready for print (if I decided to do that). For the B&W book, below you see it rasterized into Photoshop and saved as a Grayscale PSD at 300 dpi.

A Minnesota winter at home!

I agree. It's missing something in greyscale, but surely you see the point. You can do graphics like this very quickly In fact, if you have the pieces at hand, any graphic of this nature can be done in less than a minute. Fancy tables with inserted photos and complex typography can be created in a separate document and exported as a PDF to be used wherever needed at whatever size you need.

Graphic needs of the formats: Print, PDF, ePUB, & Kindle 8

The only other thing you need to understand about graphics is what works in which formats. I'm just going to list the four options and their requirements, best formats, and so on.

Greyscale print with color cover (Lulu & Createspace)

You need to be careful. This is digital printing and we are dependent upon the quality of equipment used by the vendors and the quality control exercised in their use. In general, I have had almost no problems with Lulu.

On the other hand, I have had many quality issues with Createspace. They are the 500 pound gorilla so we cannot ignore them. But, be careful and make sure your artwork is conservative. In all cases, the problem was solved by flattening Photoshop images or re-exporting PDFs with Acrobat 4 compatibility. In one case I had to rasterize a PDF at 300 dpi for a Createspace book. Don't argue. Just give them what they ask for.

- Bitmap images: 300 dpi grayscale PSDs, TIFFs, and PDFs. Lulu can handle layered PSDs with transparency. Createspace sometimes has trouble, although I've never had any issues with transparent backgrounds for either of them. Createspace sometimes drops color lighter than 10% (they have a tendency to print a little light).

- Vector images: PDFs, AIs, and EPSs. I use Acrobat 5 compatible PDFs for Lulu and Acrobat 4 compatible PDFs for Createspace. Lulu's printing of these images is much sharper.

Createspace sometimes drops light tints (I suspect they rasterize them before printing).

Createspace's books are acceptable. Lulu's books are often excellent. This is on-demand digital printing.

Cover art

- ❦ Lulu seems to prefer PDFs: I use 300 dpi CMYK bitmap images with vector lineart and type. Lulu provides a vector PDF of your ISBN artwork. You place it where needed. Their upload cover page gives you the necessary document size and spine widths. I export them with Acrobat 5 compatibility and have had no problems.

- ❦ Createspace demands Photoshop files: Their recommended workflow starts with assembling a layered PSD on their template. Their template has a guides layer showing bleed trim areas and maximum area for type. You are required to leave a specific area for the ISBN and they imprint the ISBN into that area.

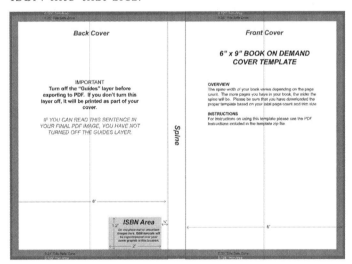

They leave very little room for type on the spine and enforce their rules strictly. They require 300 dpi RGB. Once you have all the type and images in place and saved as a layered PSD, you then flatten a copy and save it as a Photoshop PDF. They accept nothing else.

This required rasterization does soften the type (and often fattens it up quite a bit) and they can have problems printing rules thinner than three-quarter point (though normally they can print half-point rules with no problem). Make sure your type is large enough and clear enough to handle this.

Color printing throughout (Lulu & Createspace)

I haven't done much full-color printing. When I have, I've used Lulu. Every thing I said about greyscale printing still applies. Lulu works well with CMYK. My best guess is that Createspace likes RGB better (they might require it).

Downloadable PDFs (Lulu & Scribd)

Now that Lulu has separated the downloadable PDF from the printed version, there is no reason not to go full-color. The same is true with Scribd. Lulu can easily handle everything that you can print. Scribd is geared more toward the Word user and has trouble with fancy stuff. For example, Scribd has trouble with paragraph rules, in general, and ruins rules with gradients. Scribd seems to be using a non-Adobe PDF reader, but I have no proof of that.

The bottom line is that you need to be much more careful proofing Scribd's online PDFs. Also Scribd does not seem to do well with sales. They are more geared to free stuff. But they can give you a lot of eyeballs.

Lulu has always sold a lot of downloadable PDFs for me. That has slowed quite a bit now that they've moved PDFs to their own pages (they used to be a downloadable option on the print pages).

- RGB color

- Vector if possible

- Go for 300 dpi bitmaps: unless the file size gets too large. Scribd seems to have problems with files sizes much over 5 MB. Lulu does not seem to have those issues.

- Acrobat 5 compatible seems to work for either

ePUBs and Kindle books will change radically in the next few years...

EPUBs (Lulu, & Nook)

Think of this as Web design. It'll help. All graphics are bitmaps—no vectors allowed. The spec supports SVG, but that has not happened yet in reality.

- Maximum image size: 600x800 pixels: this has become the interim standard. In specific, image sizes are a bit more complex. The iPad full page image size is 600x860. Who know what will happen if the new iPad get a Retina display? Most are guessing 1200x1800 pixels. Nook takes 600x730 pixels. Kindle uses 600x800.

- RGB: Use color to help

- JPEGs or GIFs: Supposedly PNGs work, as far as I know, but use the Save for Web option to help control sizes.

Kindle (Kindle Direct Publishing)

If you have an Amazon account, you have a KDP account to publish your books on Kindle. They have the most current requirements listed there. The new format is called Kindle Format Eight [KF8], and it was developed for Fire. The problem is that the specs were only released the 2nd week in January, 2012. At present , use the same basic options as you use in ePUBs. Thge only realchange isthat KF8 can now handle embedded fonts.

In fact, the best advice I can find now is to use the new InDesign Export to Kindle plug-in supplied by Amazon. At this point, I have not seen the new CS6 plug-in. Basically KF8 is ePUB2 so the normal standards apply.

C2: Cover design

This area of graphic design has been going through major changes lately because of the nature of selling books online. Most of the traditional rules of cover design were geared toward displays at book & mortar bookstores or magazine and book racks at supermarkets and the large discount houses like Walmart and Target.

The problem with that is that as an author you have no choice in your cover designs if you are going with a traditional publisher. We are talking about self-publishing on-demand. This means that virtually all your books will be sold online. Online sales mean that you need to have a cover design that reads well at very small sizes.

A list of thumbnail sizes in pixels

- ❦ Lulu: List size: 94 x 140
  Detail page size: 212 x 320
  Approximately 2x3 proportion but they
  specify a cover dimension of 612 x 792 pixels
  which is closer to a 3x4 proportion

- ❦ Amazon: List size: 60 x 90
  Detail page size: 164 x 242
  Their image specs are: Image dimensions of at
  least 500 by 800 pixels; A maximum of 2000
  pixels on the longest side is preferred; Ideal
  height/width ratio of 1.6; Save at 72 dots per
  inch (dpi) for optimal viewing on the web

- ❦ Nook: List size: 128 x 192
  Detail page size: 300 x 450
  A 2x3 proportion but their specs are: "Please
  make sure that your cover image is a JPG file
  between 5KB and 2MB. The sides must be
  between 750 pixels and 2000 pixels in length."

- ❦ Scribd: List size: 129 x 167

As you can see, all of these images are very small in size. Worse yet, you do not get much control of them. As you can see you upload them at wildly varying sizes. These uploaded images are then downsampled into very small sizes by the Website. So, what are we supposed to do?

I'll admit I do not have a definitive answer yet. But trying to explain this to you is giving me some insights as to what I am going to try with this book.

What do we know for sure?

Many covers are close to 2x3: Amazon says the ideal is 2x3.2, a 6x9 book is 2x3 in proportion. So let's start with that.

The other standard is 3x4: We need to leave top and bottom margins which allow for adjustments: Lulu's ebook covers, for example, are specified to be 612x792. That divides out to 77% or about 3x4, as I mentioned. In practical terms, this means that I must take my 6" x 9" cover and reduce it to 6" x 8" to get the proper proportions. That's interesting because most people tell us that the maximum image size for an ePUB is 600 x 800 pixels [which is the same proportion].

We need color to the edges: If we leave a white background on the cover, the thumbnails get lost on the page. In fact, several of the companies specifically warn about covers with no background color.

At the small sizes the typography needs to be extremely readable and legible: This is not an problem solved by fancy, swirling type overlaying a complex photo. We really need to work at the legibility of the type. Basically we need to follow the dictum of billboard design: 8 words maximum, sharp contrast between the type and the background, nothing subtle, because all subtlety will be lost as you whiz by the billboard at 60 miles per hour.

We are left with two possible solutions.

- ❦ One: We can design the cover to be pure type reversed out of a dark background so we can freely resize it as necessary. The type block should be separate from the back ground so we can avoid type distortions as we resize the background to fit the various proportional needs.

- ❦ Two: We must carefully redesign the cover to fit each particular circumstance. This is going to be a particular problem if our book simply requires a photo or image on the cover. Obviously, any images used must be sharp enough and with enough contrast so the image is discernible at a half inch or so. Or, they must be so lacking in contrast that we can overlay the type without loosing legibility.

There is no easy solution

First of all we must reduce the copy to a minimum. Online covers are no place for lengthy epistles listing all the content. All there is really room for at these small sizes are the book title and your name. Even a subtitle can be a problem if it is too long. Let me show you a book I did last year and the two covers I finally used. It gave the start toward what we are talking about here. The actual covers are in rich royal blue gradients

 &

The cover on the left was the original designed for print. I really like it in color on the printed books. But in the online listings, it was always broken up pretty bad. As you recall, even the large image on a Lulu detail page is only 212 x 320 pixels. At that size the color still looked very good, but the type was starting break up to the point where readability was bad & I risked poor reader reactions.

Yes, the capture on the next page looks a bit better than this on the computer screen—but not much. So, when I went to the ePUB version I did the image on the right above. Is that as pretty? No. But it is legible, readable, clear in concept, and probably produces a much better reader reaction when it is seen in a list on the screen.

Looking now I can see I should have made my name larger. (I've been told that it's gauche and a sure sign of amateurism to use the word "By" in front of my name. I fully believe that is a mere fashion of the day, but what do I know?)

I now believe that the real solution is on the side of the ePUB version, but I would want to do a bit more to it and tweak the typography a bit. What is in no doubt is that the second version has much more impact at small sizes.

Here's image captured on the detail page converted to greyscale

InDesign 7.5 On-Demand

By David Bergsland

View this Author's Spotlight

Part of the Wattpad Marketplace

Paperback, 154 pages ☆☆☆☆☆ This item has not been rated yet

Price: **$12.95**

Ships in 3–5 business days

Help for authors & teachers publishing in the new millennium
The focus of this book is very sharp. It is designed for people who are designing books and booklets with very limited capital and few personnel resources. It is a sharing of techniques for the new wave of author/pastor/teacher/designers who need to get their work published digitally & online.

Finally, make sure you look at the covers used by your competition. It's likely they'll show you a design style you should use to look appropriate. But the entire process of cover design is an art, not a science. No one has definitive answers—merely informed opinions.

A cover tutorial

Something has come to my attention I should have noticed long ago. People do not have any idea how to apply effects to type because they have no experience with being able to add radical styling to live type.

Stylizing live type—only in InDesign

I forget that no one else allows you to even apply a gradient to live type. Illustrator requires you to convert your type to outlines and Photoshop requires you to rasterize it. InDesign lets you simply select it and apply a gradient—of any kind. In fact, in InDesign you can apply all the Effects available in InDesign—and that is quite a few.

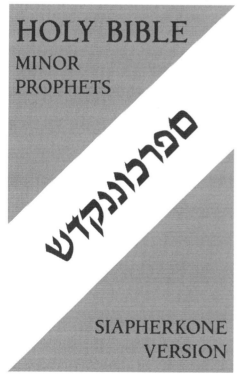

But this goes quite a bit further. So, what I want to do is that a small real world example to give you some ideas what can be done.

Over the weekend, I received a tentative proof of an idea for a book cover. The man who sent it is brand-new to designing in InDesign. He is actually doing very well—given his lack of training.

I critiqued it quite hard. I sent him back an annotated PDF with a dozen or so suggestions for improvement. I told him I thought it looked mid-century modern, and wondered if that would be effective for his audience (I have no idea as I have not looked into that market).

He wrote back that he was going for a similar look to one of his old King James Bibles with a black leather cover—though he had switched things around a bit. I had no real idea what he was referring to, but I tossed off a quick idea to send back.

It turns out that stunned him, He had no concept of what could be done along these lines. I suggested some Photoshop tutorials and he went to look at some of them. His response was that he was amazed at what could be done, and he would let me know what he decided. He also suggested that I add this tutorial—so here goes.

One] Make new document with bleed

This is simple, but not often thought of before you do it awhile. I commonly make my graphics documents square and the same width as my column. But for this one I am doing a 6x9 cover and I want the ink to goto the edge of the printed cover. So, I need a bleed.

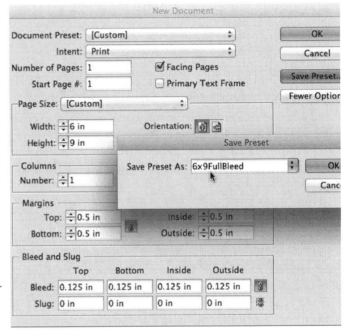

In addition, I made a New Document Preset by clicking on the Save Preset button. This opened the Save Preset As: dialog. I called the new preset: 6x9FullBleed—so I could recognize it in the list of presets.

Two] Add background layer for a template

Next I added a new layer, clicked on its name in the :Layers panel and dragged it below Layer 1. Into that layer I placed the PDF proof I was sent. Then I selected the actual graphic by clicking on the little selection donut in the center of the graphic window. I resized the PDF to fit the new margins of my document. I hit Command+Option+C to make the frame fit the resized content. I do not care at all that the original PDF is distorted quite a bit.

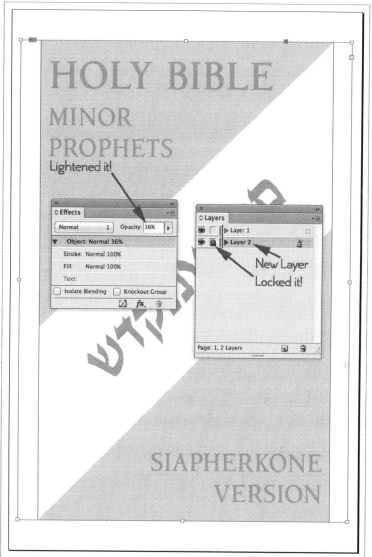

With the resized graphic selected, I went to the Effects panel and lightened it significantly by changing the opacity. I do not want the template graphic to confuse me as I draw on top of it. The final step was to lock the new layer.

Three] Find some leather

One of the things often forgotten when you are doing your own designs for the first time is the simple fact that your background does not have to be blank paper. You can add anything you like as a background color. If you look at the cover of this book, for example, you will see that I have put a computer keyboard as a background image. I couldn't find what I liked, so I laid my keyboard in the scanner and scanned it.

For this tutorial, my friend said his concept was an old KJV leather Bible. So I need an image of black leather. There are countless sources for images—and you can easily pay $300 for an excellent one. However, in this instance we are merely looking for texture. We will not get into copyright issues, but you need to be sure you understand this. So, where shall I look?

Sources for free images

- ❧ Wikimedia Commons: This visual adjunct to the open source online encyclopædia is filled with free images [well over 12,000,000 images at this point]. If you need an attribution, the page will tell you and give you the copy to use.

- ❧ MorgueFile: This site, morgueFile, is not ghoulish. A morgue, in designers parlance, is the collection of images you build to use for reference as you draw you illustrations. This site has over 250,000 free images plus images for sale.

🍒 My camera: If you can shoot photos, you have the best images you can use, because there is no question about copyright, at all. Just make sure you have any people used your images sign a model release. This will give you permission to use their image without problems.

For this tutorial I went to morgueFile. I searched for leather textures and quickly found a photo of black leather which will work perfectly for what we need. I downloaded it. Opened it in Photoshop, and cleaned it up—saving it at 300 dpi for print use.

Four] Place leather in bottom layer ▦

It will be the foundation for everything we build. At this point, I add a new layer (by clicking the little new layer button at the bottom of the panel) and drag it just above the leather. I unlock the original template on top of the whole pile and relock it.

I move the leather into position, so it covers the entire page including the bleed. I then adjust the handle of the frame enclosing the leather image to mask it to the exact size of the bleed.

Five] Draw the top triangle ▦

With the template on top and the leather on the bottom—both locked—it is a simple three click process to trace the triangle with the Pen tool. I choose a strong brilliant yellow-gold to color the triangle. I make it strong and bright because I am going to be making it transparent and additive to the leather texture. This will radically tone down the color. If I do not make it strong enough, it will disappear when I adjust it.

Six] Adjust the transparency ▦

With the new triangle selected and colored, I open the Effects panel and make the triangle 36% transparent—adjusting the look by eye. I also use the Multiply mode which takes the colors of the triangle and adds them to the underlying leather texture. The result is something that looks like a transparent gold covering of the leather. To make it look more real I need to deboss it a little to make it look like it is slightly stamped into the surface of the leather.

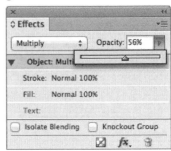

Modes in Effects (from Photoshop)

Modes change how layers interact. A mode will cause the selected object to interrelate to layers and objects below it. Let's look at some quick definitions.

Normal: What do you think? Everything remains normal and the layer does not interact with the layers below it. I think of it in terms of overprinting, but then that is probably just my experience.

Multiply: This basically adds the color of each pixel of the layer to the colors of the pixels under that pixel. In other words, it makes the image darker. This is the way to darken and add detail to a very light image. Simply copy the image into a duplicate layer (drag the layer to the New Layer icon) and apply the Multiply mode. For severely light images, you might have to do this several times with varying opacities in the various layers. For some reason, several light transparent layers often work better than trying to do it all in one layer. It is an extremely handy mode.

Screen: This mode is the opposite of Multiply. You can use this to lighten areas. I have seen scans that looked totally black on the screen reveal astonishing detail through the application of Screened duplicate layers and/or the History brush. This is also a good way to add highlights.

Overlay, Soft Light, and Hard Light: These three modes apply different combinations of Multiply and Screen using 50% gray as neutral. In other words, they apply effects to the highlights and shadows. Overlay, for example, uses the dark tones to darken the dark areas while the light tones lighten the light areas. Hard Light really exaggerates the highlights, often causing a "plastic" look. These modes can be used very well with filters like Emboss where the flat area is 50% gray.

Color Dodge or Burn: These two modes increase contrast by intensifying the hues or increasing the saturation (same thing). Color Dodge lightens as it brightens. Color Burn mainly deepens and intensifies the shadows.

Lighten and Darken: These modes work by comparing the pixels in the upper layer with those in the lower one. They do this channel by channel for all the channels. Lighten only makes changes when it finds a pixel in the upper layer that is lighter than the ones in the lower layer. Darken works oppositely by changing only pixels that are darker.

Difference: Here's one of those mathematical wonders. It compares the upper layer and the image below it using black as a neutral. If there is no difference in color between the two, those pixels are changed to black. It usually results in more saturated color, often psychedelic. It's great for professionally ugly stuff. As you can imagine I rarely use the filter.

Exclusion: This is a more subdued version of Difference that creates much less saturated colors (that is, they are grayed out).

Hue, Saturation, and Luminosity: Here we have computer geek speak. For those of you with fine art training, these would be hue, saturation, and value. In each case, the mode takes that particular information from the overlying layer and applies it to the image beneath. Hue changes the colors only. Saturation changes the intensity only. Luminosity changes the value (or grayscale info) only.

Color: This mode applies both the hue and saturation — everything except the value.

The key is remembering that all of these modes can be applied to anything selected, and it can be applied transparently. One thing where InDesign again demonstrates it superiority is that you can have separate modes and transparency for the fill, stroke, type, and/or the object as a whole. This is immensely helpful and no other application has anything that comes close.

They remain editable: Effects can always be edited. They work with live type, text frames, graphic frames, and/or the contents of graphic frames. InDesign effects are immensely powerful and very useful to add graphic touches to your designs. Don't go overboard—only add them if they help your readers.

But before I can do that there are two more things I need to do.

First, I copy the new triangle and paste. I click the flip vertically and the flip horizontally buttons in the Control bar—and drag the triangle into position.

Second, I drag the layer with the transparent triangles down to the new layer icon and release it there. This makes me a duplicate of the layer on top of the first one. As you will see this will intensify the color [because it is in multiply mode. Every time you do it, you basically double the intensity of the Multiply effect in its interaction with the leather texture. Then I select  both the triangle layer and its copy (by holding down the shift key and clicking on each layer). Finally I select Merge Layers from the Option menu of the Layers panel. This will save the look I have developed and make it into one layer.

As you can see to the right, this looks surprisingly realistic—even in grayscale.

Finally, I click the little *fx* button at the bottom of the Effects panel to add an effect to the selection. Then I chose Bevel and Emboss and made the settings you see at the top of the next page for a subliminal debossing into the leather.

I want it very subtle to keep it realistic. The only trick here is that the lower triangle is rotated, so I need to make

288

the embossing up instead of down to keep the shadows on the right edges.

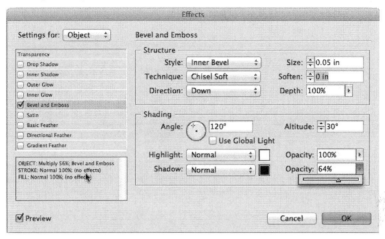

Seven] Set the type

I added the type into the two triangles. I carefully kerned it to get the letterspacing looking professional. Then I added a slight deboss (emboss down, remember).

It was still not enough to set off the type. So, I added a quarter-point white stroke to the type. This is so thin that it is almost subliminal—but you'll be surprised at how much it makes the type pop out.

The type still did not have enough contrast to I went to the leather layer and lightened that a bit. I made it 75% opaque (which I later changed to 80%). I think it would work better in color if I made the leather brown also.

Eight] Add the Hebrew

I have the type in a separate file in Illustrator where I can simply copy/paste the type into the InDesign document. If I had the font I could set it in Hebrew—but all I have is the original PDF. So I drop it in and it looks like what you see at the top of the next page.

The next thing I want to do is give this type an illusion of metal—gold in the color version.

We start by making the type a pale yellow. For, as you know, gold is basically a yellow. It needs to be a clean yellow

with no blue or greenish hints. I used a new swatch set at
0 cyan, 20 magenta, 90 yellow 0 black. After I color the type
this color I set it for a 35% tint.

Next I add a set of effects by clicking on the fx button
at the button of the Effects panel. When it opens, I choose
Bevel and Emboss set to 100%, up, and the rest of the settings you see at the top of the next page. In addition, as
you can see I added a slight softening with the Satin effect.
Finally I added a little bit of inner shadowing. The only

thing I should mention is adding colors to the highlights and shadows. If you look closely to the following capture, you'll notice that I changed the highlight and shadows to a gold and brown respectively.

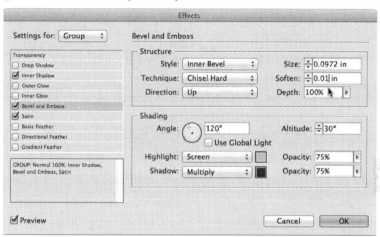

I did the same thing with the inner shadow. When I clicked on the colored box to the right of the mode popup, I opened the Effect Color dialog. It opens to Swatches, but you can change this to RGB or CMYK and pick the color you like. You can see I picked a warm brown: 15 cyan, 64 magenta, 100 yellow, and 20 black.

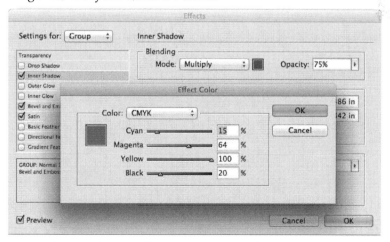

The final result looks pretty good, considering it was all done in InDesign. Yes, I can be much more fancy in Photoshop. But it is not necessary. As you can see on the next page, even in greyscale this will do.

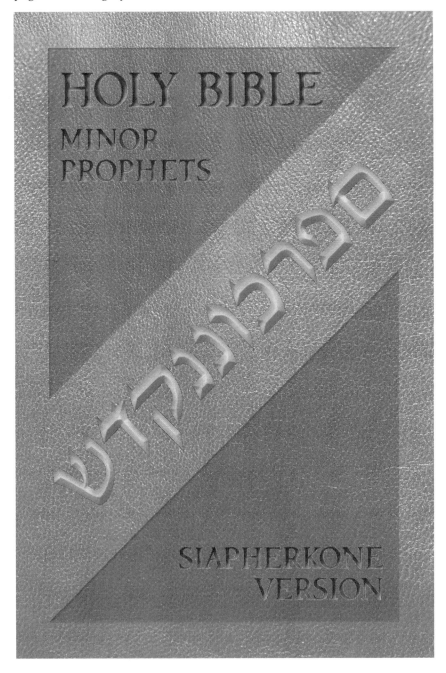

D: Uploading to suppliers

Once your book is completed: formatted, edited, and proofed. The graphics are in place—what comes next? Getting it ready to upload. Every company had slightly different requirements, but the basic procedure is the same. You can start the process any time and take it up where you left off at a later date.

Let's start with print

Lulu's procedure for paperback books

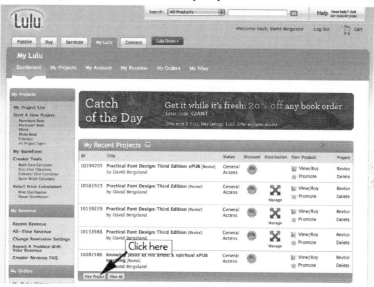

You begin by clicking on the new project button in your Lulu Dashboard

Select Paperback books: That brings up the page to name your book. Name it with care. Make sure you check the "Make it public and assign an ISBN to your title to sell your book on online bookstores like Amazon…" You'll need that ISBN# before you upload your book because it needs to be added to your copyright page. The title is extremely important, but you can revise it later, if necessary.

Working Title InDesign On-Demand: professional publishin

You will have a chance to change this later.

Author David | Bergsland

First Name — Last Name

What do you want to do with this project?

○ **Keep it private and accessible only to me**
You can change this later if you decide to sell

○ **Make it public to sell in the Lulu Marketplace**

◉ **Make it public and assign an ISBN to your title to sell your book in online bookstores like Amazon as well as the Lulu Marketplace.**
Learn more about ISBNs and distribution

Click the save & Continue button when you have it filled out. That will bring up the bindery options page.

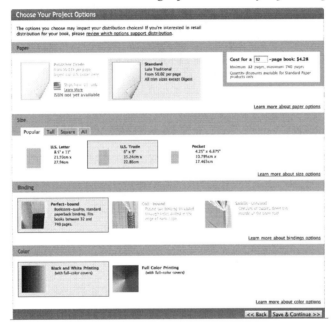

For this sample, I set it for Standard, U.S. Trade (6x9), Perfect-bound, with a black and white interior and a color cover. Then I clicked Save & Continue. I can still change this later, but this is where I usually start. This brings up the ISBN# choices. There are three options.

✢ Get a Free ISBN from Lulu
✢ Add an ISBN I already own
✢ Do not add an ISBN

I choose to get a free one, click save and continue and I am presented with this:

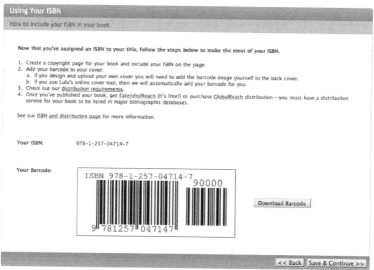

I click on the Download Barcode button. And a vector version of the barcode is downloaded. I save that to my CoverArt folder in the Book folder.

Now I have the barcode and ISBN# I need to publish professionally with distribution. I take the ISBN# and add it on the copyright info on page iv. The vector barcode is added on the outside back cover so it can be scanned by the bookstore when the book is sold.

This is the great change Lulu and Createspace have added—free ISBN#s. Createspace never gives you a vector version. They just give you the number. You send them a 300 dpi Photoshop PDF. You must leave a specified blank rectangular area for Createspace to insert your barcode when they print the book. But that is it.

When I click Save and Continue now, I am brought to the upload files page.

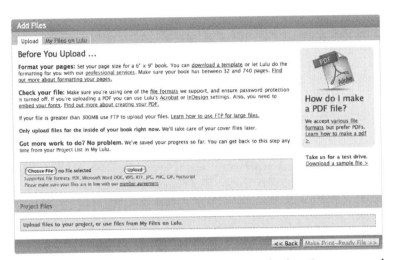

Here are all the instructions and the Browse and Upload buttons that enable me to upload the PDF for the book. Notice that I can upload a PDF up to 300 MB (I've never had a file anywhere near that large). I can upload up to 600 MB (I think), but I'll need to use their FTP server to do that.

Once this is done, click Make Print-Ready File.

When that is complete and saved, you go on to making a cover. You can use Lulu Cover Creator or you can make your own PDF by clicking on the use Advanced One-Piece

Cover Designer. This one-piece designer page allows you to build an InDesign page with a specified spine width that will work for Lulu. This spine width is calculated using the number of pages you uploaded. All the sizes are listed where it says One-piece cover requirements.

You take their specs and build the cover you like as a separate InDesign document. Notice that the sizes given include the bleed—so you might need to add guides for bleeds and columns. You have to put the vector barcode you downloaded on the back page. If this level of graphic design is a bit much for you, use their cover designer which gives you templates to work with and images to choose from.

After you click upload you need to carefully examine the preview. You'll be able to see if you messed up the bleeds or poorly sized anything.

Once you have that complete, you save it and move on to the describe your project section.

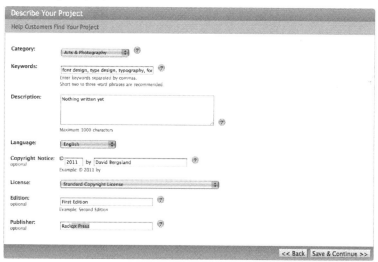

This is a very serious point in your production. This is the information that will be used by the search engines, and the Websites selling your book. So, take it seriously. Study what others do. Get it right.

Put your name as the copyright holder. Put your company as the publisher. Make it the first edition (if it is the first edition). Pay special attention to the description and keywords. Do your research. Practice good SEO techniques. If you do not know what that is, you have some more research to do on Search Engine Optimization (SEO) techniques. When you've done the best you can, pray it will work well for you, and move on. Save & Continue.

Next you set your pricing

Lulu gives you lots of help and a great deal of freedom here. The only confusing area might be the Lulu price versus the Elsewhere price. Elsewhere has the standard 100% retail markup. Amazon requires this, for example, as do all the retail sellers. I usually set a discount for buyers at Lulu that keeps my profits at about the same as they are at retail but gives my readers a break if they go to my Website to buy the book. But be careful. Amazon has been known to reprice books on Amazon to reflect the lowest price anywhere.

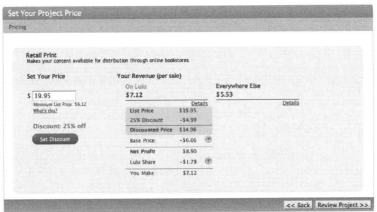

This is used to be where you set the price for the PDF download. You need to set this up. But under the present procedures, you need to add the PDF as an ebook with no ISBN. This has cut PDF sales, as I mentioned, but we have to deal with reality. At Lulu, I still sell as many PDF downloads as I do printed books—plus I get a larger royalty. I set the download price at the same as I am going to price my ePUBs.

When you have your pricing set, click the Review Project button. If that is OK, you are ready to publish. You can see the Review Your Project page at the top of the next page of this book. Click Save & Finish and you are done!

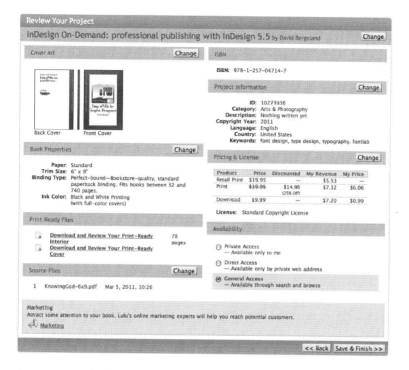

After it is finished page

On the next page, after you are finished, you get the opportunity to generate a preview. The only problem I have ever had is getting a preview to please me. I usually end up making a separate PDF for that to upload, but you need to be careful because Lulu's preview generator does not support transparency (it has the same limitations as Scribd) and you will get unexpected results if you are not careful. But you can look over your generated preview and redo it until you are happy. If you use Lulu's preview it will show the reader all of your front matter and very little of the actual book. It pays to take a little time with this. But this is a clear case of: "Do what I say, not what I do."

Getting it distributed

Now you get to deal with getting it distributed and selling some copies. This is not the place for authors who have places to hand out books, sell them, or distribute personally. There are cheaper ways to print if you need a couple thousand copies.

The good news is that you can get basic distribution from Lulu for free. They usually require you to buy a proof. Of course, it is very wise to purchase a proof to find obvious stupid errors or flaws in the printing process. But getting it distributed on Lulu is simple. You click on the four-arrowed X. It gives you the choices you have made available depending on the size and options you have chosen.

If you used a Lulu ISBN#, ExtendedReach is free. You do need to "purchase it" though. So go through the routine and order a proof. Now we get to your part.

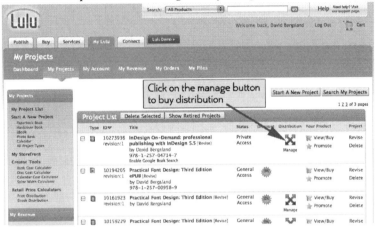

Marketing is up to you

A lot of it is done by the cover you designed, the description you wrote, and the keywords you chose. The title is very important. But the rest of it is also up to you, unless you want to purchase a marketing package.

The marketing packages from Lulu start at $2900 and go up to nearly $10,000. There is no right or wrong here. For me, it would be a waste of money for many reasons: size of niche, lack of media focus, and the list goes on. Many of you will be in the same position as I am.

Some of you will have a product that will market well to businesses, or a specific denomination, or whatever. Some of you are writing mass market stuff. You will need a massive push at some time. There is no right or wrong. But if it is a large market print job, you need a printer who can give you better pricing in bulk (though Lulu has bulk pricing).

Events

Lulu also offers display space at specific library events on the state level and other large events like the Beijing Book Fair. If you see an event that targets your potential audience, this may work well for you.

They'll also help you write a professional press release for several hundred dollars, and/or sell you a targeted list of media contacts for just under $1,000. You can also purchase book reviews for several hundred dollars. The list goes on.

Createspace's publishing routine is similar

Remember, for printed books Amazon is king of on-demand. It sells more ebooks [Kindle] than iBooks sells ePUBs and it sells more on-demand printed books than Lulu. Amazon's in-house books [Createspace] are marketed the best by Amazon—of course.

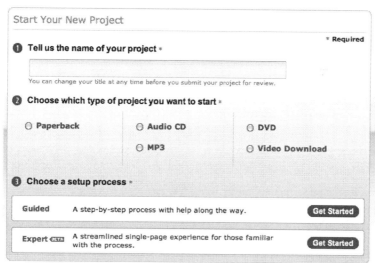

Starting a new book

I would use the guided step-by-step process to start. Createspace is much more careful of their preflighting process. They will give you more requirements than Lulu. But this is neither good nor bad, it just is.

The Title page

Next you add the title of your book as well as the name of the primary author. It is very important that you get this right because you cannot change these items after you have assigned an ISBN to this book.

Next comes the description—which they say it is optional. It most certainly is not. After the title, there is nothing more important to your book than a good description that will help people searching Amazon to find a book like yours. Unless it is the keywords, but they come later.

ISBN Number

We covered all of this when discussing what you need to do to get your publishing business set up. Now you make the choice based on the decisions you made. For your first book, I would not hesitate to recommend you choose the free ISBN# offered by Createspace. All of the other choices are for books with larger sales or they are merely ego-boosters.

However, make sure you have researched where you are going to be selling your book or books. In the Christian portion of the industry, for example, none of the distributors or retail outlets will deal with you unless you do what is necessary to get yourself listed with Bowker as an official publisher. Without that, you are limited to Amazon, Barnes & Noble, iBooks, Lulu, and the like. You know what you need.

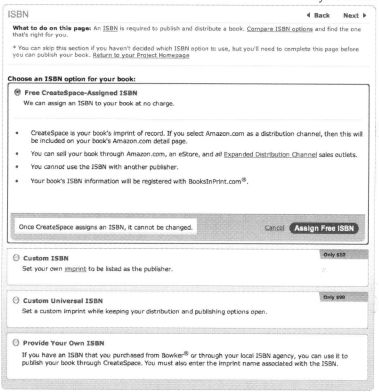

Once you have made your choice you get this page. Notice that it tells you clearly, amazon [Createspace] requires an ISBN#. So you must choose one of the options.

The other thing about ISBN numbers is that they cannot be changed once you have a title, author, and ISBN# tied together for a book. If you make changes [including different sizes, different binding, and so on] you'll need an additional ISBN# for that version. Notice on the next page that Createspace specifically states that you are not allowed to use their number with another publisher. That is their rule, but then they own the ISBN#.

Interior

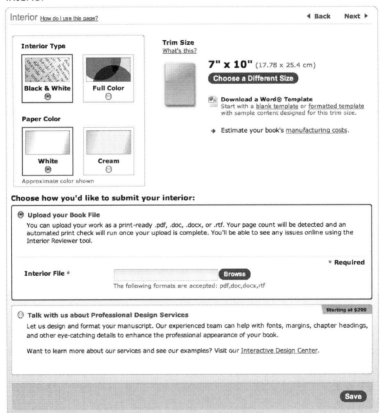

Now you have an important choice to make. Here you need to pick the page size for your book. I would suggest something different from what you release in Lulu. As you can see above, I tend to use 7x10 for Createspace, but the choice is yours. If you remember that you probably need a 4-inch column for your type to help readability, and you should use ¾" margins as a minimum, this makes 5.5" widths the minimum also. CS requires a ¾" interior margin. If you wish to use the smaller sizes, you will have to make the type smaller which really compromises readability.

The cover

Here you need to go with the flow. I suggest you let Createspace build a template for you. They say they take PDFs, but the truth of the matter is that they really want fully rasterized Photoshop PDFs. I've never even been able to get them to accept a PDF directly from InDesign. Their new instructions say they can, so I'll try again. But I expect to need to use their PSD template, regardless. I talk about these issues in more detail in Appendix C: Image Production & Formats.

Submit for review

After you have the interior PDF and the cover PDF uploaded, you submit your files for review. Remember, the majority of files they receive are Word documents or clumsy conversions of Word documents. So, they assume that you know nothing. I have made the mistake of trying to argue with them [because it is obvious that I have more experience]. That was a real mistake. I have learned to simply make any changes they require with no fuss.

Order a proof

Once your files are approved, you need to order a proof. If you have printed this book already through Lulu, you know that it is OK. In that case, you can skip the proof and release it immediately. However, I always order a copy of it after I approve it for production. I seem to get a more "normal" quality of proof doing it this way. I have had book quality issues where I have had to get them to send me a new copy of the book.

General issues with Createspace

I find they flag little things that I know about but do not consider a problem. They have a terrible time with screen captures, for example, always flagging them as too low in resolution. Of course they are, but there is no way to improve them.

As I have mentioned, their printing quality is simply not as good as I would like. My suggestion is to avoid subtlety in your designs. I am starting to eliminate subtle gradients in my Createspace books, for example. There is a real possibility that these will not print consistently and that will affect the reading experience of people who buy the Amazon version.

Here's an example of what you deal with: In my edition of Practical Font Design which I was releasing in Createspace at the time I am wrote the first edition of this book, I received the following instruction:

> *"The interior file submitted for this title contains text referencing Createspace as the publisher on PDF page 18. Please remove all text and/or logos which reference Createspace as the publisher. If you would like to include information regarding the publisher, you may include information regarding your own Imprint."*

I had no idea what that was about, but I knew I must fix it. I went and looked. All I said was that I was going to publish the book through Lulu and Createspace. I finally removed most of the discussion of Createspace in the version I released through them. It is not important, and I did it without any issues. I may have to do it here also. For one thing, it made the Createspace book different from the Lulu book and that justifies the additional ISBN#. I commonly change my Createspace books to an 7x10, 8x10 or a 5x8 which are two other sizes I tend to like better than 6x9.

 I always feel like I am dealing with bureaucrats at Createspace: They have procedures and policies, and it does not matter how that matches with reality. You learn to not fight the system and do what they ask. Just do what you need to do to make the book satisfy them while somehow maintaining the level of excellence you require. This can be a tricky balancing act on your part, but that is why you are doing this yourself.

Services which provide designs for you will not take the time to make special versions for the different printers. So, you simply work through the hassles.

They need a proof (but they now have a good digital proofer). No problem! As I have said several times, you really need a proof—especially if you are just starting out and cannot afford a proofer or a copyeditor. I still cannot afford that service and I have several dozen books released now.

Createspace's Editing & Marketing Services

They provide everything you might need from simple copyediting for $175 per ten thousand words to $5,000 for a complete package (though you only get a few graphics for this and they obviously want a Word document).

They do very good work and are a very valued resource for me. What I am doing in on-demand publishing would be much more difficult without them.

Extra distribution options for $25

This is the best distribution deal I've seen. You get better royalties and much wider distribution. The only quibble is that if you want a Library of Congress Catalog Number, you need to purchase this ($75 at present) before you approve the proof. But they may have changed that also.

Producing a downloadable PDF

PDFs for Lulu

In Lulu you start a new project again for an ebook this time. You go through the same procedure in naming the book and all that. Lulu's ebook process is specifically geared toward ePUBs. They are downplaying the printable PDF. However, I find that my downloadable PDFs still sell well through them. I add PDF to the name of my book so I can tell which ebook I am talking about. Otherwise the PDF and the ePUB look the same in the project list.

The rules for the ePUB are quite stringent and we'll talk about them in Appendix E. For the downloadable PDF you can simply use the same interior PDF and the same cover design as the printed version. The only problem you'll have is with the Preview. I would make a special preview PDF to upload. As with Scribd, this PDF preview has issues if you let them do it for you.

You may want to follow the procedure I list below for Scribd. There is no reason why you cannot make your downloadable PDF on Lulu in full color. Lulu does not seem to have the file size restrictions that Scribd has, because they are not presenting your PDF in a screen reader.

PDFs for Scribd

Scribd offers a very good service for people to take a look at a sample of your book. You can also sell the PDF for a complete version. They have a very good PDF reader for the screen. The only problem is that they seem to have trouble with PDFs much over 5 MB. Or rather, my iMac with 4 GB RAM has trouble with PDFs larger than 5 MB on Scribd. So, I would try to keep the file sizes down, if possible. You are pushing the envelope if you offer very complex PDFs with large and/or very complex graphics.

The process is very simple, but do it carefully.

1. Package your book into a new folder for conversion to Scribd

2. Replace the graphic links with the color graphics you saved in the ePUB folder: I recommend you simply copy/paste the color graphics into the new links folder and replace all the greyscale graphics. This is why I mentioned that I have an Originals folder with all my graphics in color using exactly the same names as I use in the Links folder.

3. Relink all the graphics: If you used my naming technique you can simply Option+Click on the Update Link button at the bottom of the Links panel. Then go through the document and check that they all look good. You'll need to make some adjustments, of course.

4. Check "Create PDF Bookmarks" in your TOC: Radically simplify & update your Table of Contents. Make sure you check the "Create PDF Bookmarks" box

under Options in the Edit Table of Contents
Style dialog box under the Layout menu.

5. Eliminate as much front matter as possible: you want
    your readers to get to the good copy as quickly
    as possible. You may want to move it to the back
    matter. Then all you need is a page that tells
    the reader where to look for the information.

6. Make page one a full bleed, full color cover: You
    need color to the edges to make a thumbnail
    that is easy to see. Make sure the title reads
    well in the thumbnail. Note: If you are not sure
    how to revise your cover for digital thumbnails,
    go to Appendix C on Graphic production.
    There's a section on cover design there.

7. Adjust your paragraph styles: Scribd cannot handle
    gradient strokes for paragraph rules, for example.
    The only way you are going to know about any
    problems is to carefully examine the book on
    Scribd after you upload it. The likelihood is
    that you will find some issues with your style
    of formatting. You will find things that do not
    work for Scribd. So make those changes now.

8. Export a printable PDF: Proof it carefully—
    take the viewpoint of an online reader.
    Scribd is designed for reading online.

9. Upload your PDF to Scribd: Take a look at
    it on Scribd and make any adjustments
    necessary. When it looks good, add the
    marketing copy, & share it with your
    FaceBook page and Twitter feeds.

Using Smashwords

I used to do this quite a bit. The problem with Smashwords is that they require a Word document and they simply
smash it into submission. So, you start with something
typographically inadequate and lessen the quality. They do
sell quite a few books, but you get no typographic options
and they cannot handle many graphics. They are limited to
a 5 MB file size. For all of this follow their formatting guide

exactly. Smashwords may work very well for you if you have a text-only book.

Now get to work on your ePUB!

E: ePUB Design

Designing & formatting your ePUB & Kindle book without coding

At this point I am assuming that you have a finished, formatted and uploaded book for print and probably a downloadable PDF. The question is how do we take this and convert it to an ePUB and a Kindle book?

Coding is anathema: Again, I must assume some things. My experience is that people like us can handle a little simple Web coding like XHTML and CSS (actually, most of us have been forced into it for our Websites). However, most people who do what we do really dislike coding.

Important announcement! This is current as of April 2012

This field of design is changing so rapidly that anything a month old is at least a bit out of date. The good news is that the methods I will cover here will still work. The bad news is that some of them may no longer be necessary. This week we are dealing with image size issues for the Retina display of the new iPad, for example. I found new information about dealing with lists this morning and I have to test it before I can write that portion of this chapter.

Fancy ePUBs require fancy coding

At this point in the development, ePUB design is commonly produced by coding specialists. Even though InDesign can export good validated ePUBs, a lot is still missing. It's not just missing from InDesign but from all WYSIWYG applications. This is because of one simple issue. In order to do simple things like text wraps (CSS: alignments), sidebars (CSS: divs), and all the rest, you must be able to crack the compressed ePUB file and mess with its innards (many files and folders) [see Appendix F for instruction about these things]. CS6 has made major strides to solve the text wrap and sidebar issues. However, it is still not clean and simple. Plus, there are many purely design issues which suggest that text wraps and sidebars do not work well in ebooks, regardless.

There is no simple program that allows you to do this visually. Dreamweaver is the obvious candidate for this capability, but nothing has been done yet by Dreamweaver. As a result, all of these things must be done on the code level and most of us are simply not ready to do that. It is possible to do the editing in Dreamweaver, but it is not pleasant and it is certainly not a good design experience. You are going to make some tough decisions about your ebooks.

InDesign CS5.5 can produce validated ePUBs: but you must rethink your book layouts severely.

InDesign CS6 has done quite a bit to write better code: but it still takes a lot of setup on your part. Many of the excellent design possibilities of print are simply not available in ePUBs. What I intend to do is give you a list of changes you must make to get a validated ePUB. The good news is that several things that I would have had to mention for CS5.5 are no longer necessary for CS6.

Digital books are a very different world. You must rethink your concept of a book in order to design one that will work for ePUBs and Kindle books. Let's talk about some of these necessary changes.

Why are ebooks so different?

The most important factor is adjustable type: The reader controls font sizes globally and can override your font choices. At this point, even as a designer you don't get much control over font choice, font style, font size, font spacing, or typography in general. These critical typographic concerns are downgraded to CSS capabilities—but with far fewer fonts even on the iPad. OpenType features are not available. We are back to the very limited 256 character choices.

 This is changing as you read this: As I am writing, it is now recommended that you embed fonts for Nook and Kindle. I have worked with the Kindle export and it seems to work well for Fire, but the Mac readers are still the old capabilities. I can only see the embedded fonts in Amazon's Kindle Previewer. I tried with Nook, but the embedded fonts encrypt the ePUB, and Nook will not accept it. I'll post this in my blog as soon as I can get something worked up. I'll need to release this book before I can do that.

As a reader, you get a few fonts with up to four styles, a dozen sizes (maybe), and that's it. As a designer, you get the number of fonts available (usually just serif and sans serif, unless you're on an iPad), four typestyles, largely unlimited sizes & line spacing, alignments, indents, nested styles, a couple of list styles, six headline styles plus unlimited classes, and all of this directly out of InDesign.

The second major factor is the single column layout: Without coding—cracking the ePUB to edit the raw code—there is nothing that can be done about this. There is a real hope that the CSNext version of InDesign will deal with this. InDesign and Dreamweaver CS5.5 were supposed to be interim versions to prepare the way for the full implementation of HTML5 and CSS3—whatever that means in software capabilities. CS6 made some radical steps forward in this, but Liquid Layout with its automatic column additions and graphic resizing and remasking for various ereaders and smart phones has no real bearing on ePUBs. It's developed for use in app design for magazines with tablets—where multi-column pages are the norm. For now, we are not there with ePUBs unless you are a better than competent coder.

 CS6 will now export floating graphics: It is possible to set up graphics in an Anchored Object with an Object style which will float your graphics to the right or left. The margins still cause trouble, and you must do the graphics as a fixed size, so far. But the capability now exists—more on this in a bit.

How much do we change? Everything.

So, it is obvious that we must rethink our book designs. The real question is how much do we want to change in the conversion from print to ebook? The unavoidable answer, at present, is that we need a complete redo. This goes quite a bit beyond simple repurposing.

Designing for repurposing: This can certainly be done. What it requires is a clear idea of what is going to be needed for the conversion. So what we need to do is talk about what you will need to set up in your print versions. In order to make your ePUB look as good as possible we need to think reasonably about how to set up our documents so they can be converted quickly.

Document size

At present for ePUBs I am using a document with a Digital Publishing intent: iPad vertical (768x1024 pixels), with 84 pixel margins right and left; and 82 pixel margins top and bottom. This gives me a Primary text frame of 600x860 which is the maximum image size for an image in an ePUB on an iPad2. The Retina resolution (double the iPad2) has no standardized techniques, yet. I'll cover Kindle later.

Graphic format, size, and resolution

This one is rough. They always look horrible when compared to print. What you basically need to understand is that you will be using relatively large Web graphics—but 72 dpi not 300 dpi. This is obviously a serious conflict with the way we have been working for the past decade. Basically you need 600x860 pixel [iPad2 maximum], RGB JPEGs. The Nook and Fire have different image size requirements as we'll see in a bit.

This obviously takes some planning ahead as you will be using grayscale images (vector PDFs if possible) in your print documents—in most cases. You'll have CMYK images if you print in color. So from the beginning, as you write and create, you need to save RGB versions of your color images.

This obviously takes some planning ahead as you will be using grayscale images (vector PDFs if possible) in your print documents—in most cases. You'll have CMYK images if you print in color.

So from the beginning, as you write and create, you need to save RGB versions of your color images.

At this point, even though the ePUB3 spec accepts SVG, which is a vector form of graphic, none of the ereaders do—with the possible exception of Kindle Fire and iBooks2 books produced with Apple's iBooks2 Author.

Everything in one story

Eliminate all separate stories

> **The problem isn't with the ePUB standard**
>
> The problem is with the software we have available to implement that standard and with the dedicated ereaders available to read what we publish. I am always saddened when I read my ePUBs in Ibis (a browser-based ereader). They look so much better than is possible in Kindle, or Nook. This is a brand new capability. All I have to do is remember how limited PageMaker 4.2 and Quark 3 were when I began in digital publishing in 1991.

Remember that everything in an ePUB must be in one story and inline. This is a radical conversion in many cases. And you will need to do it by hand. The new Articles Panel is supposed to be a help, but in my experience it takes longer to order things in this way and it is certainly not a flawless conversion. So, I drag'n'drop any separate stories into a location that makes sense—rewriting as necessary to keep the copy flowing well. Again, simply repurposing is not a good idea. ePUBs are a very different reading experience and we must adapt to it.

What I find is that concepts which can be easily shown with typography are completely lost in an ePUB. I commonly need to rewrite copy to deal with this fact. Type in an anchored sidebar usually needs to be rewritten and placed into a different location to make sense as a part of the one story. Many sidebars can be simply eliminated.

Very limited anchored graphics: convert most to inline

For very graphic books like mine with the wrapped graphics, I simply redo the object style for the graphics so that it drops them in inline in their own paragraph with auto leading. Moving graphics around to make the most sense becomes easy with the new drag'n'drop anchoring controls built into the frame edge—upper side, right corner. Simply drag them into position and convert them to inline with a shortcut.

Wrapped graphics are definitely doable, but you'll need to read Appendix F where we'll take a brief look at editing the XHTML files and the CSS. In CS6, anchored graphics can be set to float right or left, but the margins are messed up. The biggest missing capability is in setting sizing to percentages. Now, all you can do is set the pixel width.

 Dealing with captions: It will really help you work on the ePUB code generated by InDesign if you group your captions with your graphics instead of inserting them inline. This is the only way InDesign adds a div automatically at this point, for those of you who know what a div is.

Be patient with all of this. Adding ebooks to the publishing repertoire is a very complex operation for Adobe. InDesign CS6 has laid much of the groundwork for HTML5 and CSS3 plus the beginnings of ePUB3 support and the CSNext version (a year or so from now) will do even better. We have been assured by Adobe that ePUB3 is very high on their priority list. They have a good reputation of bringing these things online—and for doing it better than we expected. I know I certainly did not expect Liquid layout, yet we got that for CS6. It may only apply to magazines, but ePUB3 support is coming—both in InDesign and in ereaders. The iPad reads simple ePUB3 docs now, in fact.

Fixing the styles

Eventually we are going to edit the exported tags. But for now I want to talk about how the styles need to change. The easiest way is to simply start editing the copy and changing the styles as we get to them. We must bear in mind that sidebars or anchored graphics require hand code work at this point—unless you convert them to inline text and graphics (which I recommend).

Again, I often find I need to rewrite copy to deal with the reality of the ePUB reading experience. Do not hesitate to do that. Your ePUB will have a different ISBN# anyway, if you get one.

Font changes

Even though the ePUB spec says we can embed fonts, this is still very tricky. My current recommendation is to choose fonts that are available on the iPad. For the Nook and Fire, we can embed fonts but you must make sure that you are using fonts with the proper licensing. **No font supplier I know of is dealing with this yet.**

With iOS5 the iPad supports 58 font families

However, out of these 163 fonts 37 of them in 17 families are Hebrew, Indic, Thai, Tibetan, Chinese, Japanese, or Arabic. So, there are really 126 fonts in 41 families which we can use for English and the rest of the European languages.

Font choices are always a highly personal thing. I'm going to suggest my personal tastes and give you reasons. You make up your own mind. I'm going to just mention the ugly ones you should never use: Courier or New Courier. These eight fonts should never be used unless you are trying to evoke a period or make a historical statement or something strange. `But almost everyone believes they are hideous fonts (not to mention very difficult to read).`

Fonts with compromised reader reactions

Next we have fonts that are not bad designs, but they have issues—some of them fatal. I don't use them.

- **Arial + a rounded style:** There are five choices here—regular, italic, bold and bold italic plus the Rounded Bold. Arial is the ugly cousin of Helvetica used to avoid the royalties (as far as I know). These fonts plus Times make up the core of some of the most overused fonts in existence. Plus they are the default for bureaucracies.
- **Helvetica [6] & Helvetica Neue [11]:** Both of these families are available in regular, italic, bold and bold italic, plus many more. There is nothing really wrong with these fonts for heads and subheads. But readability

is a real issue. The main problem is the bureaucratic
overtones that these fonts share with Arial.

✤ **Times New Roman:** This family has regular, italic,
  bold and bold italic. Though the bold pair tend to
  be too narrow and ugly with plugged counters, the
  real problem is the bureaucratic associations.

Bureaucratic fonts: These are the fonts that have been the
defaults in Office, Publisher, and similar non-professional
page layout tools for decades—Arial, Helvetica, Times, and
Times Roman. They are not very pretty fonts.

The true situation is that non-professionals who use
nothing but software defaults are the only people who use
these fonts. In fact, most bureaucracies have standardized
them and require their use. The result is that they trigger
our *bureaucratic drivel* filter.

For example, if you watch when you open your mail
or when you receive handouts, you will see that bureaucratic
output is quickly consigned to the trash—usually without
being read. We know that there is no content in these things.
Bureaucratic output is produced purely to prove to adminis-
trators that something was done—even though we all know
that nothing was done except some committee meetings.
Our experience tells us these are a waste of time to read.

So also, almost everyone simply tosses obvious Word
output without reading it. Beyond that, default Word and
Publisher output is barely readable. The default typography
settings are very bad and obvious. There are simply too
many really bad associations with these fonts to use them.

Versatile fonts for typography

The iPad gives us several quite good choices here.
These are font families that are relatively easy to read and
comfortable for the reader. There are several fine serif choices,
and a lesser selection of sans serif families. However, there
are enough choices for you to be able to make your ePUBs
unique, stylish and very readable.

For body copy you need at least regular, bold, and
italic versions for your typographic needs. A bold italic is
nice—but not often needed. You'll need these fonts installed
on your machine to use them in InDesign. If not you'll be

forced to add them by hand in the code. These are installed with Lion (OSX.7).

Serif choices for body copy

The copy in brackets and sans serif are the font names as you need to write them in the CSS code. In most cases CS6 will do this correctly for you.

- **Baskerville:** There are six choices—[Baskerville, Baskerville-Italic, Baskerville-Bold, and Baskerville-BoldItalic, plus Baskerville-SemiBold & Baskerville-SemiBoldItalic]. This is an extremely elegant font, very readable—a little cool and distant. It's a bit formal for my taste now, but it was my first font purchase back in 1991 when I started using PageMaker.
- **Bodoni 72:** This is the ITC translation of Bodoni's Papale (or Papal) version of his fonts. These fonts are extremely elegant but a bit difficult to use in smaller sizes because of the extreme modulation (contrast in stroke widths). There are seven fonts here, including a true small cap version of book [BodoniSvtySCITCTT-Book].
  Bodoni 72: [BodoniSvtyITCTT-Book, BodoniSvtyITCTT-BookIta, & BodoniSvtyITCTT-Bold]
  Bodoni 72 Oldstyle: [BodoniSvtyOSITCTT-Book, BodoniSvtyOSITCTT-BookIta, & BodoniSvtyOSITCTT-Bold] The Oldstyle version has lowercase figures which is very nice.
- **Cochin:** There are four choices—[Cochin, Cochin-Italic, Cochin-Bold, and Cochin-BoldItalic]. This has been my choice recently—largely because of the uniquely splashy italics. I suspect it is a fad on my part, but I like this family.
- **Didot:** There are three choices—[Didot, Didot-Italic, and Didot-Bold]. This is a more uptight and mechanically crafted Bodoni. I'd call it prickly and scrawny, but then I don't like it.
- **Georgia:** There are four choices—[Georgia, Georgia-Italic, Georgia-Bold, and Georgia-BoldItalic]. This font has oldstyle figures and is very solid and readable. A Web-safe font family
- **Hoefler Text:** There are four choices—[HeoflerText, HeoflerText-Italic, HeoflerText-Black, and HeoflerText-BlackItalic]. This font has oldstyle figures and is very solid and readable. It is more traditional in form than Georgia.
- **Palatino:** There are four choices—[Palatino-Roman, Palatino-Italic, Palatino-Bold, and Palatino-BoldItalic]. This is a very good looking and extremely readable font with a chiseled, calligraphic look. It uses uppercase

figures. Its only problem is some overuse because it was one of the original PostScript fonts when desktop publishing first started. A Web-safe font family

New for iOS5

Baskerville and Cochin have been removed from the iBooks menu on your iPad. But you can still specify these fonts in your CSS. Charter, Iowan, and Seravek have been added, but I can find nothing out about using them in your ePUB style. If it's important to you, try it. But they are not very distinctive fonts. So, I'm not even trying to use them at this point.

Sans serif choices for body copy

✤ **Futura:** There are two choices— [Futura-Medium & Futura-MediumItalic]. Futura is barely usable for body copy. This font is a standard in some areas (like here in southern Minnesota). But it is very hard to read, so my recommendation is to use it only for heads—sparingly.

✤ **Futura:** [Futura-CondensedMedium & Futura-CondensedExtraBold] You will not be able to choose a bold version with a character style but will have to choose both of these as separate fonts.

✤ **Gill Sans:** There are six choices—[GillSans-Light, GillSans-LightItalic, GillSans, GillSans-Italic, GillSans-Bold, and GillSans-BoldItalic]. This is the only iPad sans family with any sense of style. It is also more readable that any other sans offering other than Optima [which is nearly a serif design].

✤ **Optima:** There are five choices—[Optima-Regular, Optima-Italic, Optima-Bold, and Optima-BoldItalic—plus Optima-ExtraBlack]. This font is one of the most readable sans serifs. There is a little flare at the ends of the strokes. It's been overused in my experience so I no longer use it (but that's just me).

✤ **Trebuchet MS:** There are four choices—[TrebuchetMS, TrebuchetMS-Italic, TrebuchetMS-Bold, and TrebuchetMS-BoldItalic]. This is a good-looking easy to read sans that is slightly chunky. A Web-safe font family

✤ **Verdana:** There are four choices—[Verdana, Verdana-Italic, Verdana-Bold, and Verdana-BoldItalic]. This is an excellent font for headers. The large x-height makes it a lot larger than the rest of these fonts, but it reads well. A Web-safe font family

Stylish display options

Finally we have a group of fonts that are quite stylized and really only usable for larger headlines. They are usually too hard to read in smaller sizes—or, they have limited style choices. They do make excellent style statements for various demographics. You just need to be careful.

- **Academy Engraved LET:** [AcademyEngraveLETPlain] Very elegant, almost bankish or financial
- **American Typewriter:** [AmericanTypewriter-CondensedLight, AmericanTypewriter-Light, AmericanTypewriter, AmericanTypewriter-Condensed, AmericanTypewriter-Bold, AmericanTypewriter-CondensedBold]. The only reason this is here and not in body copy is that there are no italics.
- **Bradley Hand:** [BradleyHandITCTT-Bold] A slightly uptight script that looks like modern cursive printing—a little.
- **Chalkboard SE:** [ChalkboardSE-Light, ChalkboardSE-Regular, and ChalkboardSE-Bold]. A handwriting font.
- **Chalkduster:** [Chalkduster] More loose than Bradley Hand
- **Copperplate:** [Copperplate-Light, Copperplate, and Copperplate-Bold]. The de facto standard for lawyers and bankers. It only comes with small caps.
- **Marion:** [Marion-Regular, Marion-Italic, and Marion-Bold]. Described as being like Century Schoolbook, sorta. What this actually means is that it looks a little heavy and has relatively heavy serifs. This one is not installed with Lion.
- **Marker Felt:** [MarkerFelt-Thin & MarkerFelt-Wide]. A narrow, dark and more structured hand-written script
- **Noteworthy:** [Noteworthy-Light & Noteworthy-Bold] This is an upright handwriting style reminiscent of Tekton.
- **Papyrus:** [Papyrus & Papyrus-Condensed]. A raging fashion, but elegant and pretty.
- **Party LET:** [PartyLetPlain] Sixties junk [in my humble opinion]but then the sixties were why I dropped out [says the old hippy].
- **Snell Roundhand:** [Snell Roundhand, Snell Roundhand-Bold, & Snell Roundhand-Black] Standard formal script
- **Zapfino:** Very flashy calligraphy—the sizing is messed up so there are a lot of overlaps from line to line. Use with care. It will take a lot of extra line spacing and/or margins to work well.

Remember! Apple can change these at whim: I've heard rumors of some new fonts for the Retina Display in the new iPad.

Plus, the reader can change fonts at will: Reflow is the goal. That trumps typography in an ebook. Also remember, that an ePUB on an iPad is the typographic wonder of the ebook world. Even Kindle Fire and Nook now support ePUB and have tablets with slightly better font options. But there is nothing like the choices built into iOS.

According to an article on ireaderreview.com the following fonts are available on the older ereaders. You quickly see that the iPad and iPhone give us exceptional choices. The Kindle Fire is certainly headed in that direction. It has eight fonts, but I can't find out what they are. I don't even know if this is eight font families or eight individual fonts. So things are indeed getting better, but slowly.

- ❦ Kindle uses PMN Caecilia a condensed version of Caecilia, and a sans serif option: this is a very readable slab serif but I haven't found out what the sans serif is.

- ❦ Nook uses Helvetica Neue (sans-serif), Amasis (serif), and Light Classic (serif): Amasis is a more humanist slab serif.

- ❦ Sony uses Dutch 801 and Swiss 701: A Times variant and a Helvetica variant.

- ❦ Android OS has three font families: Droid Sans, Droid Sans Mono and Droid Serif and this includes the Nook Tablet and Kindle Fire.

The Kindle, Nook, and Sony choices may be easily readable on their devices. But they certainly do not provide good typographic choices for a designer.

Your only real font choices [outside the iPad & iPhone] are serif or sans, plus you can add italic and bold: The problem, of course, is that serif or sans were not a font choice in InDesign 5.5 or earlier. The good news is that InDesign CS6 now adds those choices automatically when you export to ePUB.

Embedded fonts: Nook and Kindle Fire both take embedded fonts, but licenses which cover ePUB use are virtually non-existent at this point. It will come though.

However, we must remember the ebooks using the currently limited choices are selling like crazy. Kindle has a huge majority of the overall market. If you want to sell to that market, you need to make a book that fits their paradigm. In my case, non-fiction about InDesign and font design sell about equally on iBooks and Kindle (plus print is still about a third of sales).

Size & Leading changes

We have quite a bit of control here. In an ePUB the font sizing and spacing must be specified in ems or pixels. InDesign is doing it in ems in CS6 [5.5 not so much]. Basically, 12 point type is converted to one em. Leading is converted to a multiple of that em. On the iPad's high resolution screen, one em is actually 16 pixels high (I guess that's 32 pixels for the Retina). [But the reader can change it all by whim—though the size proportions will remain.]

Sᴍᴀʟʟ Cᴀᴘs & All CAPS now work

Of course, the fonts used do not have true small caps, in most cases. So, any typographically excellent true small caps would have to be in fonts that have them like Copperplate & Bodoni 72 Small Caps.

No special fonts: convert to graphic

If you need a special font, you need to make it into a graphic. Sometimes selecting the words and choosing Create Outlines will do it. But the resulting rasterized graphic will likely be a bad size and very pixilated. Normally, it is necessary to make a separate PDF graphic with that type to rasterize into Photoshop. Then save as a Web graphic and place into your ePUB document. You will be doing this a lot—at least until ebook readers & distributors accept SVG vector files.

Embedding fonts has many legal issues: You need to be careful which fonts you use. Though you can embed any font you have on your computer—there are two major problems. First, it is not likely that any font you have has been hinted for 72 dpi use. Second, none of the major distribution sites like MyFonts have decided on an ePub license. So, if there is any doubt (and believe me there is), do not embed fonts unless you are sure you own the rights and that it will look good.

Remove all indents, left and right: from lists

Lists still do not translate well. All you can do is delete all special indents you set up. Make it a numbered or bulleted list (with no special bullet) and let InDesign do the translation. Not good, but anything else requires you to crack the code and set up special CSS rules for the ol and ul tags. You cannot even make li classes in the export tags dialog to control fonts and such. InDesign ignores all of this for lists. [Waiting for CSNext]

Eliminate fancy bullets: from lists

You must crack the ePUB and change the CSS to use special bullets—either from CSS choices or graphics.

Add chapter breaks before a section gets over 300K

Supposedly graphics are not counted here. But long files with no chapter breaks will not work. You must set up a H1 style (usually your headline) and specify it as the chapter break.

Eliminate all soft returns.

You must crack the ePUB and change the HTML to add the soft returns. You will get rid of all of them when exporting the ePUB.. **But understand,** soft returns are a real problem when the reader can change fonts and font sizes at will while he or she is reading.

Eliminate all OpenType feature use

Nothing can be done about this. Current ebook readers do not support OpenType features—yet. However, they will. It is part of the HTML5/CSS3 scenario and therefore usable in the ePUB standard.

Eliminate tabs & tables: or rework the code

Put your tabular materials in a separate InDesign file and export it as a PDF to rasterize and place into your ePUB document. The resulting pixilated type is the same problem we have been dealing with throughout this exercise. HTML/CSS does not support tabs so you'll need to do tables in the code.

A table is a set of zero leading returns to add a new text frame with a specified offset. InDesign 5.5 will export the tables, but they will look bad with all borders and backgrounds deleted or changed. CS6 does better and HTML/CSS do good tables, but InDesign isn't excellent yet. You will probably want to edit the code or set up an InDesign doc for the table, make a PDF, and rasterize it in Photoshop 600 pixels wide.

InDesign CS6 has improved table export quite a bit: I have not worked much with this so far, but here is the official Adobe word on this feature. They have added support for converting InDesign's table cell styles to CSS in the exported EPUB. The EPUB table dimensions now include attributes for column width and row minimum height. I'll blog about this once I get time to try it. So far, simple tables seem to work well

Eliminate paragraph rules

HTML/CSS does not support rules though you do have border controls. InDesign drops any rules upon export at this time. The only rules you have available are Underline and Strikethrough without any customizing allowed.

If you need the rules, you can create graphics that you can place before and/or after your paragraphs. The only problem with that is the lack of spacing control. Plus there is no way to do an overlap so you cannot have a rule as a bar from which the type reverses out to white. For that you need to edit the code and set the background, alignment, and padding for the paragraph

Eliminate borders

You can only use borders on a graphic. The ePUB readers cannot put borders on a frame. For CS5.5, to add a border to a paragraph or group of paragraphs you need to edit the HTML and often add a div in the code. For CS6, you can add a stroke, fill, and corner options to your frames holding your graphics. InDesign still rasterizes them into graphics, but at least the look is there.

CS5.5 & better now work with nested styles

Prior to 5.5, we had to hand format any character styles by selecting the type and applying the style. Now you can use nested styles. In the exported ePUB they are converted to spans which you can control with the Export Tags dialog. Of course, you need to do all the changes to make those character styles work in an ePUB.

Making these changes & proofing

What needs to be done now is to go through all the styles used in your print document and convert them to work within ePUB limitations. Then export your ePUB and open it in Adobe Digital Editions—Adobe's free ePUB reader and Ibis—Safari Books Online's online browser reader. Ibis shows many things that ADE doesn't. Calibre works also. But none of these options compares with what you will actually see in the ereader. You can set the export options to automatically open your ePUB after it is exported.

 If you own an iPad, Nook, and/or Kindle [Fire]: open the ePUB in it to see how it will look there. Make sure you import a copy of the ePUB into your iPad. Letting iTunes get a hold of your original ePUB adds some sort of plist code that negates the validation of the ePUB [that may be fixed in iBooks2, I haven't checked]. It is especially important to check out the graphics and see how they fit. Adjust spacing as well as you possibly can.

If you are typographically trained and visually sensitive, this first attempt at an ePUB will be a horrible shock: The typographic ugliness of HTML after you have so carefully crafted your typography is a major hit to the senses. No kerning, tracking, or careful spacing. All the controls are very crude—displayed on a low resolution screen.

Take a deep breath!

Now get on with it: You've learned to deal with the low quality as far as Websites are concerned. [If you haven't—shame on you!] This is the reality of ePUB. Now your goal is to make it as easy to read as possible. Make the window narrow enough to be readable and go to it. It is likely that your first attempts will require you to fix several of your styles. Thankfully, they control the entire document globally because everything is formatted with no local formatting. This is yet another reason why the use of styles is so critical.

Deal with reality

Do not hang on to impossible requirements. The more simple you make your typography, the better it will work in this greatly restricted environment. There is nothing wrong with ePUB and the ePUB standard. It is simply different and requires a new sense of design. As InDesign improves we will have more control.

ePUB does give us much more

If we quit looking at ePUBs from the background of the printed book and start looking from the background of ebooks, then we can see how much we have available in an ePUB—especially in iBooks2 and Ibis. Just focus on readability: go easy on the bold, italic, and small type. If your readers have to work at reading your book, they'll try changing the size—but more likely they'll just quit reading.

Setting the TOC (THIS IS REQUIRED)

This is a very important part of setting up your styles. ePUBs do not support page breaks—with one exception. If you have a style set up as a headline, with the keeps set up to start on the next page, the ePUB will start a new chapter when you use that paragraph style. But you must choose it when you export the ePUB. You find this choice in the ePUB

Export Options dialog box: Break Document at Paragraph Style with a popup menu to pick the style.

> **One problem I have had:** Because I have h2 & h3 based on h1, I have found that I need to make sure that the styles chosen for h2 and h3 (used in the TOC) have the "starts on new page" option turned off in Keeps. Otherwise, every time h1, h2, or h3 is used you will get a page break. I'm starting to base h1 and h3 on h2 which solves the problem. I can then turn on start new page for H1 without affecting h2 or h3.

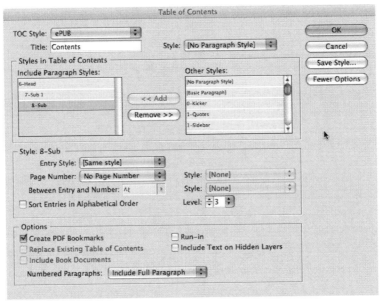

You do need to set up a TOC (Layout>> Table of Contents). You will chose this Table of Contents style in the ePUB Export dialog. The styles you choose for your TOC will be added to the bookmarks in the column to the left of your ePUB. You do not do leaders or page numbers as leaders do not work and page numbers do not exist in ebooks [more accurately the page numbers change all time as the reader changes fonts and/or type size].

Practicality rules in these things. You can spend time and money trying to figure out why these things are so or you can publish books.

I publish.

Another potential problem: I originally had two styles I have mapped to h2 and two styles mapped to h3. I also chose No Page Number, which also turns off the leader. However, the ePUBs would not validate. I kept getting cryptic messages about TOC entries missing. I finally had to delete all the TOC entries except for h1, h2, and h3 to get the ePUB to validate. [It turns out it was actually a bug. Lately I have eliminated all TOC listings except for the chapter heads.] You simply need to test your results.

Writing the metadata (THIS IS REQUIRED)

You need to write the metadata before you export the ePUB. As you can see below, this is just partially completed in most cases. The important things here are the title,

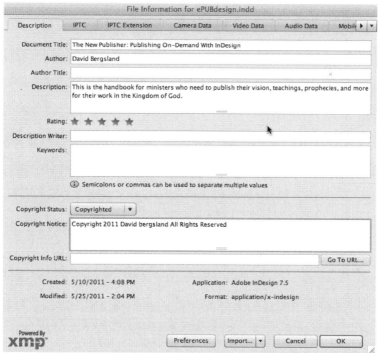

description, and keywords. Hopefully, you worked all this out when you released your book for print. You find this dialog in the File menu under the File Info command. It is required to fill out this description page. It contains the information primarily used by the search engine spiders.

There are some new strict rules

These rules are Apple's rules, as far as I can tell. However, some of them may be Lulu paranoia. It doesn't matter. Do what they ask. You do want to sell your ePUBs, right? They include things like the metadata title must be identical to the copy found on the cover. It must be in title case except for a half dozen or so tiny words. There are several others things like this.

Here are just a few from Lulu's page:

- **Title must match everywhere:** metadata, cover, and book's title page
- **No advertisements or links.**
- **No mention of included materials that don't exist in the digital product (Example:** CD, poster, etc.).
- **Cannot up-sell to a version of the product that is more complete.**
- **Do not use character which require entity references in the description (Example:** &, -, or –, etc.)
- **Do not use font sizes in the description (Example:** <font face="Helvetica" size="3">)
- **Cannot mislead buyers or misrepresent the ebook (Example:** An illustrated guide containing no illustrations or pictures).
- **Subtitles are particularly important for differentiating multiple books in a series that share the same title.**
- **Improperly formatted HTML tags in the description can cause a garbled description in retail channels.**
- **Titles and Subtitles incorrectly capitalized. The first letter of all words in the title and subtitle should be capitalized, except for the following words:** a, an, and, for, from, of, or, the, to. The first and last word of the title and subtitle should always be capitalized.
- **Use of HTML lists in description**
- **Titles beginning with articles should display properly. EX:** A Tale of Two Cities, not Tale of Two Cities, A
- **Must have a valid description. Ex:** Do not use the title.
- **Multiple blank pages. Especially at the beginning of the book. Please remember to remove blank pages before converting to ePUB**

There are many more like this on the *eBook Retail Distribution Guidelines* page of the Lulu site. If you do not follow all of them precisely, they will not publish your book.

Setting the Export Tags

New to InDesign CS5.5: As mentioned, this new ability to open a single dialog box and set all the HTML tags and add the CSS classes for each style is huge. It is a real disappointment that we cannot edit these class rules, but it makes it much easier to edit the CSS. CS6 is good enough for me, now.

Edit All Export Tags

Show: ● EPUB and HTML ○ PDF

Style	Tag	Class
[No Paragraph Style]	p	none
¶ [Basic Paragraph]	p	basic
¶ 0–Kicker	h5	kicker
¶ 1–Quotes	p	quote
¶ 1–SidebarBody	p	sidebar
¶ 2–body	p	standard
¶ 2–Description	p	indented
¶ 2–No first	p	nofirst
¶ 2–run–in	p	nested
¶ 3–bullet–tabbed	li	tabbed
¶ 3–Bulleted	li	sans
¶ 3–Numbered	li	serif
¶ 4–BoldSideHead	h4	side
¶ 5–Tips	p	nestedindent
¶ 6–Head	h1	chapter
¶ 7–Sub 1	h2	normal
¶ 8–9(WavyRule)	h3	italic
¶ 8–Sub	h3	normal
¶ TripleNested	p	triple
A Blue	strong	blue
A 1–bodyBOLD	strong	serif
A 1–Head Bold	strong	bold
A 2–Italic	em	italic
A 3–ListRegular	strong	regular
A 3–Version	strong	small
A Page#	em	small
A Red	strong	red

OK

Cancel

I still suggest Automatic, with no class but the word is that CS6 has fixed lists.

You can use what you see I set to the left as you experiment. I'll post more specific techniques in Font Design & Typography On-Demand.

Forcing InDesign to write usable CSS

Sometimes I feel so stupid. The solution to the incomplete CSS in exported ePUBs for 5.5 and 6 is so much more simple than I thought. Your mind just seems to turn a little corner and the solution pops up in front of you.

My beef with InDesign CS5.5's ePUBs was the need to edit the CSS. I've posted several times on my blog and published a couple free booklets about fixing the ePUB CSS (It's also in Appendix F, if you are still in CS5.5). What I wrote was accurate. It's not difficult, as long as you know HTML and CSS and can work in Dreamweaver to fix this stuff. But my frustration is that I don't think you should be forced into DW to make an ePUB. It turns out that what I wrote simply is not necessary in most cases.

You can easily force InDesign CS5.5 to write good CSS ▪

Well, that's a bit of an overstatement. The Web developer purists will be shrieking. But, you can easily make InDesign write CSS that controls all of your type in the ePUB. The problem is that InDesign does not define the basic tags: h1-6, p, ol, ul, and so on. It may in CS6, but I still use the tag.class naming procedure described below.

What I suggested before is that you map your tags so that all you need to do is open the CSS in Dreamweaver and add definitions for all the basic tags you need. That still works. And in many ways that is still the way to go for reasons we'll mention in a bit.

However, you can easily force InDesign to write CSS rules that will control all of your type without the need to edit the CSS afterward. What you need to do is make sure that you specify a class for all your styles as well as a tag. Let's take a look at what I just exported for the ePUB for Writing in InDesign. I opened the Edit All Export Tags… dialog and set up the tags and classes you can see them on the previous page.

Notice I added tags for all the styles. For the lists I was using li plus classes, but this is still dropped upon export in CS6. InDesign adds the ul and ol tags for CSS lists, but we have no way to edit them in InDesign. You need to leave them as [Automatic] for now.

The same is true with all the tags for tables (though CS6 captures Cell Style data). If I want any fancy sidebar rules with backgrounds and reversed type and all of that, I'll still need to edit the CSS.

But this will work, and it will look remarkably close to what I see in InDesign. I'm waiting for CSNext to get more control. I'm tired of editing the CSS in Dreamweaver.

What changed are the basic tags

I used to make my heading h1 with no class. Now I have added a class of chapter. I used to make my first level of subhead (Style 7-Sub 1) h2, now I add a class of normal. Even my basic paragraph tag (Style: 2-Body) is now given a class of standard (or normal).

Why add the classes?

That's simple. InDesign will not define p, my basic paragraph tag. But it will define p.normal. It will not define h2, but it will define h2.normal. Is the result wonderfully sleek and elegant XHTML code? No. But it works and all of your typography is controlled. If you do not do this, you are forced to crack the ePUB, open template.css and add the basic tags.

So, the choice is yours. You can now design your ePUB edition of your book in InDesign and directly upload the resultant ePUB with no modifications. The results will look very good.

It is never quite that easy: bad fonts

The problem is that during the massive conversion from your print version to your ePUB version it is extremely likely that you have many styles or locally formatted type that use fonts you cannot use in an ePUB. I was looking at the CSS for the first proof of the ePUB and at the bottom I found many spans asking for fonts I was certain I was not using.

Here we see the Find Font dialog box (Type>> Find Font...) for the InDesign file I used for one of my font design ePUBs. As you can see, the top listings (there were actually sixteen of them) are fonts I didn't want to use in my ePUB, *because* almost every ereader would substitute them out into its defaults. Obviously this is real problem with an ereader like the Nook which only has three fonts available. More importantly, you must be sure it is legal for you to use them. None of these sixteen fonts are available on any ereader unless I am using a browser-based ereader (like Ibis) on my own computer where these fonts are installed.

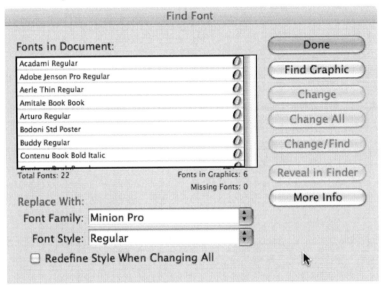

For this ePUB there were about ten of these errant fonts. I carefully decided what to do with each one of those instances. If I click the More Info button you can see on the opposite page in the Find Font dialog, it will show me the page location of the font use. Once I locate the font flagged in the actual copy of the book, I find I have three choices:

- ❦ It may be in a paragraph or character style that was never redefined: In that case I can redefine the style and eliminate the font usage very easily.

- ❦ It may be in a graphic: In this case it is usually large enough to convert to outlines and then make a rasterized version of the graphic.

- ❦ It may be part of the copy: This will probably not happen to you unless you are like me and write about typography and fonts. In this case, I can select the type and Create Outlines—leaving the outlines type inline in the copy. That will work, but InDesign will convert that outlined type into a coarse bitmap that looks pretty chewed up. Your best choice (for quality) is to rasterize that type in Photoshop and save it as a high quality JPEG at 300 dpi. You can then place that high resolution bitmap graphic inline in your copy and it will look as good as possible.

Many of these things will be solved in CSNext or CSNext+1. But for now. This is what you need to do. Once you have your fonts cleaned up and your export tags set, you can export your ePUB. Type Command+E and select ePUB for your format.

The ePUB export box

With InDesign 5.5, the ePUB export dialog gives us a lot of tools and options as we fight to control our output. There are three pages and many things you need to set. CS6 ramps it up even higher with the choices for EPUB 2.0.1, EPUB 3.0, and EPUB 3.0 with Layout.

At this point, only ePUB 2 works because that is all the distributors are accepting. This will change though. EPUB 3.0 with Layout uses all the possibilities of Liquid Layout and the other new HTML5/CSS3 capabilities added in CS6. No one can read this yet except for a vaporware Adobe Reader which is not available yet.

I am including captures which are set up the way that is working for me currently. This entire area is changing by the week, so any updates will be mentioned in my blogs.

The general page

Let's go through these in order

This has all changed radically since CS5.5. Things are moved. New options are available. Adobe is working hard to keep current with a field that is changing so rapidly.

Version: EPUB 2.0.1: This is still the standard and nothing else is accepted by Lulu or Nook. This will change.

Setup

Cover: The choices are None, Rasterize First Page and Choose Image. Once you choose an image that changes to From File as you see above. I design a specific front cover to be used and link it here. That way I can set it up in vector with live type and so on. Just remember to use a JPEG for the cover, at this point. I also place a copy of the cover on page one of the book so it shows up as the first page in the ePUB. TOC Style: You need to choose the one you have set up for your ePUBs. As you can see I call mine ePUB.

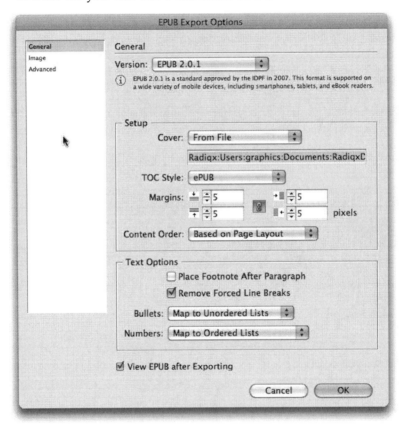

Book margin: I set this at 5 pixels, but no one actually seems to use this setting [so leaving it at 0 is probably all right]. I've heard that Nook requires specific settings, but I've heard no complaints about the ePUBs I give them and they are still a small part of my market. I'll change if they ask me to.

Content Order: I use based on page layout. I can do this because I completely re-layout the ePUB version in a new document. Also I do not write XML. I find the articles panel does not give me the control I want. I always place my graphics, for example, in specific locations to read as part of the copy. I do the same with the converted sidebars and all the rest. If your book is simple, you may not need to do this. You'll need to experiment and carefully proof the resulting ePUB to see if the other options work best for you.

Text Options:

Remove Forced Line Breaks: That's what they are calling soft returns. You must remove them because the type re-wraps horribly when the readers change the size and font (and they will). When InDesign CS6 removes these soft returns it replaces them with a space. That is almost always what you want. But check and make sure.

Bullets & Numbers: Leave them at the defaults [letting InDesign do the mapping]. This is the choice which InDesign uses to add the ul and ol tags. As mentioned, you really need to eliminate all special indents and tabs and let the defaults carry the day. Other than that, you will need to crack the ePUB and edit the CSS file.

View after Exporting: Always check this. Always look over the exported ePUB in ADE or Calibre before you validate and upload. You also need to check in iBooks. Increasingly, I check it out in Ibis, the browser-based ereader from Safari Books Online. It seems to show me the best I can hope for until we get better ereaders. I am still regularly surprised by something that needs to be fixed.

This is not a smooth process yet. It is really good that InDesign can now export ePUBs that can be validated. But it is not smooth yet—and probably not be uneventful until InDesign 9 or 10. But then that is still true for the print versions also and I've been doing that for decades.

The image page

There are no real changes here from 5.5. Again, 5.5 was a large improvement about these things. But there is really no direct guidance. I will share what I know from experience. You may well find new information available by the time you buy this book. I will keep this info updated whenever I hear of new data. Please share it with us if you hear anything.

Finding out information on images is like trying to pull hens' teeth (and no, they don't have teeth). No one seems to want to admit how bad the images really are. The best I can find is that the iPad and most smart phones require 600x800 pixels or less.

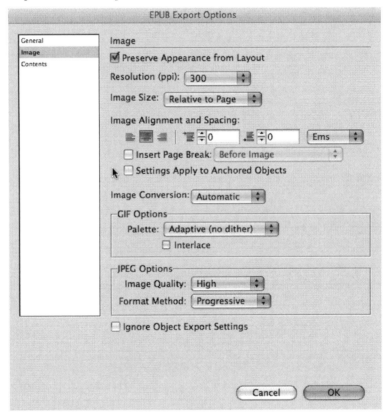

The iPad maximum is 600x860 pixels. Nook's maximum size is 600x730 pixels. For Fire it is 600x800. At this point, I make my images to size, and JPEG [in most cases]. I make them wide enough to fit the column of type and place them as inline graphics (unanchored). I do this to get as much help as I can with image sharpness. For photos, you can make them smaller and have them work OK. But, if you need detail make them as large as possible, and that is 600 wide portrait, and 800 wide landscape. The InDesign automated conversion processes trash the graphics. So, I open them in Photoshop and use Save For Web... to save them as JPEGs.

For print, I use PSDs (Photoshop's native format) at 300 dpi. I keep the original PSDs in case I want to go back to the way the image was before the JPEG compression. Then I save JPEG versions at 600 pixels wide to use in the ePUB. This doubles for iPad with Retina (if you can afford the larger file sizes).

Preserve Appearance from Layout: I check this but I am not sure why. It seems to help certain images in iBooks. However, I am continuing to experiment with it. I'll post new knowledge in The Skilled Workman. You need to experiment also.

 Remember, ebook graphics are ghastly: I continue to fight the good fight, but you really need to question why you are even including graphics. The iPad does a good job, but the ePUB format itself does not support graphic excellence. The eventual support of SVG (vector) graphics should help solve these problems. But that's only available in iBook Author, at this point. Of course there is now the hope that the high resolution of the new iPad will really help.

Resolution (ppi): 300—you need the highest resolution possible to look good on the better machines like the Retina Displays of the iPad and the iPhones. I imagine the other tablets won't be quite as good, but they will be getting better. If the file size gets too large, I cut it to 150 ppi.

Image size: The choices are Fixed and Relative to Page. I now use Relative to Page, and this seems to make good graphics that are the width of the page. I want them the width of the page because they are basically low-res bitmap images. I want them as large as possible to be readable.

Image Alignment and Spacing: Because my images are all inline the alignment is controlled by the paragraph style used and that is flush left, so I don't expect any changes when I click the Left button here. It doesn't make any difference as I make all my images the width of the column. I leave the spacing at the defaults and use auto leading for the special paragraph style I set up to hold my images.

Insert page break: Before Image, After Image, or Both Before and After Image. I've never used it, but I can see its utility.

Image Conversion: I leave this at automatic, and set the JPEG options to High. The image quality in ePUBs is bad enough without any JPEG artifacts produced by compressing the JPEGs too far. However, for my font design book (with nearly 300 graphics) this made my ePUB nearly 20 MB. So, I changed the quality to medium and set the resolution at 150 dpi. Because the images are almost all screen captures, the new ePUB looks very good on the iPad. You must do what you need to do to get the best images possible.

Ignore Object Export Settings: I leave it unchecked because I do not set custom settings for any image—yet. The problem is

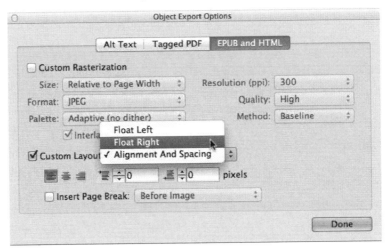

that Object Export Settings are needed to control anchored objects as sidebars. This is where you add a float to an object to make it align on the left or right margin of your ePUB. The problem is that the control are still rudimentary in CS6. Plus, you usually need a full-sized graphic to get enough pixels to make it readable.

These will be the controls for anchored text frames used as sidebars. But they are not quite ready for prime time yet. You still have to crack the ePUB and edit the CSS.

Advanced page

This last page is very important and it's changed radically from 5.5. It used to be called Contents.

Split Document: You need to pick your headline style or whatever style you use to start your chapters on a new odd page. This is working well.

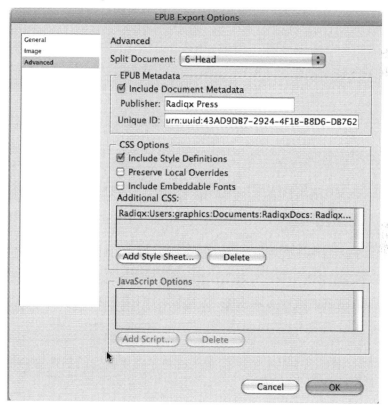

EPUB Metadata

Check Include Metadata: For Publisher:, use your company name. Let InDesign generate the Unique ID.

CSS Options

Check Include Style Definitions: This will write the styles you are using into CSS.

Make sure you uncheck "Preserve Local Overrides" and "Include Embedded Fonts": The local overrides will greatly complicate your code. It will add a lot of spans. That said I may start using this as I go ahead. Only Nook and Fire support embedded fonts—yet (and there are bad licensing issues). However, as embedded fonts are the only hope for Android machines, they are coming quickly.

Additional CSS: This requires coding. It may be the best solution but I haven't done much with it yet. But as you'll see in Appendix F, I was working on it hard. My hope was to have a sample CSS file you can use with the sample styles I have you set upon the Website. I'm not making any promises because I really dislike Coding. If InDesign gets good enough I want to be able to simply export and end up with usable ePUBs. At this point, it is close enough so I am no longer worrying about this.

If you link to a CSS file, I would uncheck the "Include Style Definitions" option. You wouldn't want to confuse the poor program.

Click OK and you've got an ePUB

It will open in ADE, Calibre, (or your reader of choice). Proof it carefully. Redo as necessary. By now you'll have a good idea what is translating well.

Edit the CSS if you can (or don't if you can't)

If this is possible for you, (or if you are still using CS5.5) read Appendix F for some basic instructions.

The problem is that even with CS5.5 the resulting CSS has some major issues. With CS6 things are much better. Of course, you must know CSS to do anything about it. But some of the things are relatively easy.

- Make sure the font choices are good: I would double-check to at least make sure that the serif and sans serif names are correct. Then make them work for the fonts in the iPad list.

- Define the basic HTML tags: InDesign does not do this in CS5.5. It defines all the classes you set up in the Export Tags dialog, but the basic tags are not defined (unless you force it to with classes as I mentioned earlier).

☙ Do anything else you can figure out from Castro's *ePUB Straight to the Point*: It all depends on how comfortable you are with code, HTML, and CSS. You can open the whole folder as a site in Dreamweaver. Edit carefully, and work on a copy if you are not good with the code.

Validate it ▪

Redo the proof as often as necessary. When you have what you like, go to: http://validator.idpf.org/

It should validate. The only real problem is that Lulu is still using ePUB Check 1.2 and the validator site is using the beta of version 3. I finally gave up and found an older version of ePUB Check 1.2 (googled it). But both Lulu and validator. idpf.org are getting much better about this and increasingly they let you know what is causing the problem in a manner you can understand (this was not true a year ago).

Upload to Lulu

If it does validate, then you can start a new ebook project at Lulu. As I've mentioned they are an official aggregator for iBookstore. They will give you an ISBN# and get your ePUB listed on iBookstore.

Upload to PubIt!

You can use the same ePUB you produced for Lulu. But now I recommend a new version. I'm going to try embedded fonts. [I won't have a technique for that until InDesign On-Demand 2nd Edition With CS6 comes out in the Summer of 2012.]At the least, you should check your graphics to make sure that none are taller than 730 pixels. You cannot use Lulu's ISBN (but PubIt does not require one). You'll need a cover with a different resolution.

Converting to Kindle

Until very recently, I gave some very explicit instructions for the construction of the HTML and CSS needed to step back in time to Amazon's MOBI format. It was extremely limited in what was allowed.

Designers are rarely good coders, and writers even less so. InDesign is the best tool we have at present, but there's still a long way to go until some of the typographic niceties we rely on in print are actually available in an ePUB without a lot of hand-coding.

I used Calibre to convert my ePUBs

But this was before I could embed fonts. Now I'm using the Amazon InDesign plug-in for CS5.5 [at the time of this release the new plug-in for CS6 has not been released. If you do not embed fonts, you simply add your ePUB to Calibre and use it to convert your ePUB to MOBI. Google Calibre. It's a free app (shareware, actually).

This week I am experimenting with embedding my own fonts. If you embed fonts, you cannot use Calibre to convert your ePUB. It is locked (to protect the fonts from theft) and Calibre thinks it has DRM. So this book's Kindle version used the plug-in for CS5.5.

For the Amazon InDesign plug-in

You need to start by doing all the conversions we talked about for building an ePUB. The KF8 format is a Kindle/Amazon proprietary product, and therefore, it is not Adobe's responsibility to build around it. It is entirely Amazon's responsibility to provide any necessary plug-ins to work with InDesign (which they have done but the CS6 plug-in is not released yet, April 2012).

The Kindle plug-in for InDesign works well for what it does, but it is only useful if you are using ID to build a document with the single purpose of exporting that file to MOBI for use on the Kindle (Legacy e-ink and Fire). You can use the document you created for ePUB export to start with.

- ❧ The plugin only recognizes the most basic of text formatting and anchored images: (but we've already covered that with ePUB design).

- ❧ It cannot handle nested styles: so all run-in heads will need to be formatted by hand.

- ❧ It does do a good job of creating working hyperlinks: based on properly built cross-refs, hyperlinks, ID-generated TOC, and footnotes.

- ❧ It does do a good job of embedding fonts: Of course, this assumes that you have fonts with a license which allows you to embed them in an ebook.

- ❧ The plug-in will add eBook section breaks based on separate InDesign files only: It does not recognize InDesign's ability to add breaks via Paragraph style. This is a big problem for those of us doing larger graphically intensive books. We'll need to break our ePUB file in pieces and use the Book panel again.

- ❧ The plug-in will also only recognize content order based on the old-school way of ordering: single text thread with inline images. It does not recognize the use of the Articles Panel.

Bottom line for kindle plug-in use:

- ❧ The Kindle plug-in for InDesign is ONLY useful if your document/project is intended for Kindle only: For that purpose, it works well.

I still recommend Calibre conversions unless you are embedding fonts for the Kindle Fire

You need to download a copy of the Kindle Previewer from Amazon to see the fonts (unless you own a Fire). The Kindle apps for OSX and iOS5 do not show the embedded fonts. So, it's still iffy.

If I release this book before I come up with a new procedure, subscribe to The Skilled Workman or Font Design & Typography On-Demand. I'll keep you up to date on these blogs as new things develop.

F: ePUB CSS Repair

Once you have your ePUB

It will open in your default ereader (Adobe Digital Editions?). Proof it carefully. Redo as necessary. Then drop a copy of the ePUB file onto iTunes and sync it into iBooks on your iPad to read it in iBooks. The reason you need to use a copy is that iTunes adds some weird plist file that prevents the ePUB from validating. This may no longer be true with iBooks2, but I have not bothered to check yet. Then open it in the Ibis reader at ibisreader.com. Then check it out in Calibre. Ibis and Calibre will give you a very good idea about what is really in the file. ADE and iBooks will not do this. But you need to know what ADE and iBooks look like because many people will be reading your ePUB in those apps. For example, Nook is a variation on ADE. By now you'll have a good idea what is translating well.

Editing the CSS if you can

Or don't if you can't. For CS6 I don't find it necessary. You do not have to edit the CSS, but until InDesign gives us controls within the app to control font use, styles use, div construction, text wrap, and all of that, fixing the CSS is a good idea.

You use Dreamweaver. It does not do much to help us either. EPUBs are like a little orphan child at this point where no one wants to deal with it on the software development level. Hopefully for CSNext...<sigh>

The first problem is compression

The problem with this has been the difficulty with decompressing the .epub file and then recompressing back into .epub. Evidently this is no real problem on a PC, but I'm not going there. On the Mac, some of the files which must be saved within the archive cannot be compressed. For that you will need a script. I recommend that you Google and download "ePUB Zip 1.0.2". It's an AppleScript that will let you simply drop the ePUB folder you get when you uncompress the ePUB onto the script icon to recompress it into an ePUB again. It has worked flawlessly so far. There are other solutions and you can research them, but this is the most simple at this point in time.

Looking at the uncompressed folder

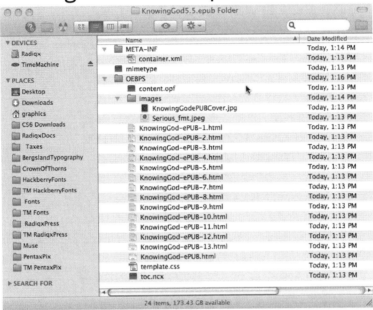

An ePUB is simply a zipped folder with a special extension. When you decompress the ePUB (I use StuffIt), it opens into a Folder.

The content looks something like what you see above.

Mimetype: As mentioned, one of the things within this folder cannot be compressed when you recompress it back into an ePUB. It is the mimetype file (which is just a single line of code—application/epub+zip—a coder thing). This is why you need the script just mentioned.

META-INF folder: You do not have to worry about this either. It works and that is all we care about. Coding purists like Liz Castro suggest some possible changes, but they are not necessary. InDesign CS5.5+ writes a file that works fine.

All the real content is in the OEBPS folder

Because the rest of the stuff in the ePUB does not concern us here, I ignore it when I open the ePUB pieces into a site in Dreamweaver. I open Dreamweaver; go under the site menu to Manage Sites...; make a new site with the OEBPS folder as the root folder; and click done. Dreamweaver will open this up so I can edit all the files I need to edit within the ePUB

Fonts folder: This is there if you embed fonts, but only Nook, & Kindle support embedded fonts. I have yet to find a list of fonts which are licensed for this. For example, MyFonts tells me they haven't decided how to handle this yet. So, we will not deal with that here.

Graphics folder: This folder contains all the linked graphics and the cover image.

The toc.ncx & content.opf files: Thankfully, CS5.5 seems to be writing good ones now. This is coding on a level I can't handle [or won't]. Do not touch is a good word here.

All the HTML files (XHTML for CS6)

These are the files generated upon export. They are supposed to have a .xhtml extension. You don't need to change it, but the coders are freaking. There is a new XHTML file for every chapter break headline you used. As you recall, one of the choices you made in 5.5 on the Contents page of the EPUB

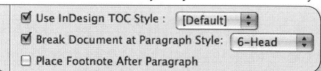

Export Options dialog was which paragraph style to use to break your document. As you can see above, I used 6-Head for my chapter/page breaks.

The result of that was a new XHTML file for each use of the chosen style. We did this because it is the only practical way to make page breaks in a variable media like an ePUB. The good news is that the resulting HTML documents are good, clean code. There are other ways to do this by editing the code. Check Liz Castro's book if this is a biggie for you.

Fixing the code

The first thing to do is take a look at the XHTML and see if it used the tags you wanted to use. If it did not you need to go back and fix the issues in the Edit All Export Tags... dialog box. This will set all the basic tags. The problem is that even with CS6 the resulting CSS has some major issues. Many of the issues are very obvious. And they come about because of the flexibility demanded by the paradigm. My problem is that I want more control than that.

Fixing the CSS if you didn't set the classes [PG 299]

When I look at the CSS file in Dreamweaver I immediately notice that several key rules are flat missing. For example, I had assigned my 8-Subhead2 style to h3. My 4-BodyHeads style is assigned to h3 with a class of small. When I look at the CSS generated, I see the rule for h3.small—but there is no definition for h3.

This is true throughout. No wonder my ePUBs were never what I expected. None of the twelve basic tags used (p, h1, h2, h3, h4, h5, h6, ul, ol, li, strong, or em) are defined unless you added a tag in Export Tags. So, the first thing I do is add definitions for those tags in the template.css file.

Make sure the font choices are good

Before I can do that, I need to change the font lists in Dreamweaver. The DW default font lists give us no real choices of any good-looking fonts [except for Palatino]. My suggestion is that you build your font lists out of fonts available to the iPad plus the Web-safe fonts.

We must remember that at this point, the big 3 ereaders all support embedded fonts (to some degree). The problem is getting fonts with a license that allows embedding in ePUBs. The Nook and Kindle (including Fire) defaults basically have only serif and sans-serif. But the iPad has 37 font families available in a reasonably versatile set.

First let's review the iPad list

With iOS5 the iPad supports 58 font families. However, out of these 163 fonts 37 of them in 17 families are Hebrew, Indic, Thai, Tibetan, Chinese, Japanese, or Arabic. So, there are really 126 fonts in 41 families which we can use for English and the rest of the European languages. The more complete descriptions and suggestions are in Appendix E, pages 269–274. Here I am just going to list them.

Not to be used:

Courier or New Courier. These eight fonts should never be used unless you are trying to look like a typewriter and do not care about reading the copy.

Fonts with compromised reader reactions: Bureaucratic fonts

Here are fonts that are not bad designs, but they have issues. I don't use them: Arial + a rounded style; Helvetica [6] & Helvetica Neue [11]; Times New Roman: This family has regular, italic, bold and bold italic.

Serif choices for body copy

* **Baskerville:** There are six choices—[Baskerville, Baskerville-Italic, Baskerville-Bold, and Baskerville-BoldItalic, plus Baskerville-SemiBold & Baskerville-SemiBoldItalic].
* **Bodoni 72:** [BodoniSvtySCITCTT-Book].
  Bodoni 72: [BodoniSvtyITCTT-Book, BodoniSvtyITCTT-BookIta, & BodoniSvtyITCTT-Bold]
  Bodoni 72 Oldstyle: [BodoniSvtyOSITCTT-Book, BodoniSvtyOSITCTT-BookIta, & BodoniSvtyOSITCTT-Bold]
* **Cochin:** [Cochin, Cochin-Italic, Cochin-Bold, & Cochin-BoldItalic]
* **Didot:** [Didot, Didot-Italic, and Didot-Bold]
* **Georgia:**[Georgia, Georgia-Italic, Georgia-Bold, & Georgia-BoldItalic]
* **Hoefler Text:** [HeoflerText, HeoflerText-Italic, HeoflerText-Black, and HeoflerText-BlackItalic]
* **Palatino:** There are four choices—[Palatino-Roman, Palatino-Italic, Palatino-Bold, and Palatino-BoldItalic]

Sans serif choices for body copy

* **Futura:** [Futura-Medium & Futura-MediumItalic].
* **Futura:** [Futura-CondensedMedium & Futura-CondensedExtraBold]

- ✤ **Gill Sans:** [GillSans-Light, GillSans-LightItalic, GillSans, GillSans-Italic, GillSans-Bold, and GillSans-BoldItalic]..
- ✤ **Optima:** [Optima-Regular, Optima-Italic, Optima-Bold, and Optima-BoldItalic, plus Optima-ExtraBlack]
- ✤ **Trebuchet MS:** [TrebuchetMS, TrebuchetMS-Italic, TrebuchetMS-Bold, and TrebuchetMS-BoldItalic]
- ✤ **Verdana:** [Verdana, Verdana-Italic, Verdana-Bold, and Verdana-BoldItalic]

Stylish display options
- ✤ **Academy Engraved LET:** [AcademyEngraveLETPlain]
- ✤ **American Typewriter:** [AmericanTypewriter-CondensedLight, AmericanTypewriter-Light, AmericanTypewriter, AmericanTypewriter-Condensed, AmericanTypewriter-Bold, AmericanTypewriter-CondensedBold]
- ✤ **Bradley Hand:** [BradleyHandITCTT-Bold]
- ✤ **Chalkboard SE:** [ChalkboardSE-Light, ChalkboardSE-Regular, and ChalkboardSE-Bold]
- ✤ **Chalkduster:** [Chalkduster]
- ✤ **Copperplate:** [Copperplate-Light, Copperplate, and Copperplate-Bold]
- ✤ **Marion:** [Marion-Regular, Marion-Italic, and Marion-Bold]
- ✤ **Marker Felt:** [MarkerFelt-Thin & MarkerFelt-Wide]
- ✤ **Noteworthy:** [Noteworthy-Light & Noteworthy-Bold]
- ✤ **Papyrus:** [Papyrus & Papyrus-Condensed]
- ✤ **Party LET:** [PartyLetPlain]
- ✤ **Snell Roundhand:** [Snell Roundhand, Snell Roundhand-Bold, & Snell Roundhand-Black]
- ✤ **Zapfino**

Remember! Apple can change these at whim. Plus, the reader can change fonts at will: Reflow is the goal. That trumps typography in an ebook.

Setting up Dreamweaver with usable sets

I can't even show you the default sets because I have deleted all the ones that use bureaucratic fonts and fonts I don't like. I suggest you do the same.

As you can see below, after I delete the ones I do not use I really only have four choices left (and I should delete the Courier choice also as I never use it).

There are a couple of things you need to understand here. First of all you need to add the font names as I listed them on the previous pages. If there are two or more words, you need to enclose them with quotes like this: "Gill Sans".

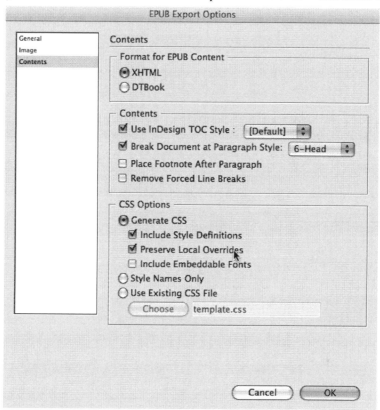

Secondly, you need to plan these things out. As you know, these lists give the browser or ereader font choices to make in order of priority. For example, in the Palatino default above (as set up by DW), I only get Palatino on my computer because I do not have Palatino Linotype or Book Antiqua installed. You need to help the reader here. The lists are much more simple in an ePUB, because only the iPad has any real choices.

Thirdly, DW does not allow you to reorder a list once you have added the font. If you do not like the order, you'll be forced to delete and start over.

Other than that the process is obvious. You simply type in the font name and click the double left arrow (<<).

To remove a font you click the double-right arrow button. If you are like me it will take a few trial runs for each list.

Some recommendations

- ✤ Always include a Web-safe font: depending on the ereader used, you may well be on either a Mac or a PC. If you are using a browser-based ereader like Ibis (one of the best) then your choices will be governed by the fonts installed on your computer.

- ✤ Always include a generic choice: Remember, Nook and Kindle (and other dedicated ereaders) only have two choices, serif and sans serif—unless you embed fonts [and that's very iffy at this point]. So even if you use cursive or fantasy for your generic, I would always add the sans/serif choice last.

My current Dreamweaver lists are shown below. I modify these quite regularly as I find more fonts available. Eventually, I will be adding special, custom fonts when I get fonts I can use. CS6 now does a good job with @font-face and will embed whatever you want it embed. But the licensing issues are not nearly resolved.

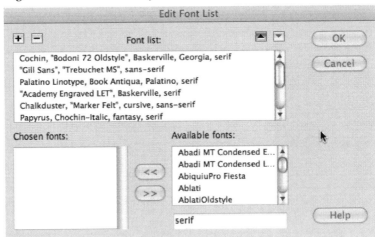

Repairing the CSS

The first thing to do is decompress your ePUB and take a look at the rules defined by InDesign upon export. As you are looking, remember that you can fix much of this by going back and adjusting the Export All Tags dialog box and reexporting your ePUB. This is a long process as you begin to get control over your ePUBs.

My goal is to make it more simple for you. But there will be many things you try that do not work in actual practice. Do not be discouraged, try and test until you are satisfied. Eventually, our goal is to have a standard set of files in InDesign with consistent remapping to the exported tags and a standardized [named].css file you can use in the Export ePUB dialog box in InDesign. But that will take a little bit of time and effort. I'm not there yet. This book will be my first attempt at standardization for me. To be honest, CS6 has enabled me to not worry about this at all.

Here are some mapping tricks

- Lists: You cannot map to ol or ul. You will be adding these definitions to your CSS file, but when mapping from InDesign you map to li.

  If you are like me and use your sans choice for numbered lists and your serif choice for your bulleted lists then you might want to map your exports to an li with a class of serif or sans.

- Multiple lists: I have a bulleted sidebar list style, for example, that is smaller. So, I am mapping that to li.small to give me control over that.

- Character styles: You do not want to use span as your choice in the Export Tags dialog. You want to use strong and em with as many classes as you need.

- Heads & subheads: You can be creative with your formatting of the h1–h6 tags, using multiple classes as necessary.

Check it out thoroughly

I really have a tendency to be lazy about this. As you go through this process, make sure you check out your ePUBs in various readers. ADE may be rough so far, but it is common and you need to see how your book looks in that environment. But the most important are the iPad and Nook (which uses an ADE variant). Kindle is much more limited, but the Fire has really ramped things up. [KF8 (Kindle Format 8) is basically an encapsulated ePUB]. But also check out your book in a good reader like Ibis. It's browser-based and it is good. Calibre also shows almost everything. Bookle is a new Mac-based browser ereader app that has people interested.

Most of the ereader options only show part of the CSS instructions. That is one of the most frustrating things about the current state of ePUB design. But it will surely get better quite quickly. There are too many ePUB sales to ignore.

Fixing the CSS

If you know CSS this is pretty straight forward. However, my books assume that you do not know a lot about coding so I will go through some simple explanations of some things the more advanced among you may find tedious.

❧ Adding the basic tags: you need to add p, h1–h6, ol, ul, li, strong and em unless you decide to use InDesign export to tags with classes capability. InDesign also does nothing for tables, when you need them.

You need to define them pretty tightly, but there is a difference here. We are talking about ePUBs, not Websites. You really need to be concerned with allowing enough reader freedom to modify the copy as they read.

On the other hand, you want to make the first impressions good, comfortable and easy to read [before they "mess things up" with their personal settings in their reader]. Remember the basic conceptual world of the book designer and typographer:

Your reader has far too much to read and will drop your writing as soon as possible unless it is easy to read & relevant to his or her life

356

Some things you may need to change

 Before we start, I must define an em for those of you who have forgotten: An em is a typographic blank space that is the square of the point size. In other words, 34-point type will have an em that is 34 points wide. It was used to define a size for characters and spacers that vary proportionally with the point size. Now you know how large an em space or em dash is. [An en is half as wide, but the same height.]

When exporting ePUBs, InDesign defines an em as 12 point type or leading. Everything is specified as a multiple of 12 points (even though the iPad uses 16 points to render that 12-point em).

❦ Type size: This is a variable for the person who is reading. But more than that, it varies by device. The actual size of the type will differ a lot between, iPhone, iPad, Blackberry, laptop and desktop. **So, you need to use ems for sizing & leading.** In CS6, this is covered for you.

❦ Spacing: For margins, padding, and indents we again need variable spacing. The width of devices changes radically.

For top and bottom measurements, ems work best. For right, left, and first line margins and indents you need to use %. Percentages are based on the window width and work much better for smartphones and the like.

❦ Indents: You may well need to adjust the first-line indent. In fact, for things like poetry and certain types of lists, you may need to go back to an old standby of early desktop publishing, making hanging indents by hand using code in a variation of this.

```
{font-size: 1em;
    margin: 0;
    margin-left: 10px;
    text-indent: -8px;
    }
```

- Divs are rare & tied to text location: It is really not possible to do double columns or anything approaching that with divs. All you can use are Float: Left, and Float: Right. Div widths need to be in percentages again.

  Divs are essential for images and many types of sidebars which need to be more narrow than the column width. You have to add them by hand to the HTML docs with one exception. InDesign defines a div for a group, as in an image grouped with a caption.

- Graphics are not Web graphics: It's XHTML, remember. So, for now, you are stuck with GIF, JPEG, and PNG. But you can do them high resolution. You need to do them in Photoshop.

  We talked about this earlier, but you must keep it in mind. InDesign's conversions are abysmal for the designer accustomed to print. For the high resolution JPEGs and PNGs I use Save As instead of Save For Web in Photoshop. It seems to give me better quality.

- Text wraps require HTML editing: You need to add a div to do it. Then you can set the alignment for the div.

- Headers as inline-blocks: This must be done because there is no widow or orphan control that works in all ereaders.

- Keeping captions with images requires a div: You also have to set those divs to display as an inline-block to keep a caption tied to its image.

 InDesign defines far too much: You need to understand that to maintain a cascade of styles (the ePUB variation of based-on styles) you should probably delete all properties that do not change from the parent rule (according to Liz).

Creating Sidebars

You can make inline sidebars by setting up borders, backgrounds, padding and so forth with an inline block. Or You can make separate divs with alignments for text wrap.

Inline sidebars

This is very easy to do in CSS. Set up a style in InDesign that you can map to one of the headers, say h3. Map it as h3.sidebar. Set up your indents, a background, margins and so forth. Make sure you set the padding to keep the type from getting too close to the edges. Proof and redo as needed. Ereader support varies.

You can do some of the fancy coding available in CSS3 like round corners, drop shadows, and gradients, But at this point you must do a lot of special coding for webkit and mozilla. That's a level of pain I don't want to deal with. You'll find that iBooks supports some of this, but most dedicated ereaders do not. This is one of the reasons I have been using Ibis a lot more recently.

Floating sidebars

Here you need to enclose your sidebar with a div. Set the div to float left or right. Set up the div as a percentage width of the ereader screen. Images within the div need to be set at a width percentage relative to the div—commonly 100% or close to that.

Mainly, you need to remember that while you have a fair amount of real estate on the iPad and similar tablets, for smart phones the width is a lot narrower. The iPhone Retina display helps a lot, but there is still very limited screen width.

Keeping the CSS as a default

This is still tedious. Gone are the days when you can simply design loosely—going with the flow, as it were. To get any real production speed, you need a set of styles you can add to your InDesign documents that will met all your normal needs. In fact, it should even cover regularly used uncommon needs like kickers, quotes, and such.

Then you need to have a standard set of mapping choices so that the exported styles are converted to CSS rules that are already defined in your CSS template. Your best hope for production speed is a personal common usage that you can remember habitually.

 This is still a work in process for me: As I have said repeatedly, the software and hardware has not nearly reached its potential at this point in early-2012. It will. There are many societal forces that will ensure it happens soon. **Keep current:** These things are changing all the time. I try to mention new changes at my blog: The Skilled Workman. Liz Castro does the same at hers: Pigs, Gourds, and Wikis. A List Apart and many others are good also. Twitter helps a lot. I use @davidbergsland for my typography & book design tweets.

Test, Proof, & Validate it

Redo the proof as often as necessary. Check it out in a variety of readers. Make sure that when you have what you like, you remember to validate the ePUB. I go to the validator at the International Digital Publishing Forum. It even validates ePUB3s: http://validator.idpf.org/

It should validate. If it does not, all I can do is pray you will be given information that will enable you to figure it out. The failure messages tend to be very cryptic. But both Lulu and IDPF are getting much better about this and letting you know what is causing the problem.

This is why CSS is not in my first book

This has all changed since I released *InDesign 7.5 On-Demand*. I'm not even going to bother to update that book until the next version of InDesign comes out. That is our best hope as far as I can see. CS6 has helped a bit, but there's a long ways to go.

All of this is much more pain and time spent than most designers are willing to put up with. You can sub-contract these conversions. But that costs money as well as time. My suggestion is that while we are waiting for transparent software solutions, the techniques mentioned here will get you by. But you should know that I just use export from InDesign CS6, at this point. When InDesign adds better features, I'll start using them then. They should be coming in CSNext—whenever that shows up.

Colophon:

This book has been written in my small office at the back of our 130 year old, two-story framed home in southern Minnesota—Mankato to be specific. It is a beautiful old section of the city with streets lined with large, mature trees, brick and framed two and three story homes, near the bottom of the large (200–300 foot) bluffs lining the Minnesota River valley in this area. This is part of the view through the window next to my built-in desk.

I have an aluminum iMac running Lion with 4GB RAM, an old Epson scanner, an older Xerox wax printer, and cable modem access to the Web. I'm using Adobe's Creative Suite Design Premium CS6.

For the fonts, I designed the basic fonts used in this book in FontLab 5—though my most recent fonts have been designed for my new book on font design using Fontographer 5.1. The fonts were designed as part of my personal best seller, *Practical Font Design 3rd Edition*. The serif faces are from the eight font Contenu family and the headers are from the companion font family I designed for Contenu: Buddy.

As usual, it has been great fun putting this book together for you. I pray it's helpful for you in your work.

Index

A

academic versions 26
accents 208
Acknowledgments 120
Afterword 122
aggregator 135, 136, 343
Alignment 96, 103, 239, 339
alignments 19, 82, 116, 311, 359
all caps 43, 188, 195, 196, 205, 222, 230
Amazon 7, 30, 46, 52, 53, 58, 59, 133, 136, 137, 138, 141, 293, 298, 301
anal 185
anchored graphics 82, 188, 315, 316
Anchored Object Character 234, 235
anchored objects 81, 233, 234, 235, 236, 239, 240
anchored object settings 234, 239
Android 140, 322, 342
apostrophes 193
Apply Master to Pages 129
arabic numerals 127
artwork 30
ascender 45
autoflow 77
auto-formatting your writing 83
auto leading 106, 315, 340
automatically formatted 80
automatic layout control 221
automatic text wrap 81

B

back matter 118, 121, 123, 128, 133
backup hard drive 51, 54
Barnes & Noble 140, 141
based on 55, 82, 94, 96, 98, 212, 240, 328, 337, 357
baseline shifts 214, 228
Bible 2, 11, 24, 100, 123, 226
billboard 103
bindery options page 294
bitmap 4, 255, 258, 260, 265, 266, 274, 335, 339
blank pages 127, 129
bleed 57, 64, 65, 309
blog 6, 24, 77, 80, 124, 332, 360

body content 128
body copy 33, 42, 47, 68, 80, 81, 82, 91, 92, 94–106, 149, 182, 186–188, 192, 195, 198–200, 202–206, 212, 220, 222, 233, 318, 319, 320, 321, 351
body copy styles 95
book design 36, 42, 44, 47, 49, 124
book designers 11, 42, 46, 47, 356
book folder 49
Book panel 128, 129, 130, 131
book publishing 56
book review 18
borders 325, 326, 359
break for sense 101, 202
Bringhurst 46, 194, 200, 204
British usage 194
bulleted lists 82, 101, 185, 192, 202, 203, 228, 355
bullets 100, 101, 202, 203, 204, 215, 228, 324
bullets, decorative 100
bureaucratic output 318

C

Calibre 142, 347, 356
callouts 104, 203
camerawork 255
cap height 45, 68, 234
captions 12, 43, 81, 82, 99, 100, 120, 184, 203, 316, 358
chapter break 324, 349
character color 229
Character panel 213, 214
character style 212, 215, 225, 226, 228, 229, 235
character styles 81, 84, 85, 86, 87, 88, 91, 93, 107, 219, 225, 226, 227, 240, 326, 334
cheap clip art 67
C&lc 196, 222
CMYK 50, 51, 315
coil bound 32, 136, 137
Colophon 122, 363
color versions 51
column 67, 68, 69, 96, 97, 101, 107, 108, 182, 185, 186, 190, 200, 201, 202, 211, 219, 220, 224, 232, 233, 234, 313, 328, 338, 340
column width 67

comb binding 59
computer 1, 7, 24, 27, 47, 192, 228, 334, 353
minimums 25
copyediting 307
copyeditors 14, 16, 18, 33
copyright page 118
cover designer 15, 18
covers 3, 4, 120, 136
Create Outlines 323, 334
Createspace 2, 4, 7, 52, 59, 133, 137, 138, 139, 149, 295, 301, 306, 307
Creative Suite 5.5 26
CS3 26, 211, 213, 226
CS4 26, 116, 211, 212, 213, 226, 227
CS5 26, 27, 141, 211, 223, 224, 312, 326, 332, 342, 349, 350
CS5.5 26, 211, 312, 326, 332, 342, 349, 350
CS6 25, 26, 32, 56, 57, 70, 72, 76, 78, 79, 117, 125, 127, 130, 141, 149, 350, 354, 355, 357, 360, 361, 363
CSNext 27, 72, 347, 361
CSS 4, 143, 316, 324, 325, 331, 332, 333, 337, 342, 343, 347, 350, 354, 355, 356, 359, 360

D

Dedication 120
default styles 91, 118
default tabs 192
derivative styles 82, 94
descender 46, 222
desktop publishers 17
desktop publishing 7
digital books 312
digital publishing 10, 14, 18, 40, 315
dingbats 202, 203, 204, 228
direct deposit 139, 142
discretionary hyphen 201
Discretionary Ligatures 230
distribution 31, 32, 58, 59, 135, 136, 137, 138, 139, 141, 295, 300, 307
divs 311, 358, 359
Document Setup 55
document size 57, 314
double returns 184, 186

Made in the USA
Lexington, KY
29 June 2012